Problems as of 3/2000
1. Printing default to Black
2. Full Justify + Right Align do not show on tool bar

SO-BFI-632

The Learning Guide to Word for Windows 95

The Learning Guide to Word for Windows® 95

Gini Courter
Annette Marquis

SYBEX®

San Francisco ▪ Paris ▪ Düsseldorf ▪ Soest

Associate Publisher: Amy Romanoff
Acquisitions Manager: Kristine Plachy
Developmental Editor: James Sumser
Editor: James A. Compton
Technical Editor: Michele Petrovsky
Educational Consultant: Shari V. Cohen
Production Coordinator: Robin Kibby
Technical Illustrator: Dan Schiff
Book Designer: Seventeenth Street Studios
Page Layout and Composition: Seventeenth Street Studios
Indexer: Linda Facey
Cover Designer: Ziegler Design
Cover Illustrator/Photographer: Otto Eberhard
The cover photograph appears courtesy of FPG International Corp.
Screen reproductions produced with Collage Complete.
Collage Complete is a trademark of Inner Media Inc.
SYBEX is a registered trademark of SYBEX Inc.

TRADEMARKS: SYBEX has attempted throughout this book to distinguish proprietary trademarks from descriptive terms by following the
capitalization style used by the manufacturer.

Every effort has been made to supply complete and accurate information.
However, SYBEX assumes no responsibility for its use, nor for any
infringement of the intellectual property rights of third parties which
would result from such use.

Copyright ©1996 SYBEX Inc., 2021 Challenger Drive, Alameda, CA 94501.
World rights reserved. No part of this publication may be stored in a
retrieval system, transmitted, or reproduced in any way, including but not
limited to photocopy, photograph, magnetic or other record, without the
prior agreement and written permission of the publisher.

Library of Congress Card Number: 95-72869
ISBN: 0-7821-1824-0

Manufactured in the United States of America
10 9 8 7 6 5 4 3 2 1

To Charlotte for her unwavering faith in our dreams

Acknowledgments

The suggestion that we co-author this book started with Jim Sumser, our developmental editor. Despite our initial trepidation, it's been a fabulous experience. Thanks, Jim, for believing in us as a team.

We want to give special thanks to Jim Compton, our editor, who kept things moving at a brisk but manageable pace. Jim's hard work and flexibility have helped to keep us on the right track. Shari Cohen, our academic editor, provided us with invaluable feedback about the book's application in the classroom.

Some times it is easy to get focused on the words and forget about how an entire book will come together. Thanks to Catalin Dulfu, the Book Design Supervisor at Sybex, for being so willing to involve us in discussing the design of this book. We also can't forget to mention Ina Ingenito for her work on the spectacular cover design.

And, as always, it's been a pleasure working with Kristine Plachy, who took care of our contracts and made sure that we had access to software in record time. Thanks, Kristine, and thanks to everyone at Sybex for your encouragement and support.

Contents at a Glance

Introduction	xxi
Part I: Getting Acquainted with Word	**2**
Session 1: Getting to Know Windows 95 and Microsoft Word	3
Session 2: Creating Your First Word Document	15
Session 3: Foolproof Editing Techniques in Microsoft Word	29
Session 4: More Editing Techniques for Word	47
Part II: Formatting Documents Using Word	**64**
Session 5: Enhancing Document Text	65
Session 6: Inserting Dates and Working with Indenting	81
Session 7: Lists, Lines, Numbers, and Symbols	97
Session 8: Document Formatting	111
Part III: Word Tables and Tools	**126**
Session 9: Polishing the Writing in Your Document	127
Session 10: Constructing High-Quality Tables	139
Project A: Paint the Town	154
Session 11: Customizing the Word Environment	157
Part IV: Greater Efficiency for Repetitive Tasks	**176**
Session 12: Working Efficiently in Word	177
Session 13: Entering and Managing Data in Word	195
Session 14: Creating Customized Merge Documents Using Word	209
Project B: Merging	228
Session 15: Working with Outlines	231
Session 16: Harnessing the Power of Word Macros	241
Part V: Publishing Tools and Techniques	**254**
Session 17: Defining and Using Columns	255
Session 18: Adding Impact with Graphic Objects	269
Session 19: Advanced Graphic Features in Word	281
Session 20: Putting It All Together: Publishing with Word	297
Project C: Creating an Electrifying Newsletter	310
Project D: Producing High-Impact Promotional Materials	311
Glossary	313
Index	321

Table of Contents

Introduction   **xxi**

PART I: GETTING ACQUAINTED WITH WORD   **2**

Session 1   **Getting to Know Windows 95 and Microsoft Word**   **3**

1.1: Understanding Windows 95 Applications   4
1.2: Starting Microsoft Word for Windows 95   5
1.3: Working with Windows   8
1.4: Ending Your Word Session   11

Session 2   **Creating Your First Word Document**   **15**

2.1: Changing the Primary Mouse Button   16
2.2: Features of the Word Window   17
    The Word Menu Bar   17
    Toolbars   18
    Which Method Should I Use?   19
    The Status Bar   19
    The Document Window   20
2.3: Entering Text in Word   21
2.4: Saving Your Document   22
2.5: Closing Your Document and Creating a New Document   24

Session 3:   **Foolproof Editing Techniques in Microsoft Word**   **29**

3.1: Opening Previously Saved Documents   30
3.2: Using Special Keys   33
3.3: Moving the Insertion Point in Word   34
    Moving the Insertion Point   34
    Inserting and Deleting Text   35
3.4: Selecting Text   37
3.5: Moving and Copying Text in Word   39
    Moving Text   39
    Copying Text in Word   40

Damage Control in Word   41
3.6: Saving Your Document as a Copy   42
3.7: Using Print Preview to Examine Your Document   43

Session 4   ▇ **More Editing Techniques for Word**   **47**

4.1: More about Move and Copy   48
Move and Copy with the Pop-up Menu   48
Dragging and Dropping Text   49
4.2: Working with Multiple Documents   51
Moving and Copying Text Between Documents   53
4.3: Using Spell-Check   55
A Word about AutoCorrect   55
Is the Spelling Tool Always "Right"?   55
Checking Spelling on the Fly   56
Spell-Checking an Entire Document   58
4.4: Printing Documents   60
Setting Print Parameters   61
One-Step Printing in Word   61

PART II: FORMATTING DOCUMENTS USING WORD   **64**

Session 5   ▇ **Enhancing Document Text**   **65**

5.1: Formatting Text   66
5.2: Font Basics   66
Typefaces   67
Font Sizes   68
Font Style   69
Font Attributes and the Font Dialog Box   71
Underline Styles and Special Effects   72
Font Color   73
Setting the Default Font   74
5.3: Using Highlighting to Add Emphasis   75
5.4: Painting Formats on Other Text   76
5.5: Aligning Text   77
5.6: Using Horizontal Lines for Added Emphasis   78

Session 6   ▧ **Inserting Dates and Working with Indenting**   **81**

6.1: Inserting Dates and Times   82
6.2: Using Tabs   84
    Viewing the Ruler Bar   85
    Setting and Using Tabs   85
    Setting Tab Stops Using the Ruler Bar   86
    Setting Tab Stops Using the Tabs Dialog Box   88
6.3: Indenting Paragraphs   90
    Creating Indents Using the Ruler Bar   91
    Indenting Using the Toolbar   91
    Indenting Using the Menu Bar   92

Session 7   ▧ **Lists, Lines, Numbers, and Symbols**   **97**

7.1: Numbered and Bulleted Lists   98
    Creating a Numbered List   98
    Creating a List with Bullets   99
    Modifying the Bullet or Number Format   100
7.2: Using Symbols in Your Documents   103
7.3: Changing Line Spacing   104
7.4: Managing Text Flow   106
7.5: Adding Borders and Shading to a Document   107

Session 8   ▧ **Document Formatting**   **111**

8.1: Viewing Documents in Word   112
    Zooming In on a Document   112
    Displaying Nonprinting Characters   113
8.2: Changing Margins   114
8.3: Changing Paper Orientation   116
8.4: Adding Page Numbers   117
8.5: Creating Headers and Footers   118
    Editing or Deleting Headers and Footers   121
8.6: Vertical Centering   122

PART III: WORD TABLES AND TOOLS **126**

Session 9 ▓ **Polishing the Writing in Your Document** **127**

9.1: Changing Spelling options 128
9.2: Using the Thesaurus 130
9.3: Searching for Text Using Find and Replace 131
Finding Text 131
Replacing Text 134
Altering Formats Using Replace 135

Session 10 ▓ **Constructing High-Quality Tables** **139**

10.1: Creating a Table in Word 140
Creating a Table Using the Table Wizard 141
Creating a Table Using the Table Menu 141
Creating a Table Using the Toolbar 141
Entering Text in the Table 142
10.2: Formatting a Table 143
Using AutoFormat 143
Selecting and Formatting Table Cells 145
Inserting and Deleting Rows and Columns 146
Changing the Width of Columns 147
Merging and Splitting Table Cells 148
10.3: Simple Math in Tables 150

▓ **Project A: Paint the Town** **154**

Session 11 ▓ **Customizing the Word Environment** **157**

11.1: Displaying Toolbars 158
11.2: Customizing Toolbars 161
Adding or Deleting Toolbar Buttons 161
Creating a New Toolbar 163
11.3: Customizing AutoCorrect 164
11.4: Setting Options in Word 166
The General Options 167

The Edit Options 168
File Location Options 169
Compatibility Options 169
User Info Options 169
View Options 170
Revision Options 171
Save Options 171

PART IV: GREATER EFFICIENCY FOR REPETITIVE TASKS 176

Session 12   **Working Efficiently in Word** 177

12.1: Wizards and Templates 178
Using a Wizard to Create a Document 178
12.2: Document Formatting with AutoFormat 182
12.3: Creating and Applying Styles 186
Creating a New Style 188
Viewing a Paragraph's Style 189
Creating a Style from Formatted Text 190
12.4: Using AutoText 191
Creating an AutoText Entry 191
Pasting AutoText in a Document 191

Session 13   **Entering and Managing Data in Word** 195

13.1: Understanding Mail Merge 196
Creating a Table Data Source in Word 196
Creating a Delimited Data Source 198
Using the Mail Merge Helper 200
Entering Records 202
Using the Database Toolbar 204
13.2: Sorting a Data Source 205

Session 14   **Creating Customized Merge Documents Using Word** 209

14.1: Creating a Main Document 210
Creating a Main Document from Scratch 210
Previewing the Merged Document 213
14.2: Converting an Existing Document to a Main Document 213

14.3: Merging Documents   215
    Specifying Records to Merge   217
    Using And and Or   218
    Sorting Records in a Query   219
14.4: Creating Envelopes and Labels   221
14.5: Troubleshooting Merge Problems   224

Project B: Merging   **228**

Session 15   **Working with Outlines**   **231**

15.1: Creating an Outline in Word   232
15.2: Editing an Outline   234
15.3: Collapsing and Expanding the Outline   236
    Changing Views and Printing   236
    Numbering the Headings   237

Session 16   **Harnessing the Power of Word Macros**   **241**

16.1: Understanding Macros   242
16.2: Recording a Simple Macro   242
16.3: Running the Macro   246
16.4: Placing Macros at Your Fingertips   246
    Assigning a Macro to a Toolbar   246
    Assigning a Macro to a Keyboard Shortcut   248
16.5: Deleting Macros   251

PART V: PUBLISHING TOOLS AND TECHNIQUES   **254**

Session 17   **Defining and Using Columns**   **255**

17.1: Working Column-Wise   256
17.2: Creating Equal Columns   258
17.3: Adjusting Column Widths   260
17.4: Mixing Column Formats   261
17.5: Balancing and Breaking   262
17.6: Using the Column Dialog Box   263
    Locked Equal Columns   264
    Entering Specific Column Widths   264

Session 18 ■ **Adding Impact with Graphic Objects** **269**

18.1: Using Graphics 270
18.2: Using Clip Art in a Document 270
   Placing Clip Art 271
   Sizing and Cropping Pictures 272
   Copying, Pasting, and Deleting a Picture 273
   Adding Borders 273
18.3: Importing Other Graphics 275
   Linking and Embedding Pictures 275
18.4: Faster Work with Graphics 276

Session 19 ■ **Advanced Graphic Features in Word** **281**

19.1: Positioning Objects in Documents 282
   Relating Frames to Text and Margins 284
19.2: Adding Pictures and Text to Frames 286
19.3: Drawing Your Own Graphic Objects 287
   Creating and Formatting Lines and Shapes 288
   Text Boxes and Callouts 291
   Selecting and Manipulating Objects 292
   Editing the Picture 293

Session 20 ■ **Putting It All Together: Publishing with Word** **297**

20.1: Special Effects for Text 298
20.2: Text Spacing 301
   Applying Kerning 302
   Using Leading 303
20.3: Desktop Publishing in Word 304
   Guidelines for Desktop Publishing 305
   Rules for Page Layout 305

■ **Project C: Creating an Electrifying Newsletter** **310**

■ **Project D: Producing High-Impact Promotional Materials** **311**

■ **Glossary** **313**

■ **Index** **321**

Guide to Quick Steps

Session 1   ▪ **Getting to Know Windows 95 and Microsoft Word**

To Start Windows 95 5
To Launch Microsoft Word for Windows 95 7
To Minimize the Word Application Window 9
To Size the Word Application Window 10
To Resize and Move the Word Application Window 10
To Maximize Word 11
To Close Microsoft Word 11
To Shut Down the Computer 11

Session 2   ▪ **Creating Your First Word Document**

To Open the Mouse Properties Sheet and Change the Mouse Settings 16
To Browse the Menu Bar 18
To Browse a Toolbar 19
To Save Your Document on a Floppy Disk 24
To Close the Document Window 24
To Start with a New Document Window 25

Session 3   ▪ **Foolproof Editing Techniques in Microsoft Word**

To Open a Document Using the Menu 32
To Edit and Close a Document without Saving Changes 33
To Open a Document Using the Toolbar 33
To Move the Insertion Point 35
To Add and Delete Text 36
To Move Text Using the Menu Bar 39
To Move Text Using the Toolbar 40
To Copy Text 40
To Undo an Action 41
To Save Your Document and Keep the Original 43
To Preview Your Document 44

Session 4 ▨ **More Editing Techniques for Word**

To Move Text Using the Pop-Up Menu	48
To Move and Copy Text Using Drag-and-Drop Techniques	49
To Copy Text between Document Windows	54
To Correct a Single Misspelled Word	56
To Correct All Flagged Words	57
To Use the Spelling Tool	60
To Print a Document	62

Session 5 ▨ **Enhancing Document Text**

To Change a Font Using the Formatting Toolbar	68
To Change Font Size	69
To Bold, Underline, and Italicize Text	70
To Change Fonts Using the Font Dialog Box	73
To View Font Attributes in a Document	74
To Change the Default Font	75
To Highlight Text in a Document	76
To Paint a Format onto Existing Text	77
To Align Text in a Document	78
To Add a Horizontal Line	79

Session 6 ▨ **Inserting Dates and Working with Indenting**

To Insert Date and Time as Updatable Fields	83
To Insert a Date and Time as Text	83
To Set Tabs Using the Ruler Bar	87
To Set Tab Stops Using the Dialog Box	89
To Indent Paragraphs Using the Ruler Bar	92
To Indent Paragraphs Using the Paragraph Dialog Box	93

Session 7 ▨ **Lists, Lines, Numbers, and Symbols**

To Number Paragraphs Automatically	99
To Create a Bulleted List	99
To Modify a Numbered or Bulleted List	102
To Change Line Spacing	105
To Manage Text Flow Between Pages	107
To Add a Border to Text	108

Session 8   ■ **Document Formatting**

To Change Document Views   113
To Change Document Margins   115
To Change Paper Orientation   116
To Number Pages   118
To Create a Document Header   120
To Edit a Header   121

Session 9   ■ **Polishing the Writing in Your Document**

To Change Spell-Checking Options   129
To Use the Thesaurus   131
To Find Text in a Document   133
To Change Document Text Using Replace   135
Using Replace to Change Formatting   136

Session 10   ■ **Constructing High-Quality Tables**

To Create a Table from the Toolbar   142
To Enter Text in a Table   143
To AutoFormat a Table   144
To Format Selected Areas of a Table   145
To Insert Rows and Columns   146
To Delete Rows and Columns   147
To Adjust Column Width   148
To Merge or Split Cells   149
To Add Totals to a Table   151

Session 11   ■ **Customizing the Word Environment**

To Display Toolbars   160
To Add or Delete Toolbar Buttons   163
To Create a New Toolbar   164
To Set AutoCorrect Options   166
To Set Options   172

Session 12   ■ **Working Efficiently in Word**

To Create a Document Using a Wizard   182
To AutoFormat a Document   185

To Apply a Style 187
To Create a Style Using the Style Dialog Box 189
To Create a Style from Formatted Text 190
To Create and Use AutoText 192

Session 13   **Entering and Managing Data in Word**

To Create a Tabular Data Source 197
To Create a Comma-Delimited Data Source 199
To Create and Enter Records in a Data Source File 203
To Sort a Data Source 205

Session 14   **Creating Customized Merge Documents Using Word**

To Create a Main Document 211
To Preview the Merged Document 213
To Convert an Existing Document to a Main Document 214
To Merge a Main Document with a Data Source 216
To Select and Sort Records to Merge 220
To Create Labels Using Mail Merge 223

Session 15   **Working with Outlines**

To Create a Simple Outline 233
To Edit an Outline 235
To View and Print Specific Headings of an Outline 237
To Apply Heading Numbering to an Outline 237

Session 16   **Harnessing the Power of Word Macros**

To Create a Macro 245
To Play a Macro from the Macro List 246
To Create a Toolbar Button Macro 247
To Create a Shortcut-Key Macro 250
To Delete a Macro 251

Session 17   **Defining and Using Columns**

To Create Columns for New Text 258
To Create Columns for Existing Text 260
To Adjust Columns Widths and Gutter Position 261

To Balance Column Length 263
To Create or Adjust Columns Using the Columns Dialog Box 265

Session 18 ▇ **Adding Impact with Graphic Objects**

To Insert Clip Art 271
To Size and Crop a Picture 273
To Add a Border to a Picture 274
To Hide Graphics for Faster Scrolling 277

Session 19 ▇ **Advanced Graphic Features in Word**

To Move a Picture 283
To Attach a Frame to Text 285
To Insert Text in a Frame 287
To Draw Lines and Objects 290
To Send Objects to Back or Bring Them to Front 293
To Frame a Drawing 293

Session 20 ▇ **Putting It All Together: Publishing with Word**

To Create a Drop Cap 299
To Create WordArt 301
To Apply Kerning 302
To Add Leading to a Heading 304

Introduction

Microsoft Word for Windows 95 is a full-featured word processing program you can use to do everything from simple letter-writing to dynamic desktop publishing. The possibilities are limited only by your imagination and your willingness to learn. By working through the twenty sessions in this book and completing the various exercises and projects, you will become an accomplished user of Word with skills and knowledge that you can also apply to other Windows applications.

ABOUT THIS BOOK

This book is divided into five major sections. In Part I, "Getting Acquainted with Word," you will learn how to create and edit a document in Word. Part II, "Formatting Documents Using Word," provides you with the skills you need to format and enhance your text. By Part III, "Word Tables and Tools," you'll be ready to learn some of Word's more advanced features, like how to create useful tables within your documents and customize the Word environment. Part IV, "Greater Efficiency for Repetitive Tasks," teaches you many of the time-saving features of Word, such as using templates, Wizards, and mail merge. In Part V, "Publishing Tools and Techniques," you'll discover how to put everything you've learned together with graphics and columns to create amazing desktop publishing projects.

At the beginning of each session, you will find a vocabulary list that identifies words introduced in the session. (The Glossary at the end of the book provides a definition of each vocabulary term.)

In each session, you will find descriptions of Word's major features with explanations of how to use these features. Throughout the session, you will find several step-by-step exercises that will guide you through the topics being discussed. The exercises look like this:

EXERCISE 3.5 | **TO ADD AND DELETE TEXT**

1. **To add text, position the insertion point where you want the text to be added and begin typing.** For this exercise, position the cursor between "that" and "will" in the third sentence. Remember to click it into place.

Listed in boldface type are the general steps to follow anytime you want to complete the task indicated. (Use the Guide to Quick Steps, after the Table of Contents, to find these instructions any time you need them.) Before and after the boldface text you will find instructions specific to the practice exercise. Read the entire step first, and then do what it says.

At the end of each session, you will find a series of Focus Questions about concepts covered in the session. You will also find four Reinforcement Exercises you can complete for more hands-on practice to help you integrate the new material you learned in the session with what you have already mastered. Many of the reinforcement exercises build from session to session. For example, in Reinforcement Exercise 4 of each session, you'll maintain and work with a vocabulary list.

Following Sessions 10 and 14 are projects that provide you with the opportunity to apply your skills. These projects cover major topics from multiple sessions. Use your imagination and creativity to make the projects useful to you. (And have some fun with them, too.)

STYLE CONVENTIONS

When you are making choices from a menu, the ➤ symbol lets you know that your first selection leads to a second menu. For example, an instruction to choose File ➤ Save means that the Save option will appear only after you have chosen File.

We hope you enjoy using *The Learning Guide to Word for Windows 95*. We would love to hear your comments on this book. You can contact us care of Sybex:

Gini Courter and Annette Marquis
c/o Sybex
2021 Challenger Dr.
Alameda, CA 94501
E-Mail: www@Sybex.com

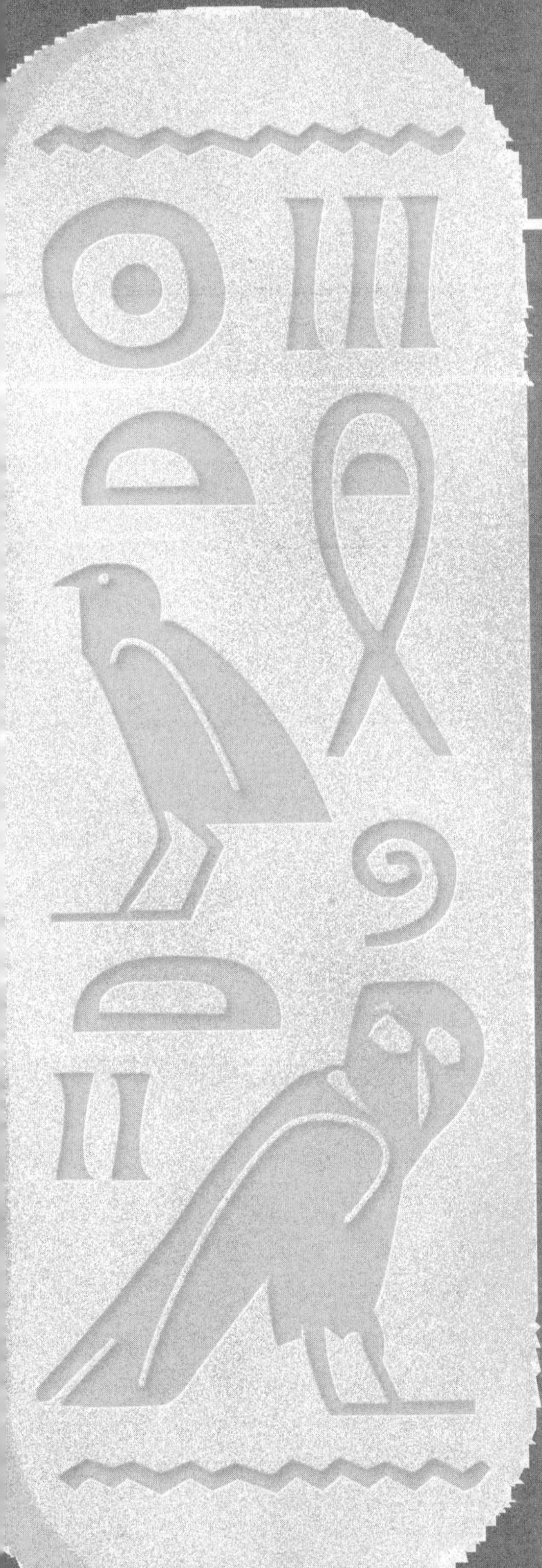

PART I

Getting Acquainted with Word

Vocabulary

- application window
- applications (apps)
- close
- desktop
- hardware
- icons
- launch
- maximize
- microcomputer
- minimize
- mouse
- operating system
- personal computer (PC)
- Shut Down option
- size
- software (programs)
- Start menu
- taskbar
- template
- wizard
- word processing programs

Getting to Know Windows 95 and Microsoft Word

THIS SESSION introduces terminology that will be helpful while you are learning Word. It also provides an overview of Windows 95, Word, and the relationship between the programs. At the end of this session you will be able to:

- Define the difference between hardware and software
- Explain the relationship between Windows and Word
- Launch Word for Windows 95
- Minimize and maximize the Word window
- Exit Word
- Shut down your computer

3

SECTION 1.1: UNDERSTANDING WINDOWS 95 APPLICATIONS

We live in a time of rapid technological change. The first commercially available computer was built less than fifty years ago. Until the 1970s, computers were so large (and expensive) that the idea of computers in homes and small businesses was a dream reserved for science fiction. In the past two decades, advances in technology have made computers more powerful, more compact, and less expensive. The **microcomputer** (also known as **personal computer,** or **PC**) sitting on your desk may be more powerful than any computer available in the 1950s—at a hundredth the size and cost.

Computer systems, including microcomputers, include two types of elements: hardware and software. **Hardware** refers to the physical parts of the computer: the components you can see and feel. There are some basic pieces of hardware included in computer systems: the screen (or monitor), keyboard, memory, disk drives, mouse, and the computer itself, the micro processor. In addition to these devices, your PC system may also include other hardware: a printer, a fax/modem, a CD-ROM drive, or a sound card.

The term **software** refers to computer programs. There are two basic kinds of software: system software and applications. System software includes **operating systems,** groups of programs that manage the computer's hardware. The presence of an operating system allows you to enter information by pressing keys on a keyboard or buttons on a mouse, print to a printer, or copy a file to or from a disk. **Windows 95** is a graphically-oriented operating system designed to help you harness the power of today's faster, more powerful microcomputers.

Once you have an operating system like Windows 95 running on your computer, you can use application programs, like Microsoft Word for Windows 95. **Applications** (also called "apps") are programs used to complete specific tasks. While application software is relatively new in a historical sense, the tasks you perform with it have been around for a long time. If you want to create a budget, you can use a spreadsheet application instead of a pencil and calculator. Database programs are used to maintain lists that were maintained manually on index cards or in file folders before the use of computers. Computerized drafting programs have replaced the pencils and templates used to create blueprints and schematics.

Word processing programs like **Microsoft Word for Windows 95** are used to create letters, memos, publicity pieces, and mailing labels—tasks that were formerly completed with a typewriter. But you can do much more than simple typing with Word. You can create professional newsletters and publications with columns and graphics, make personalized letters from a form letter and a list of names, or design customized forms for business or home use. If you need to construct a great-looking document in a hurry, you can use one of Word's templates or wizards. **Templates** are predesigned forms provided as part of the Word package that provide the basic structure of commonly used documents, like memos and reports. **Wizards** are an exciting feature of Word for Windows 95; they ask you specific questions and use the answers to lay out and format a document like a newsletter or a resume.

Word for Windows 95 and other programs written to work specifically with the Windows 95 operating system offer many advantages to you as a computer user. The Windows 95 applications run more quickly and have more built-in features than applications written for older versions of Windows. Older applications allowed you to use no more than 8 characters in file names. Word and other Windows 95 applications allow names up to 256 characters long. This enables you to give each document a name that accurately describes its contents. You'll discover more of the exciting advantages of Word as you work through the sessions in this book.

Before you can begin working with Word, you need to turn on your computer system. This will automatically start the Windows 95 operating system.

EXERCISE 1.1	TO START WINDOWS 95

1. Turn on the computer.

2. Wait while Windows 95 loads automatically.

SECTION 1.2: STARTING MICROSOFT WORD FOR WINDOWS 95

The screen shown in Figure 1.1 is the Windows 95 **desktop,** the control center for Windows 95. There are a number of **icons** (small pictures representing hardware or software) on the desktop. At the bottom of the screen is an area called the **taskbar.** The current time is displayed at the right end of the taskbar. On the left end is the Start button.

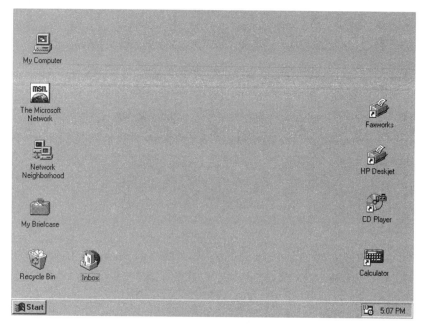

Figure 1.1

The Windows 95
desktop

Both the keyboard and the mouse provide ways to give instructions to the computer. A **mouse** is an input device that allows you to make selections or start actions by moving the pointer to an item on the screen and pressing one of the mouse buttons (if you are right-handed this would be the left or primary button). This is referred to as **pointing and clicking,** or simply **clicking on** a button. (You will learn more about the right or secondary mouse button in Session 2.) Pointing to the middle of the Start button and clicking once on the left mouse button opens the **Start menu,** shown in Figure 1.2.

Figure 1.2

Opening the
Start menu

Opening the Start menu is a way to launch programs and applications, including Windows 95 programs like Help and Find. It also provides access to two other menus: the Programs menu and the Documents menu. (A menu selection that leads to another menu has an arrow pointing right.) Moving the mouse pointer to Programs opens the Programs menu, as shown in Figure 1.3. Here, each folder containing applications has a file folder icon and an arrow next to its name. Word for Windows 95 is included in the Microsoft Office folder. Moving the mouse pointer to the right into the Programs menu and then down to Microsoft Office opens the

Microsoft Office folder. Clicking on the Microsoft Word program launches Word for Windows 95.

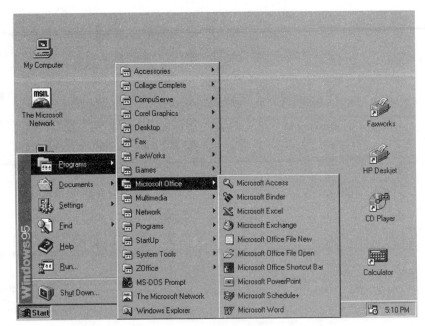

Figure 1.3

Opening the Microsoft Office folder

EXERCISE 1.2   **TO LAUNCH MICROSOFT WORD FOR WINDOWS 95**

1. Move the mouse pointer to the Start button and click once to open the Start menu.

2. Move the pointer to Programs to open the Programs menu. (It is not necessary to click.)

3. Slide the pointer into the list of programs, then up or down the list to the Microsoft Office folder.

4. Slide the pointer into the list of Microsoft Office programs, then down the list to Microsoft Word.

5. Click once on Microsoft Word to launch the application.

When you **launch** a program, it is copied from disk into the memory of the computer. Windows 95 adds a button for the program to the taskbar at the bottom of the screen and opens an **application window** containing the program, as shown in Figure 1.4.

Figure 1.4
Microsoft Word for
Windows 95

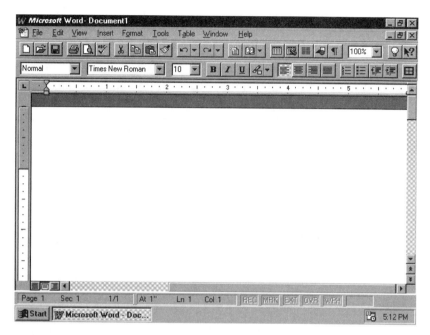

At the top of the application window is a **title bar** that includes the name of the application (Microsoft Word), the name of the current document, and three buttons:

The current document when you launch Word is called Document1. This is a temporary name assigned by Word; you'll change it the first time you save a document.

SECTION 1.3: WORKING WITH WINDOWS

The three buttons at the right end of the title bar are used to minimize, size, and close the application window.

The button with the horizontal bar is the Minimize button. **Minimizing** an application reduces it to the taskbar button, putting the application "on hold." A minimized application is still running, but is inactive. Clicking on the Word taskbar button will restore the application window to its former size, making it available to use again.

CAUTION

There is a set of identical buttons directly below the application window buttons on the title bar. Ignore these buttons for now—you'll learn to use them in Session 4.

EXERCISE 1.3	**TO MINIMIZE THE WORD APPLICATION WINDOW**

■ **Click on the Minimize button on the title bar.** This reduces Word to a button on the taskbar. For this exercise, click on the Microsoft Word taskbar button to restore the Word application window to its former size.

The Word application window fills the screen when Word is launched (unless a user has previously changed the settings).

 The middle button, which looks like two overlapping windows, is the **Restore** button. Clicking the **Restore** button downsizes the Word application window, as shown in Figure 1.5.

Figure 1.5
A sized Word window

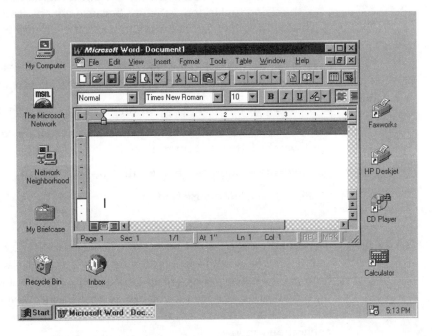

EXERCISE 1.4   **TO SIZE THE WORD APPLICATION WINDOW**

- **Click on the Restore button on the title bar to resize the application window.** Notice that the Restore button changes shape and becomes the Maximize button.

 When you've clicked a window's Restore button, you can make it larger or smaller (resize it), and move it to a new location within the display, by using the **sizing tool** in the lower-right corner of the window. Point to the sizing tool, then hold down the left mouse button while dragging the mouse pointer (and the corner of the window) to a new location. The window can be moved as easily as it can be resized. Dragging the title bar to a new location moves the entire window.

EXERCISE 1.5   **TO RESIZE AND MOVE THE WORD APPLICATION WINDOW**

1. **Point to the sizing tool in the lower-right corner of the Word window. If the sizing tool is not visible, it's because the application is maximized. Click the Restore button to resize the window before proceeding.**

2. **Hold down the left mouse button and drag the pointer to the left to make the window smaller and to the right to make it larger.**

3. **Release the left mouse button when the window is a size you like.**

4. **To change the location of the window, point to the title bar and hold down the left mouse button.**

5. **Move the window to a new location on the desktop.**

6. **Release the left mouse button.**

 When the application window does not fill the entire desktop, the Restore button is replaced with a new button showing a single window: the **Maximize** button. Clicking the Maximize button maximizes the Word window, returning it to its original, screen-filling size. You will usually want to use Word with its window maximized, allowing you to see all the features in the application window.

EXERCISE 1.6 **TO MAXIMIZE WORD**

■ Click the Maximize button to restore the application window to its former size. Notice that the Restore button changes shape and becomes the Maximize button.

SECTION 1.4: ENDING YOUR WORD SESSION

 The **Close** button appears in all application windows. Clicking the Close button ends your Word session, returning you to the desktop. It is important to close Word properly when you are finished using the program. If you create or change a document during your work session, Word will make certain you have saved the latest version of your document before closing the application window. If you have not, you will be prompted to save it. In addition, there are a number of temporary files created by Word. Closing the application deletes those files so they don't take up space on the hard disk and so they don't create problems saving files in the future.

EXERCISE 1.7 **TO CLOSE MICROSOFT WORD**

1. Click on the Close button in the Microsoft Word title bar.

2. If you pressed any keys or entered text while the document window was open, you will be asked if you want to save changes to the open documents. For this exercise, click No.

It is equally important that you shut down Windows prior to turning off your computer. The Start menu's **Shut Down** option prepares your computer to be turned off, deleting temporary files that were created by Windows 95 and ending any Windows 95 network connections created when you started the computer.

EXERCISE 1.8 **TO SHUT DOWN THE COMPUTER**

1. Click on the Start button.

2. Click on Shut Down.

CONTINUES ON NEXT PAGE

3. The button in front of *Shut down your computer?* should be selected. If it is not, click on it once.

4. Click on Yes.

5. When Windows prompts you to do so, you can safely turn off the computer.

What You Have Learned

You now understand the difference between hardware and software and how Microsoft Windows 95 and Word for Windows 95 relate to each other. You are able to launch Word from the Start menu. You know how to minimize, size, and maximize application windows. Finally, you know how to exit Word and safely shut down your computer.

Focus Questions

1. Name three pieces of hardware that are part of your computer system.

2. What are the two basic types of software?

3. What is an application?

4. What is the purpose of the Start menu?

5. List the steps you need to follow to launch Word.

6. What happens to an application when you minimize it?

7. How do you move a window to a new location?

8. Why is it important to close an application before shutting off your computer?

Reinforcement Exercises

Exercise 1   Using the Start menu, locate an application other than Microsoft Word. How can you tell that it is an application and not a folder? List the steps you followed to get to the application's icon.

Exercise 2   Launch Microsoft Word from the Start menu. Practice minimizing, sizing and maximizing the application window. Resize the window and move it so that just the title bar is visible at the bottom of the desktop. Maximize the application before you close it.

Exercise 3   List three ideas you have for documents that you would like to create using Microsoft Word.

Vocabulary

- backspace
- control
- Control Panel
- cursor
- double-clicking
- default
- dialog box
- document
- document window
- drive
- highlight
- insertion point
- margin
- menu bar
- new document
- save
- scroll bar
- shortcut key
- status bar
- Tip Wizard
- toolbar
- tool tip

Creating Your First Word Document

MICROSOFT WORD's built-in features make it easy to create and save documents. In this session, you will enter text, correct mistakes, and save your Word document on disk. *You will need a formatted floppy disk to use in this and future sessions.* At the end of this session you will be able to:

- Change the Windows 95 setting for mouse buttons
- Identify the features of the Word application window
- Enter text in a document
- Correct misspellings identified by Word
- Do simple editing using backspace
- Save a document to a floppy disk

SECTION 2.1: CHANGING THE PRIMARY MOUSE BUTTON

The developers of Windows 95 created **default** settings (preexisting settings) for your hardware. The developers' goal was to pick default settings that are acceptable the majority of the time. Since most people are predominantly right-handed, the default mouse settings are for "righties" with the primary mouse button on the left, under a right-handed person's index finger. Windows allows lefties to change the mouse settings so that the primary mouse button is the right button. If you are left-handed, you might want to start and end this and future sessions by changing the mouse settings and moving the mouse to the appropriate side of the keyboard. If you are right-handed, you should still walk through these steps without changing the default settings. It's important to know how to change them if someone inadvertently leaves them set for left-handers. Use the Windows 95 **Control Panel** to change hardware settings.

EXERCISE 2.1   **TO OPEN THE MOUSE PROPERTIES SHEET AND CHANGE THE MOUSE SETTINGS**

Turn on the computer if it is not on already.

1. Click the Start button to open the Start menu.

2. Point to Settings.

3. Click Control Panel.

4. In the Control Panel window, double-click the Mouse icon. You will now see the Mouse Properties page.

5. Under *Button Configuration*, click on Left-handed to change the setting or Right-handed to restore the default setting.

6. Click the OK button at the bottom of the dialog box to save the setting and exit.

In this book and most computer books, "mouse button" and "left mouse button" refer to the primary mouse button (under your index finger). If you have changed the mouse settings, your "left mouse button" is now on the right, and vice versa. Remember to change the mouse buttons back to the default setting at the end of your session before exiting Windows.

SECTION 2.2: FEATURES OF THE WORD WINDOW

The Microsoft Word Window (see Figure 2.1) is really two windows—the application window and a document window. The application window includes a title bar, menu bar, one or more toolbars, the Tip Wizard, and a status bar. The document window is contained in the application window.

Figure 2.1

The Microsoft
Word window

■ The Word Menu Bar

The **menu bar** provides lists of available options organized in categories:

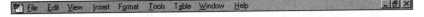

Clicking File, Edit, View, or any other menu bar choice opens a list of options within that category on a pull-down menu. (Follow the steps below to see why it's called a "pull-down.") While your mouse pointer is resting on a menu item, a description of the item appears in the status bar at the bottom of the application window.

EXERCISE 2.2   **TO BROWSE THE MENU BAR**

1. Point to a menu option and click once to open the menu. For this exercise, click on File to open the File menu.

2. Move the pointer down the menu to highlight different choices.

3. Move the mouse to the right to open other menus.

4. Point anywhere in the document window (the white part of the screen) and click once to deactivate the menu bar.

In the File pull-down, across from New, you will see the description Ctrl+N. This is a reference to a **shortcut key**: a series of keystrokes that you can use instead of making choices from the menu bar. To open a new file, choose File and then New from the menu, or press the N key while holding down the Control key (labeled "Ctrl") on your keyboard. You will notice that shortcut keys are available for some but not all menu selections.

Shortcut keys are holdovers from older (DOS) programs that did not accept instructions from a mouse. Early Windows programs listed shortcut keys for almost all menu choices. As mouse-driven programs have matured, shortcut keys are no longer available for every feature of an application. Some shortcut keys are found uniformly throughout Windows applications, such as Ctrl+B to turn on the bold feature. If you are a touch typist, it might make sense to learn these keys so that your hands do not have to leave the keyboard as often. Other shortcut keys are specific to applications. It is much easier to use the mouse than to spend a lot of time learning different keystrokes for each application. After all, consistency between applications is one of the benefits of learning Windows programs over DOS-based applications. Throughout this book, we will direct attention to the shortcut keys that are most worthwhile for you to learn.

■ Toolbars

Toolbars are groups of buttons that provide another way to access the same commands available on the menu bar. To make a selection from a toolbar, simply click the appropriate button. Instead of choosing File , New from the menu bar, click once on the first button on the standard toolbar, the New button. There are over a dozen toolbars included with Word and each of these can be customized to meet every user's preferences. (You'll learn how to customize toolbars and other parts of Word in Session 11.) The three toolbars displayed by default are the standard toolbar, the formatting toolbar and the Tip Wizard toolbar:

The Word **tool tips** feature provides a quick reference for toolbar users. Pointing to a button for a couple of seconds without clicking will cause a **tool tip** describing the button to appear.

When you start Word, the randomly selected Tip of the Day appears in the Tip Wizard. As you create a document, Word evaluates how you complete tasks. If you've done something in a way that Word considers inefficient, the Tip Wizard will let you know about a potentially better way of handling the task. Clicking the up and down arrows at the right end of the Tip Wizard will provide a review of the tips provided since the start of a work session.

EXERCISE 2.3   **TO BROWSE A TOOLBAR**

1. **Point to any of the buttons on the toolbar to see the name of the button appear below it in a tool tip.**

2. **Read a description of the button in the status bar at the bottom of the application window.**

Which Method Should I Use?

Toolbars, the menu bar, and shortcut keys all allow you to do the same tasks. This kind of redundancy is common in Windows applications like Word. You may find two, three, or more ways to complete a specific task. As you gain more experience, you will find that some methods work better than others in certain situations. Don't worry about learning all the ways Word lets you complete a task. Choose the method that is easiest for you to remember and use.

The Status Bar

The **status bar** at the bottom of the application window serves as an active information source for the user. It displays information about the current status of the document:

The numbers on the left end of the status bar indicate the current page number, section number, total page count (1/1 means "Page 1 of 1"), and position within the document in inches, lines from the top, and columns from the left margin.

The five gray buttons on the right side of the status bar access Word features that you will learn about later in this book. The type on the buttons is gray when the buttons are turned off, and black when a button is activated. A small book icon at the extreme right gives information about the status of text. The red check in the book icon changes to an "X" when there is a word in the document that is not in Word's spelling dictionary. It changes to a pencil when you are typing to indicate that text is being entered.

Besides telling you about the current document, the status bar also provides on-screen information about Word's features. The user can obtain a description of each of the toolbar buttons and menu options by pointing to the item and reading the description on the status bar.

The Document Window

The area between the toolbars and status bar is the **document window**, shown in Figure 2.2. A **ruler** showing the document's **margins** (the white space between the text and the edges of the paper the document will be printed on) appears at the top of the window. Below the document window and above the status bar is a horizontal scroll bar. On the right side of the window is a vertical scroll bar. When the text overruns the document window, either vertically or horizontally, click the arrows on the **scroll bars** to see ("scroll to") another portion of the document.

Figure 2.2
The Word
document window

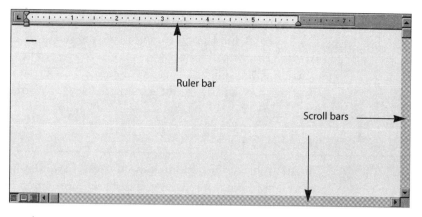

Ruler bar

Scroll bars

SECTION 2.3: ENTERING TEXT IN WORD

You type text in the open portion of the document window. A vertical flashing line called a **cursor** or **insertion point** indicates where characters entered on the keyboard will be placed in the document. Typing on a computer keyboard is very similar to typing on a typewriter. For example, to capitalize a letter hold down either Shift key while pressing a letter key. A major difference between word processing and typing, however, is that you do not hit the Return or Enter key at the end of each line. Word processors include a feature called **word wrap**, which automatically advances the cursor to the next line if the text you are entering would exceed the right margin of the document. If you change the margins later, Word will automatically adjust wrapped lines of text to fit within the new margins. To use word wrap, press the Enter key only at the end of a paragraph, not at the end of each line within the paragraph.

One of the exciting new features of Word for Windows 95 is that it automatically checks your spelling as you enter text. When you type a word that is not listed in the Word dictionary, a wavy red line will appear under the word to indicate the word may be spelled incorrectly. (The word may also be a medical or legal term, your last name, or any proper noun that is not included in the general dictionary. In Session 4, you'll learn how to train the Spelling tool to recognize such items.) This line only appears on the screen—it will not be included in a printed copy of the document. For now, if you make a mistake, press the Backspace key (above the Enter key) to erase the last letter(s) you entered until the mistake is erased. Then, enter the text correctly.

EXERCISE 2.4	CREATING YOUR FIRST DOCUMENT

1. Type the following paragraph. Remember not to hit the Enter key at the end of each line. Let word wrap do it for you.

2. Use the Backspace key if you make a mistake.

Thank you for taking the time to meet with us on Thursday. Enclosed you will find our proposal for the database project that we discussed. We are quite excited about the prospect of working with you on this project. We are confident that we can produce a quality product that will meet and possibly even exceed your expectations. Our combined experience makes us an ideal team for this venture.

SECTION 2.4: SAVING YOUR DOCUMENT

Currently, your first document exists only in the computer's memory. This memory is maintained by electricity. If the power goes out suddenly, or you turn the computer off, the document will be erased. This is, then, a good time to **save** the document—copy it from the computer's memory to a more permanent location.

As a new user, especially if you are using a computer that other people also use, it is best to save your documents on a floppy disk. You could also save them on the hard drive of the computer, but other users could accidentally alter your documents. By placing them on a floppy disk (and taking the disk with you), you retain control of your documents.

Word provides three ways to save a document. You can:

- choose File ➢ Save from the menu bar,

- click the Save button on the Standard toolbar, or

- hold Ctrl and press S.

Any of these three methods will open the Save As dialog box, shown in Figure 2.3.

Figure 2.3
The Save As
dialog box

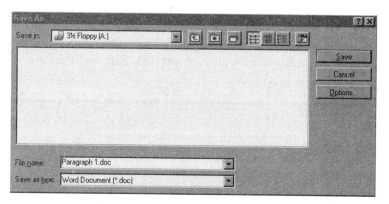

A **dialog box** appears when Windows or a Windows application needs more information from the user to complete a task. In this case, the Save As dialog box appears so that you can provide a file name and location.

Dialog boxes include one or more **controls** to set options and enter information. The Save In control at the top of the dialog box is a text box that contains a drop-down list. Clicking the arrow at the right end of the control provides a list of **drives**—hard drives, floppy drives, CD-ROM drives—attached to your computer, as shown in Figure 2.4. Moving down the list and clicking on a drive selects it as the location for the saved file.

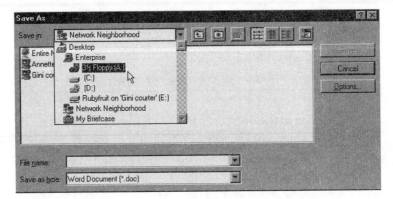

Figure 2.4

The drop-down list of drives

The File Name control near the bottom of the dialog box is a combination text box/drop down list control. This is where you will specify a **filename** for your document—the name you will use to refer to the document in the future. The filename that appears in the text box at the bottom of the dialog box is the first 50 characters of your document. This is just the suggested name, and may or may not be what you want to name your document. Word for Windows 95 file names can be up to 256 characters long and can include spaces and a mixture of upper and lower case letters.

Note: Some network software only recognizes older DOS filenames. If you are working in a network environment that does not recognize Windows 95 long filenames, your instructor will help you select filenames that meet the DOS standard: only eight characters before the period, and no spaces.

When the suggested file name is **highlighted** (meaning that the text appears surrounded by a contrasting color so that it stands out) you can just start typing a new file name over it. The suggested name will be deleted. If you select a different drive before you enter a file name, the file name is no longer highlighted. Highlight it again by double-clicking on the suggested file name. To **double-click,** press the right (primary) mouse button twice in rapid succession. Do not move the mouse between clicks or Windows 95 will interpret your action as two separate clicks.Once you have specified the file's name and location, clicking the Save button copies the file from the computer's memory to the selected location and closes the dialog box.

EXERCISE 2.5   **TO SAVE YOUR DOCUMENT ON A FLOPPY DISK**

1. **Insert a blank, formatted 3½" floppy disk into the diskette drive.**

2. **Click File on the menu bar.**

3. **Move the pointer down to Save and click once to open the Save As dialog box.**

4. **Click on the Save In control to open a list of drives available to you.**

5. **Point to the drive you want to save the document to and click to select the drive.** For the exercises in this book, choose 3½" Floppy."

6. **Move the pointer to the File Name control and double-click on the suggested file name to highlight it.** Type *Proposal* as this file's name.

7. **Point to the Save button in the top right of the dialog box and click to save the file.** The light on the computer's floppy drive should come on for a few seconds to indicate that your document is being saved to your floppy disk.

8. **Notice that the title bar no longer says *Document1*.** The new document name is prominently displayed at the top of the screen:

W *Microsoft* Word- Proposal.doc   ▬ ▣ ✕

SECTION 2.5: CLOSING YOUR DOCUMENT AND CREATING A NEW DOCUMENT

You are finished with this document, and have saved it on disk. Since you don't need to work with it any more in this session, you can close the document window. The document will be removed from the screen and the computer's memory, but you will remain in Word for Windows 95 and your first document will remain safely tucked away on your floppy.

EXERCISE 2.6   **TO CLOSE THE DOCUMENT WINDOW**

1. **Click the Close button on the menu bar. Be careful not to click the Close button on the title bar or you will close Word along with your document.**

2. **If you made any changes to your document since you last saved it, Word will ask if you want to save changes to the document. Click Yes if you want to keep your changes and No if you do not.**

Each Word document should be saved in its own file with its own file name. To start a new document, you will need to begin with a blank **new document** window.

EXERCISE 2.7	**TO START WITH A NEW DOCUMENT WINDOW**

1. **Click File ➢ New on the menu bar.**

2. **Click OK at the bottom right of the New Document dialog box.**

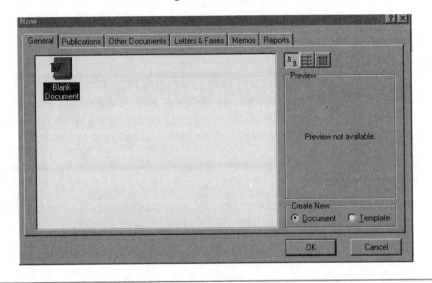

Creating this new document will give you a chance to practice the skills you learned in this session. You'll use both *Proposal* and this new document in Session 3 as you learn how to edit Word documents.

EXERCISE 2.8	**CREATING YOUR SECOND DOCUMENT**

1. Type the following paragraph. Remember to use word wrap instead of pressing the Enter key at the end of each line. Use Backspace to make any corrections.

CONTINUES ON NEXT PAGE

2. Save the document to your floppy disk as *Development*.

After careful review of the materials you presented to us and the issues discussed at our meeting, we have developed what we believe is a realistic timeline for the project. The preliminary development will be completed within the next two months. If all goes according to plan, we will be ready for piloting at one of your sites by November. We can expect that full implementation will occur by January as you had requested. In order to assure that implementation runs smoothly, we have built in adequate time for product testing and staff training.

You are now at the end of this session. If you altered the mouse settings for left-handed use, return to the Control Panel and restore the right-handed settings. Also remember to close Word and shut down Windows 95 before turning off the computer—and don't forget your floppy disk.

What You Have Learned

You now know how to enter text and you know one way to correct misspelled words using the backspace key. You also know how to change the primary mouse button for a left-handed mouse user and how to change it back for a right-handed user. You can identify the features of the Word application window including the tool bars, the menu bar, status bar, and scroll bars. Most importantly, you know how to save your documents to a floppy disk.

Focus Questions

1. Give an example of a default setting and explain why you would want to change it.

2. What are tool tips?

3. What is the purpose of the wavy red line that appears under some words as you enter text?

4. How do you access items on the menu bar?

5. What is word wrap and how do you use it?

6. Why is it important to save your document?

7. Name two ways to open the Save As dialog box.

8. List the steps necessary to save your document to a floppy disk.

Reinforcement Exercises

Exercise 1   Starting with the File menu, look at the features available under each of the items on the menu bar.

Exercise 2   Use Tool Tips to see each of the options available on the tool bars.

Exercise 3   Enter the following text. When you are finished, save the document to your floppy disk as *Orienteering Trip*. You will be using this document in future Reinforcement Exercises.

Don't forget to put the weekend of July 14-16 on your calendar for an exciting Orienteering Weekend sponsored by the Grand Traverse Wilderness Conservancy. We will spend Friday evening and Saturday morning learning about orienteering before heading out into the woods. You will need to bring a tent, sleeping bag, rain gear, compass, water bottle and good hiking shoes. Food will be provided. The fee is $35 for the entire weekend. Invite your friends to come along.

Exercise 4   Enter the following text. Save the document to your floppy disk as *Orienteering Instructor*.

Instruction in orienteering will be provided by Charlotte Cowtan, renowned wilderness explorer and orienteering expert. Ms. Cowtan will set up both a beginner and an intermediate course. So whether you are brand new to the sport or already have some experience, you are invited to join us on this exciting weekend.

Exercise 5   Open a new Word document and enter your definitions for the following terms: *hardware, applications, insertion point, save* and *shortcut key.* Define each term in a new paragraph (Press Enter after each definition.) Save this document as *My Definitions*.

This exercise will appear in subsequent sessions and will ultimately result in a personal glossary of word processing terms. Don't just copy or reword the definitions from the text (that would be plagiarizing). Write your own definitions that help you to understand the terms better. Include examples where appropriate.

Vocabulary

- block
- Caps Lock
- clipboard
- copy
- cut
- Delete (Del)
- I-beam
- Insert (Ins)
- insert
- move
- Num Lock
- open
- overtype
- paste
- redo
- revert
- reverse video
- select
- toggle
- undo

Foolproof Editing Techniques in Microsoft Word

THIS SESSION focuses on polishing existing documents using basic editing techniques. As you master these editing techniques not only will writing become easier, you'll find that your writing will actually get better. You can insert words, delete sentences, or move entire paragraphs around to your heart's content. In this session you will learn to:

- Open an existing document
- Insert and delete text
- Move the cursor and select text
- Use cut, copy, and paste to move and copy text
- Undo previous actions
- See how your document will appear when printed

SECTION 3.1: OPENING PREVIOUSLY SAVED DOCUMENTS

Before word processing software, we often had to type a document, and then retype it in its entirety just to incorporate minor changes. With Word, you can return to a document and make your changes directly to the original. This can save hours of retyping and mountains of frustration.

To work with an existing document, you must first **open** it, that is, copy it from disk to the computer's memory. If you are saving files to a floppy, you need to insert the disk into the floppy drive before you can open a document. There are two ways to open a document: using the menu bar or using the toolbar. Selecting File from the menu bar provides a list of file commands, as shown in Figure 3.1.

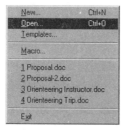

Figure 3.1

The File menu

Near the bottom of the list are the last four files opened or saved in Word. If you are the only person who uses the computer you are working on, the files listed will be the last four files you accessed. If the file you want to open is listed, simply choose it from the File menu.

Note: Even if a familiar file name appears on the list, it may not be your file if you share your computer with others. Another user may have saved a document using the same name. If you open a file that is not yours, close the file and follow the instructions below to open files from the Open dialog box.

If the file you want is *not* listed, choose File ➤ Open from the menu bar. The Open dialog box will appear, as shown in Figure 3.2.

Figure 3.2
The Open
dialog box

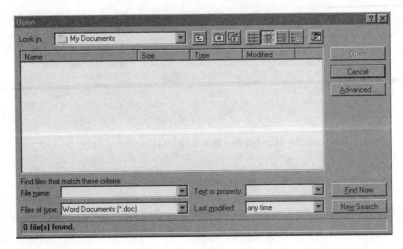

The Look In text box in this dialog box displays the default file location that was established when Word was installed on the computer. In Figure 3.2, the default location is a folder on the computer's hard drive called My Documents. The default location on the computer you are using may be the A drive, the My Documents folder, or a different drive. In Session 2, you saved documents on a floppy disk, so you need to direct Word to the 3½" floppy drive if it is not the default location. Click the arrow to display a drop-down list of drives and folders and select 3½ Floppy (A:). You'll see a list of available files on the floppy, as shown in Figure 3.3.

Figure 3.3
Opening a file from
floppy disk

Either double-click on the name of a file, or click once and then click the Open button to open the file.

| EXERCISE 3.1 | TO OPEN A DOCUMENT USING THE MENU |

To begin this exercise, launch Microsoft Word if you have not already done so, and insert your floppy in the diskette drive.

1. Click File on the menu bar.

2. Look at the list of files at the bottom of the File menu to see if the file you want is listed. If it is, point to the file name and click to open the document. In this case, you want to open Proposal, one of the files you created in the last session.

3. If the file you want is not listed on the File menu, click on Open to see the Open Document dialog box. For this exercise, go ahead and click Open even if *Proposal* is listed.

4. Check to see that the proper drive appears in the Look In text box. If it does not, click the drop-down arrow next to the text box and select the proper drive. In this case, make sure 3½ Floppy is selected.

5. Select the document you want to open from the file list that appears. Here, select *Proposal*.

6. Double-click the document name or click Open to open the document.

You've opened *Proposal*. The document on your screen is a copy of the file you saved in the last session. No matter what you do to the document on the screen, the disk copy of the file will remain unchanged until you save *Proposal* again. Saving replaces the disk copy of a file with the screen copy. The disk copy is not updated automatically as you make changes on the screen. If you want to keep the changes you make to a file, you click the Save button. If you don't like the changes you made, you can throw away the changes in the screen file and **revert** (go back) to the original, unaltered file on the floppy disk.

EXERCISE 3.2 | **TO EDIT AND CLOSE A DOCUMENT WITHOUT SAVING CHANGES**

To begin this exercise, press Enter four times to insert blank rows in your document. Even though you aren't typing any text, Word will recognize this as a changed file and ask whether you want to save the changes.

1. Open the File menu and select Close.

2. Click No when asked if you want to save the changes.

 Another way to reach the Open dialog box is by clicking the Open button on the toolbar; you'll see how to do that next.

EXERCISE 3.3 | **TO OPEN A DOCUMENT USING THE TOOLBAR**

1. Point to the Open button on the toolbar and click once to bring up the Open Document dialog box.

2. Double-click the document name or select the document and click Open to open the document. If *Proposal* is not selected, click on it to select it.

Since you did not save the changes before closing, *Proposal* looks just as it did when you opened it at the beginning of this session.

Note: Windows 95 also gives users access to recently used documents directly from the Start menu. Click on the Start menu and choose Documents. Select the Word document (with the Word icon) you want to open and it will be opened in Word. If Word is not already running, Windows 95 will first launch Word and then open the document.

SECTION 3.2: USING SPECIAL KEYS

Some keys on your keyboard aren't directly used to enter text. These include the Caps Lock, Num Lock, and directional keys. The Caps Lock key (to the left of the letter A) is what is called a **toggle** key. Press it once and it's on, press again and it's off. When Caps Lock is on, the 26 letters of the alphabet are capitalized when you type them. The letter *a* becomes *A* with Caps Lock on. If you hold the Shift key when typing with Caps Lock on, the letters will appear in lowercase.

The **Num Lock** key toggles the keys on the numeric keypad. When Num Lock is on, the keys are number keys. When it is off, they move the cursor in the direction shown. As with Caps Lock, there is a light on your keyboard that indicates whether Num Lock is on or off.

The **Ins** key toggles between Insert and Overtype modes. The default in Word is to insert; when you enter text between existing characters, those characters will move over to make room for your text. When you turn on the Overtype mode by pressing the Ins key, any characters that you enter replace existing characters. An indicator (OVR) on the status bar shows when Overtype mode is turned on. Remember that the insertion point (cursor) indicates the position for new text entered (inserted) from the keyboard. By moving the cursor, you can add or remove text anywhere in an existing document.

SECTION 3.3: MOVING THE INSERTION POINT IN WORD

You may have already noticed that the mouse pointer changes shape as you move it to different locations on the screen. The pointer looks like an arrow when it is located over the menu bar, title bar, scroll bars or toolbars.

 The pointer changes to an **I-beam** when you move it into the document window or over any text-box control where you can enter text.

■ Moving the Insertion Point

The I-beam is used to position the insertion point at a new location in your document. To move the insertion point, move the I-beam and then click once on the left mouse button. This moves the insertion point under the I-beam. It's like calling a dog—move the I-beam, whistle (click), and here comes the cursor.

You can also move the insertion point using the directional keys on the keyboard. One set of directional keys is located on the numeric keypad–the group of keys that resembles a calculator at the right side of the keyboard. The directional keys include four keys with arrows and keys labeled Home, End, Page Down (PgDn), and Page Up (PgUp). To use these keys, you must turn Num Lock off. There may also be a second set of directional keys to the left of the numeric keypad. The arrow keys move the cursor up a line, down a line, and one character to the left or right.

The Home key moves the insertion point to the beginning of the current line. The End key moves to the end of the current line. The control (Ctrl) key acts as an amplifier for the other directional keys. Holding the Ctrl key and pressing Home takes you to the beginning of your document; Ctrl+End takes you to the end of your document. Page Up and Page Down keys move the cursor up or down one screen. Ctrl+Page Up takes the cursor to the top of the screen. Ctrl+Page Down takes the cursor to the bottom of the screen.

Inserting and Deleting Text

Once you are able to position your insertion point, you can insert and delete text anywhere in your document. Insert text between words or between characters by moving the insertion point to the desired location and typing. Delete text by positioning the insertion point and then pressing the Backspace or the **Delete** (Del) key. Use Backspace to delete characters to the left of the insertion point; use Delete to del ete characters to the right of the insertion point. To delete entire words, press Ctrl+Backspace and Ctrl+Delete.

EXERCISE 3.4   **TO MOVE THE INSERTION POINT**

1. Press End to move the insertion point to the end of the line.

2. Press Home to return to the beginning of the line.

3. Press Ctrl+End to move to the end of the document.

4. Press Ctrl+Home to move back to the beginning of the document.

5. Press Ctrl+Page Down to move the insertion point to the top of the screen.

6. Press Ctrl+Page Up to move to the bottom of the screen.

7. In a multiple-page document, press Page Up to move up one screen.

8. Press Page Down to move down one screen.

9. For more practice, position the I-beam between the period after "venture" in the second sentence and "We" in the third sentence. Click to move the cursor to that position.

10. Position the I-beam before "Enclosed" in the first sentence. Click to move your cursor to that location.

| EXERCISE 3.5 | TO ADD AND DELETE TEXT |

1. **To add text, position the insertion point where you want the text to be added and begin typing.** For this exercise, position the cursor between "that" and "will" in the third sentence. Remember to click it into place.

2. **Use the Delete key to delete characters to the right of the insertion point. Press Ctrl+Delete to delete entire words.** Here, press Delete until you have completely deleted "will meet and possibly."

3. Insert the word **may**. Notice how the text to the right moves over to accommodate the new text.

4. Position the insertion point at the beginning of the last sentence.

5. Type *I'm sure you'll agree that.*

6. Delete the capital *O* in *Our* and replace it with a lowercase *o*.

Your paragraph should now look something like this:

Enclosed you will find our proposal for the database project that we discussed. We are quite excited about the prospect of working with you on this project. We are confident that we can produce a quality product that may even exceed your expectations. I'm sure you'll agree that our combined experience makes us an ideal team for this venture.

Since Word is automatically wrapping your text at the end of each line, your lines may begin and end at different places than those shown in the example. Don't worry if your document doesn't look exactly like the one shown here.

Using the Delete or Backspace keys to eliminate a few characters or even a few words is fine, but if you need to delete lots of text, there is a quicker way. You can select all the text and then press Delete.

SECTION 3.4: SELECTING TEXT

Any word or group of consecutive words is a **block** of text. There are times when you will want to change an entire block of text in some way. For example, you may want to delete a paragraph or underline a sentence. To do this, you need to **select** (pick out) the words first. When text is selected, it changes to **reverse video**—the opposite color from the rest of the text. To select one word, move the I-beam over the word and double-click. Hold the Ctrl key down and click anywhere in a sentence to select the entire sentence. To select a paragraph (as shown in Figure 3.4), place the I-beam anywhere within the paragraph and triple-click.

Figure 3.4

Selecting a
paragraph

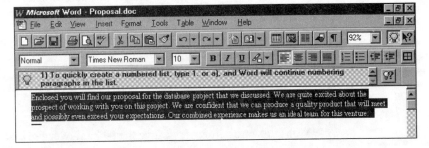

To select an entire line, move your I-beam into the left margin (past the left end of the text). The I-beam will change to a pointer pointing toward your text. Click once to select the line. If you need to select all your text, either hold Ctrl while selecting a line, or choose Edit ➤ Select All from the menu bar. Word will highlight all the text in your document.

There are two other ways to select blocks of text: dragging and using the Shift key. To select text by dragging, move your I-beam anywhere in the first word you want included in the selection. You don't need to start at the first letter. By default, Word selects whole words. If you start selecting in the middle of a word, the entire word will be selected automatically, as soon as you move into another word. Hold the mouse button down and move the I-beam to the last word you want to select. When the words you want selected are highlighted, release the mouse button to make the selection.

You can also drag to select lines of text. Move the I-beam into the left margin so that it changes to a pointer shape. Hold the mouse button down and drag down the lines of text you want to select.

Dragging is a skill you develop with practice. The trick lies in not releasing the mouse button prematurely. The selection isn't made until the button is released, so don't worry about selecting too much or too little as you are dragging. If you go too far, just back up!

To highlight using the Shift key, click on the first word you want to select. Hold the Shift key and click on the last word you want to include in the selection. Table 3.1 summarizes methods you can use to select text.

Table 3.1:

Selecting Text

To select:	Do this:
A word	Double-click anywhere in the word.
A sentence	Hold Ctrl and double-click anywhere in the sentence.
A paragraph	Triple-click anywhere in the paragraph.
An entire document	Choose Edit ➤ Select All from the menu bar, or Ctrl+click in the left margin.
A single line	Click in the left margin.
Multiple words, lines or sentences	Move the I-beam over the first word, hold the mouse button, drag to the last word, and release, or click on the first word, hold Shift and click on the last word.

EXERCISE 3.6   **SELECTING TEXT**

Experiment with each of the techniques described in Table 3.1. Try each one several times until you feel comfortable with them all.

If you select the wrong text, either too much or too little, and you've already released the mouse button, don't despair. All you have to do is click your mouse button and the text will be deselected. Then you can start over again.

CAUTION

If you begin entering text when other text is selected, the selected text will be deleted and the text you enter will replace it. This is an easy way to replace one word or phrase with another. It also works when you don't want it to—for example, when you forget you still have text selected from a previous action. When you are done working with selected text, then, it is best to click somewhere in the document to turn off the selection.

SECTION 3.5: MOVING AND COPYING TEXT IN WORD

Now that you can comfortably select text, you can move and copy selected text within your document. When you **move** text, the original text is deleted from its location and placed in a new location. You might want to move text to rearrange sentences in a paragraph or paragraphs within a document. **Copying** text leaves the original in place, and creates a copy in the new location. For example, if you have created a short form, you may want to use Copy to print three of them on a page.

Moving Text

You move text by cutting it from its current location and pasting it to its new location. When you **cut** a block of text, it is deleted from your document and moved to the clipboard. The **clipboard** is part of the computer's memory set aside and managed by Windows 95 to hold information temporarily. The clipboard can hold one piece of information at a time.

Information from the clipboard can be **pasted**—copied —into your document. By using the clipboard as a staging area, you can move text from one spot to another.

EXERCISE 3.7   **TO MOVE TEXT USING THE MENU BAR**

1. **Select the text you want to move.** Select the second sentence of *Proposal,* beginning with *We are.*

2. **Open the Edit menu and choose Cut.** The sentence will disappear from the document. In reality, it has been moved to the clipboard.

3. **Move the insertion point to the location where you want the text to appear.** Move the I-beam to the end of the paragraph following *venture.* Be sure to click the insertion point into position.

4. **Open the Edit menu and choose Paste.** The sentence reappears in the new location.

Like other frequently used Word features, cut-and-paste can be accessed from the toolbar as well as the menu bar.

EXERCISE 3.8	TO MOVE TEXT USING THE TOOLBAR

1. **Select the text you want to move.** Select the last sentence in the paragraph (the one you just moved).

2. **Click the Cut button on the toolbar.**

3. **Move the insertion point to where you want the text to appear.** Here, position the insertion point between the first and second sentence (its original location).

4. **Click the Paste button on the toolbar.**

5. So that you can practice more cutting and pasting, save the document before proceeding. (Choose File ➤ Save or click the Save button on the toolbar.)

6. Practice moving other text around in the document using cut-and-paste from the toolbar and from the menu bar.

7. When you are comfortable with cut-and-paste, close the document without saving the most recent changes.

■ Copying Text in Word

Copying text duplicates the text on the clipboard without deleting the original. You can then paste the copied text once, twice, or many times in other locations. The text will only be removed from the clipboard when you cut or copy something else, or you turn off the computer.

EXERCISE 3.9	TO COPY TEXT

For this exercise, open *Proposal*.

1. **Select the text you want to copy.** Here, select the first sentence in the paragraph.

2. **Use Edit ➤ Copy or click the Copy button on the toolbar.** Notice that the original text stays in place. A copy of the sentence has been placed on the clipboard.

3. **Move the insertion point where you want the copy to appear.** Here, place the insertion point at the end of the document.

4. **Choose Edit ➤ Paste or click the Paste button on the toolbar to copy the text to the new location.**

■ Damage Control in Microsoft Word

Word reacts quickly when you ask to have text deleted, cut, copied or pasted. If you make a mistake or if you change your mind after you have made changes to your document, don't worry. Word allows you to undo the steps you've just taken. **Undo** permits you to un-cut, un-delete, or un-paste—to cancel your last action or series of actions. Undo is accessible from both the menu bar and the toolbar.

EXERCISE 3.10	TO UNDO AN ACTION

1. **Choose Edit ➢ Undo or Click the Undo Button on the toolbar.** This will undo the copy you just made of the first sentence in *Proposal*.

If you change your mind about Undo, you can choose **Redo** to "undo the undo." Both the Undo and Redo toolbar buttons have drop-down arrows attached:

The drop-down buttons open Undo and Redo histories. The Undo history is a list of actions that have been done (and can be undone); the Redo history lists actions you have undone that can be redone. If, for example, you cut one sentence, deleted a second sentence, and then deleted a third sentence, your Undo history would look like Figure 3.5. The first action, cutting the sentence, is at the bottom of the list. The most recent action, deleting or clearing a sentence, appears at the top. When you select an action from the Undo history list, the document reverts to its state before the action was taken.

Figure 3.5

An Undo history

If you chose to undo the two deletions, the Redo history would include the two undone actions, as shown in Figure 3.6. Selecting either action from the Redo history will Redo the original action–negating the Undo.

Figure 3.6

An Redo history

EXERCISE 3.11	**UNDOING AND REDOING DELETIONS**

This exercise will let you get the hang of using Undo and Redo.

1. Select the first sentence of *Proposal* and press the Delete key.

2. Select the new first sentence and cut it using the Cut button on the toolbar.

3. Click on the down arrow next to the Undo button on the toolbar to view the history of the actions you have taken.

4. Click on the first action listed, Cut, to restore the sentence that you cut in Step 2.

5. Click on the Undo button to restore the sentence that you deleted in Step 1.

6. Click on the down arrow next to the Redo button to see the actions that you just reversed.

7. Click on the first action listed to reverse the Undo in Step 5.

8. Click on the Undo button again to restore the paragraph to its original form.

Undo is the ultimate "oops" key. Many mistakes can be corrected with just one mouse click on the Undo button.

SECTION 3.6: SAVING YOUR DOCUMENT AS A COPY

There are times you may want to change a document and keep both the revised version and the original version. Windows requires that every document in a specific location (like a floppy disk) has a different name. If you simply save a Word document that has been saved previously, the original version is replaced with the revised version. Use **Save As** to save a document with a new name and leave the unchanged original in place under the old name. You can also use Save As to save a copy of a document to a different drive by changing the Save In location.

Choosing Save As from the File menu opens the Save As dialog box—the same dialog box you saw when you originally saved the file. Specify a different name or location for the file, and then click the Save button to save the renamed copy of your file.

EXERCISE 3.12	**TO SAVE YOUR DOCUMENT AND KEEP THE ORIGINAL**

To distinguish this document from the document that you already have saved on disk, move the insertion point to the top of *Proposal* and type your name.

1. **Click on File ➢ Save As to open the Save As dialog box.**

2. **Enter a document name that is different from the original document.** In this case, enter *Proposal-2* as the file name.

3. **Click Save to save the revised file.**

 Note: If you want to preserve an original document on disk but use the contents to create another document, open it as a read-only copy. From the Open dialog box, select the document, click on the Commands and Settings button on the toolbar and choose Open Read Only. This will allow you to make changes to the document but will require you to save it under a different name.

SECTION 3.7: USING PRINT PREVIEW TO EXAMINE YOUR DOCUMENT

 Word lets you view documents in several ways. Print Preview is used to view and edit documents prior to printing. Print Preview is accessed from the File menu or by clicking the Print Preview button on the toolbar.

The preview window opens with your document displayed in full page view (at about 30–40 percent of printed size), as shown in Figure 3.7.

The Print Preview window has a custom toolbar:

When you point to the document in the preview window, the pointer becomes a magnifier. Notice that the magnifier button on the toolbar is depressed.

To examine a portion of the document more closely, click on the text portion of the document to magnify it. The preview percentage listed on the toolbar will change to 100%. Use the scroll bars at the right and bottom of the preview window to move the document. Clicking again on the document will return the document to full page view. When the document you are viewing is longer than one page, you can view multiple pages simultaneously by clicking the multiple page button. Click the Close button to close Print Preview and return to the standard document window.

Figure 3.7

Previewing a
Document

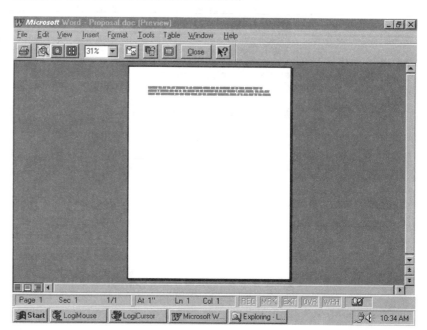

EXERCISE 3.13   **TO PREVIEW YOUR DOCUMENT**

1. Choose File ➢ Print Preview or click the Print Preview button on the Standard Toolbar.

2. Move the pointer to the text portion of the document. The pointer will change to a magnifying glass.

3. Click on the document to magnify it to 100%. Click again to reduce it to full page view.

4. Click Close to exit Print Preview.

Print Preview eliminates the need to print samples of a document simply to see what the final document will look like when printed. This is extremely useful when you share a printer with other users or when your printer is some distance from your computer. Additionally, you'll save a lot of paper using

Print Preview instead of printing draft copies. Five out of six trees surveyed recommend using Print Preview.

Before turning off your computer, please remember to exit Microsoft Word, shut down Windows 95, and take out your floppy disk.

What You Have Learned

In this session, you have learned to open a document that you have saved on disk. You are familiar with the special keys that make up the keyboard. Most importantly, you know several ways to insert and delete text, including how to cut, copy and paste. You have also learned how to use Undo and Redo when you change your mind about actions that you have taken. You now know how to save your document as a copy of your original so you can make changes and still retain your original. Finally, you know how to preview your work before sending it to the printer.

Focus Questions

1. Why might you want to close a file without saving changes?

2. Name two of the special keys on the keyboard and describe what their functions are.

3. Why is it important to know how to select text?

4. How do you select a sentence in Word? A paragraph? A single line?

5. List the steps for moving text from one location to another location using cut and paste on the toolbar.

6. List the steps for copying text from one location to another location using copy and paste on the menu bar.

7. What is the difference between using Save and Save As to save a file?

Reinforcement Exercises

Exercise 1   Write a letter to a government official about a public issue that is important to you. Save this document as *Letter* to *(name of official)*. View your letter in Print Preview. Next session you will learn how to print your documents. Close the document.

Exercise 2   Reopen the letter you wrote in Exercise 1 as a read-only copy. Delete the official's name in the letter and insert the name of another official. Make changes to the letter that are appropriate for that person. Save this document as *Letter to (second official)*.

Exercise 3   Open the document named *Orienteering Trip*. Edit the document as indicated below. Delete words that have a line through them. Insert words that are in italics. When you are finished, save this document as *Orienteering Trip Revised*.

~~Don't forget~~ *Remember* to put the weekend of July 14-16 on your calendar for an exciting Orienteering Weekend sponsored by the Grand Traverse Wilderness Conservancy. We will spend Friday evening and Saturday morning learning all about orienteering ~~before heading out into the woods~~. Saturday afternoon we will head into the woods for some real life experience finding our way with map and compass. You will need to bring a tent, sleeping bag, rain gear, compass, water bottle, and good hiking shoes. Food will be provided. The fee is $35 for the entire weekend. To register call 616-555-5555. Invite your friends to come ~~along~~ with you.

Exercise 4   a) Open the document *My Definitions*. Move the insertion point to the top of the document and type *Sessions 1 and 2*. Press Enter twice to enter a blank line between the heading and the text.

b) Move the insertion point to the end of the document and enter a new heading: **Session 3**. Type your definitions for the following terms: clipboard, copy, cut and paste, select, overtype.

c) Use cut-and-paste to move the terms and their definitions into alphabetical order.

More Editing Techniques for Word

THIS SESSION FOCUSES on advanced techniques for editing documents. In addition to learning more ways to move and copy text, you will find out how to work with more than one document at a time. Checking a document's spelling and printing documents round out this session.

In this session you will learn to:

- Cut, copy and paste using a pop-up menu
- Manipulate text using drag-and-drop
- Move text between documents
- Use the spelling checker to correct document misspellings
- Print documents

■ Vocabulary

- active window
- AutoCorrect
- context-sensitive
- Custom dictionary
- drag-and-drop
- Main dictionary
- pop-up menu
- spin box

SECTION 4.1: MORE ABOUT MOVE AND COPY

Cutting, copying, and pasting are the basic tools used in editing. (They must be, or there wouldn't be so many different ways to cut, copy, and paste.) No matter which method you use, you must always select the text to be cut or copied before performing the cut or copy action.

▩ Move and Copy with the Pop-up Menu

Once you have selected a block of text, clicking the right mouse button once opens a pop-up menu, as shown in Figure 4.1.

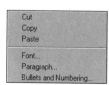

Figure 4.1

A pop-up menu

A **pop-up menu** provides you with choices based on where you are and what you are doing within Word. (Menus like this, which provide you with different choices based on your position and actions, are called **context-sensitive**.) If you have selected some text in the document window, the pop-up menu choices include Cut and Copy. After you cut or copy text, Paste appears as an option on the pop-up. If you right-click while pointing at the toolbar, the menu choices that appear relate to the toolbar.

EXERCISE 4.1   **TO MOVE TEXT USING THE POP-UP MENU**

For this exercise, open the document named *Development*.

1. **Select the text you want to move.** Select the last sentence, which begins with "In order to assure . . . "

2. **Point to the selected text and click the right mouse button to open a pop-up menu.**

3. **Choose Cut.**

4. **Move the insertion point to where you want the text to appear.** For this exercise, click between "Project" in the first and "The Preliminary" in the second sentence.

5. **Right-click and choose Paste from the pop-up menu to insert the text into its new location.**

■ Dragging and Dropping Text

You can move or copy selected text by dragging it to a new location and then dropping it in place. This method, called **drag-and-drop**, works best when you can see both the current text and its new location in the document without scrolling. (**Tip:** If you need to scroll, cutting and pasting with the clipboard is much easier.) Begin by selecting the text you want to move or copy. Move the I-beam back over the selected text so that the I-beam changes to a pointer. Press and hold either mouse button, and the message *Move to where?* will appear in the status bar at the bottom of the document window. The mouse pointer will change to an arrow with a small rectangle below it. Continue to hold the mouse button, and move the pointer to drag the insertion point to the new location for the text. When you release the mouse button, the selected text will drop into its new location.

If you want to *copy* the selected text using drag-and-drop, point to the selected text. Then, press and hold the Ctrl key while holding down the mouse button. The message will change to *Copy to where?* and the mouse pointer will change to an arrow with a plus sign (+) below it. Drag the insertion point to its new location. Release the mouse button *before* you release the Ctrl key, and the text will be copied into the new location. If you release the Ctrl key first, Word assumes you have changed your mind and wish to *move* the text.

EXERCISE 4.2   **TO MOVE AND COPY TEXT USING DRAG-AND-DROP TECHNIQUES**

First try moving text:

1. **Select the text you want to move.** Here, select the first sentence of *Development,* beginning with "After."

2. **Move the mouse pointer to the selected text and hold down either mouse button.**

3. **Move the pointer to drag the insertion point to the *desired location*. Here move to the end of the paragraph.**

4. **Release the mouse button when you can see that the insertion point is in position.** The insertion point should be following the period after "requested."

CONTINUES ON NEXT PAGE

Now try copying text:

1. **Select the sentence you want to copy.** Here, select the sentence that you just moved if it is not still selected.

2. **Move the mouse pointer to the selected text and hold down either mouse button.**

3. **Hold down the Ctrl key and move the pointer to drag the insertion point to the desired location.** In this exercise, drag the insertion point to the beginning of the paragraph.

4. **Release the mouse button when the insertion point is in position.** It should be before "In order to . . . "

5. **Release the Ctrl key.** You now have two copies of the first sentence in the document.

6. Delete the copy of the first sentence at the end of the paragraph.

7. Close the document and save the changes.

Although you have learned four methods of moving and copying text, you do not need to become proficient with all of them right away. Try each method a few times and then practice using the method or methods that work best for you. You'll find that certain methods work best in certain situations. As you become comfortable with one method, add another to your inventory. Tables 4.1 and 4.2 summarize the methods for moving and copying text.

Table 4.1:
Moving and
Copying Text
Using Cut/Copy
and Paste

Moving Using Cut and Paste	Copying Using Copy and Paste
Select the text you want to move.	Select the text you want to copy.
Choose Cut from the Edit menu, pop-up menu, or toolbar.	Choose Copy from the Edit menu, pop-up menu, or toolbar.
Move the insertion point to the new location.	Move the insertion point to the new location.
Choose Paste from the Edit menu, pop-up menu, or toolbar.	Choose Paste from the Edit menu, pop-up menu, or toolbar.

	Moving Using Drag-and-Drop	Copying Using Drag-and-Drop
Table 4.2: Moving and Copying with drag-and-drop	Select the text you want to move.	Select the text you want to copy.
	Point to the text and hold the mouse button.	Point to the text, hold down the mouse button and the Ctrl key.
	Drag the insertion point to its new location.	Drag the insertion point to its new location.
	Release the mouse button to drop the text.	Release the mouse button to drop the copied text, then release the Ctrl key.

SECTION 4.2: WORKING WITH MULTIPLE DOCUMENTS

So far you have been working with one document at a time. When you wanted to work with a different document, you closed the active document first. Word allows you to work with multiple documents simultaneously. This makes it easy to copy or move text from one document to another.

EXERCISE 4.3 | **OPENING MORE THAN ONE DOCUMENT AT A TIME**

To try out the techniques in this section, first open *Proposal-2* and then open *Development* (without closing *Proposal-2*).

Figure 4.2
Open files listed on
the Window menu

Both *Proposal-2* and Development are open, but *Development* is covering *Proposal-2*. All files that are currently open are listed on the Window menu, as shown in Figure 4.2. The active file, *Development*, is checked.

To bring another file to the front and make it active, simply choose it from the Window menu or from the list of recently used files at the bottom of the File menu. You can also press Ctrl+F6 to toggle through the open documents.

If you try to open a document that is already open, by choosing File ➢ Open or clicking the Open button on the toolbar, a message box will appear asking if you want to revert to the saved version of the document:

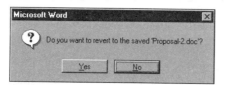

If you answer Yes, Word will close the current copy of the document, discarding any changes you have made, and open the document again from disk. This is another way to close and reopen a document without saving changes. If you answer No, Word ignores your request to open the file.

To view all open documents at the same time, choose Window ➢ Arrange All. Word will tile the document windows horizontally. Each window has its own title bar and scroll bars, as shown in Figure 4.3.

Figure 4.3
Viewing two windows simultaneously

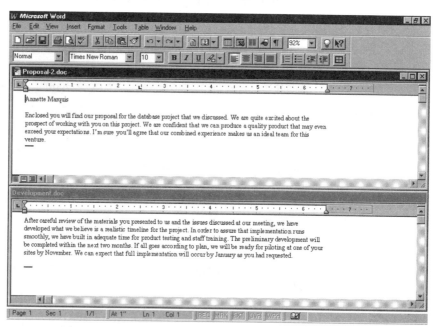

Even though you can view both documents, only one document window is active. The title bar for the **active window** is the same color as the Word application title bar and has minimize, maximize, and close buttons. The active window also contains the cursor. The inactive document window has a gray title bar and lacks window control buttons.

To work in the inactive window, you must activate it first by clicking anywhere in the window. The cursor will move to its last location in the window, and the title bar will become active.

To open two copies of the *same* document, select Window ➤ Split. When you make changes to one copy of the document, the other version changes, too. Being able to view two portions of the same document can be helpful when moving or copying text in a multiple-page document.

Word allows you to have an unlimited number of windows open at a time. (You probably won't want to arrange them all, however, since you will only be able to view a small portion of each window.) The first nine documents will be listed on the Window menu bar. If you have ten or more documents open simultaneously you will have a choice of *More Windows* on the Window menu; this will display a list of the additional open documents.

CAUTION

Opening too many documents at once could cause a drain on your system's resources. If your computer starts slowing down, remember to close the documents that you are finished with.

When you are done using the second document and close its window, the remaining document window will still be tiled. You can maximize the active window to return to work in a full-sized environment.

■ Moving and Copying Text Between Documents

You can use all of the techniques that you already know for moving and copying text *within* a document to move and copy text *between* documents. Select the text that you want to move or copy and choose Cut or Copy from the menu bar, toolbar, or pop-up menu. Activate the document you want to move or copy to. You can either tile the documents by choosing Window ➤ Arrange All or toggling from one document to the other by pressing F6. Position the insertion point in the desired location and choose Paste.

EXERCISE 4.4	TO COPY TEXT BETWEEN DOCUMENT WINDOWS

1. **Click on Window on the menu bar and select the document you want to make active.** Click on *Proposal-2* to bring it forward and make it active.

2. **Choose Window ➢ Arrange All to tile open documents.**

3. **Select the text you want to copy.** For this exercise, click on *Development* and select the entire paragraph. You may have to use the vertical scroll bar to see the text.

4. **Choose Copy from the toolbar.**

5. **Activate the document where you want the copied text to appear.** Click on *Proposal-2* to make it active.

6. **Move the insertion point to the desired position.** Move to the end of the document and press Enter twice to start a new paragraph.

7. **Click on Paste from the toolbar.** This will paste the content of *Development* into *Proposal-2.* In the rest of this exercise, you'll turn this combined document into a business letter.

8. Click on *Development* once again and close it without saving the changes.

9. Click on *Proposal-2* and click the Maximize button to maximize the *Proposal-2* document window.

10. Select the line with your name on it and delete it.

11. Press Enter twice and enter the following recipient's address:

    Mr. David Kepley

    Henry Ford Behavioral Services

    2799 W. Grand Blvd.

    Detroit, MI 48202

12. Press Enter twice and type Dear Mr. Kepley: Move the insertion point to the end of the letter, press Enter twice and type Sincerely,

13. Press Enter three times and type your name.

14. Choose File ➢ Print Preview to see how the completed letter will appear when printed. Close Print Preview.

15. Save the letter as *Proposal Letter.*

SECTION 4.3: USING SPELL-CHECK

Of the many new features in Word for Windows 95, the improved tools to check spelling may be the most impressive. Word includes a **Main dictionary** of tens of thousands of terms. You can add other words you frequently use to a **Custom dictionary**. You can correct spelling on the fly with the automatic spell-checking feature. In addition, Word will correct some common typing errors automatically with its AutoCorrect feature.

CAUTION

Automatic spell-checking uses a lot of the computer's resources. If there is not at least 8 MB of memory installed on the computer, automatic spell-checking will make Word less responsive. Word will run faster if the feature is turned off.

For this session, make sure automatic spell-checking is turned on:

1. Choose Tools ➤ Options; then click the Spelling tab.

2. Make sure the Automatic Spell Checking box is checked:

A Word about AutoCorrect

Word's **AutoCorrect** feature uses a list of commonly mistyped words to correct common typing mistakes. If, for example, you type *teh*, Word will automatically correct it to *the*; likewise, *adn* will be changed to *and*. This can be a bit disconcerting at first, especially if you are already backspacing to correct the mistyped word when Word corrects it for you. Once you get used to AutoCorrect, however, you will save time that you would have spent fixing common mistakes. In Session 11, you will learn how to add entries to the list so that other words you frequently mistype will be corrected automatically.

Is the Spelling Tool Always "Right"?

When you finish typing a word, Word automatically checks to see if the word is included in the Main or Custom dictionaries. If the word is not in either dictionary, Word flags it with a red wavy underline: Stefan Johnson and places a red "X" on the book icon on the status bar to remind you that there are questionable words in your document.

Just because a word is underlined doesn't mean it is incorrect. The Main dictionary doesn't include proper names or many terms that are jargon or specific to a particular field. For example, many computer, medical, and legal terms are not included in the Word dictionary.

On the other hand, just because a word *isn't* underlined doesn't make it correct. If a word is used incorrectly (like *there* instead of *their*), Word won't flag it. If you mean to type *from* and type *form*, don't look for a wavy underline; *form* is in the dictionary. Spell-checking, then, is not a substitute for proofreading. It's a tool to help eliminate some types of mistakes prior to proofing a document.

■ Checking Spelling on the Fly

To check a word that has been flagged with a wavy underline, move the I-beam anywhere in the word. Click the right mouse button to open the pop-up menu:

If the word is spelled correctly, you need to decide whether to add it to your custom dictionary. If it is a word you use frequently (like your first name, last name, or place of employment) choose Add from the menu to add the word to your Custom dictionary. A word you use infrequently (like a name that you will only use in this document) probably shouldn't be added to the dictionary but should instead be ignored. Choose Ignore All and the word won't be flagged again in this document.

If the word is spelled incorrectly, see whether the correct spelling appears on the pop-up menu. If it does, select it and Word will replace the incorrect word with the correct version. If the correct spelling does not appear on the pop-up menu, just click back on the word and correct the word manually.

EXERCISE 4.5	TO CORRECT A SINGLE MISSPELLED WORD

1. Right-click on a word with a wavy red line underneath it. In this exercise, right-click on "Kepley" in *Proposal Letter*.

2. Select the correct spelling from the list or choose to ignore it or add it to your custom dictionary. Since "Kepley" is a proper name it will not be in Word's dictionary. If this was a person that you wrote often, you could add "Kepley" to your custom dictionary. For now, choose Ignore All to ignore all occurrences of the name in this letter. This will close the pop-up menu.

When a word is flagged, you can choose whether or not to take immediate action. If you prefer, you can wait until you have reached the end of the document, and then check the spelling.

To check each of the flagged words in a document, begin by moving to the beginning of the document. Then double-click on the book icon on the status bar to move to the first flagged word. Correct the word, and then double-click to move to the next word. Continue until you reach the end of the document. If you double-click on the book icon and all the words are spelled correctly, you will receive the message *Spell checking is complete.*

EXERCISE 4.6   **TO CORRECT ALL FLAGGED WORDS**

For this exercise, place the insertion point after "requested" in the last paragraph of *Proposal Letter* and press Enter twice. Type the following text exactly as it appears, misspelled words and all:

We will be in tooch with you at the beginning of next weeek to to arrange for information gathering meetings wtih your staff. Feel free to call if you have an questions about the enclosed materials.

Save the document as *Proposal Letter with Errors*. You will be using it later to check your spelling a different way.

1. Double-click the book icon to go to the first flagged word. If you have no other misspelled words in the document, that word will be *tooch.*

2. Choose the correct word from the drop-down list.

3. Continue double-clicking the book icon until you have corrected all the misspelled words and you receive the *Spell checking is complete* message. Notice that the word "to" is flagged because it is a repeated word, not because it is misspelled.

CONTINUES ON NEXT PAGE

4. Reread the last paragraph. Even though Word has corrected all of the misspelled words it could find, you still have one incorrect word. Click on *an* in the last sentence and change it to *any*.

5. Resave your corrected document as *Proposal Letter*.

6. Close *Proposal Letter*.

Your letter should now look like Figure 4.4.

Figure 4.4
The finished
Proposal Letter
document

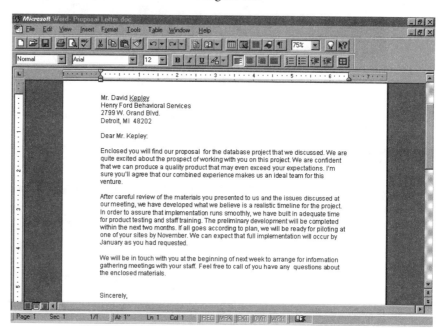

■ Spell-Checking an Entire Document

The Spelling tool can be used at any time to review and correct spelling throughout the entire document. If you have disabled Automatic Spell Check to conserve system resources, this tool becomes the only option for correcting spelling.

 To begin checking the document, choose Tools ➤ Spelling from the menu, click the Spelling button on the toolbar, or move to a misspelled word, right-click and choose Spelling from the pop-up menu.

Word will work through the document, checking each word against the Main and Custom dictionaries. When it finds a word that isn't recognized by Word from either dictionary, the Spelling dialog box will open. The unrecognized word is highlighted in the document and shown in the Not in Dictionary text box, as shown in Figure 4.5.

Figure 4.5
The Spelling
dialog box

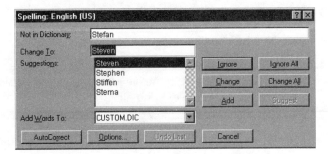

A list of Suggestions appears below the text box. One of the suggested words is shown in the Change To control. If the word is correct or the correct word appears in the Suggestions, you can:

■ Ignore this occurrence of the word;

■ Ignore All occurrences of the word;

■ replace this occurrence of the unrecognized word with the Change To word by clicking the Change button;

■ replace all occurrences of the unrecognized word with the Change To word by clicking the Change All button;

■ change to another word on the Suggestions list by clicking once on the word before choosing Change or Change All; or

■ Add the unrecognized word to your custom dictionary.

If the word is incorrect and the correct spelling doesn't appear in the suggestions, edit the word in the Change To control, then click the Change or Change All button to change one or all occurrences of the word in your document. A dialog box asks if you want to use this word. Make sure the word is spelled correctly and choose Yes.

To check the spelling on just part of a document, select the portion you want to check before choosing Tools or clicking the Spelling button.

EXERCISE 4.7	TO USE THE SPELLING TOOL

Reopen *Proposal Letter with Errors*. It should be listed on the File menu as a recently used file.

1. **Click the Spelling button on the toolbar to start spell-checking.**

2. **Correct each misspelled word.**

3. **Click OK when Spelling has completely checked the document.**

4. Choose File ➢ Save As to save this document as *Proposal Letter*. Click on the document name in the file list in the Save As dialog box and say Yes to replacing the existing file.

Now that you have finished checking your spelling, it's time to print the document.

SECTION 4.4: PRINTING DOCUMENTS

Choosing File ➢ Print opens the Print dialog box, shown in Figure 4.6. The Print dialog box allows you to specify how the print job should be completed. While you won't be changing any of the default settings at this time, you will be viewing the settings for later use.

Figure 4.6

The Print dialog box

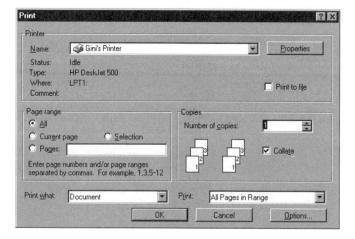

■ Setting Print Parameters

The printer listed in the Name control is the default printer established in Windows' Printer Settings. Clicking the down arrow in the Name control opens a drop-down list of printers and print devices installed on your computer. In Figure 4.7, the list includes some fax/modem devices like FaxWorks that are not printers in the traditional sense. Select the printer you want to use for this document from the drop-down list.

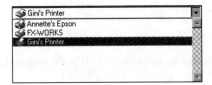

Figure 4.7

The Printer

drop-down list

The default Page Range setting is All, allowing you to print a document in its entirety. Use the option buttons to print only the current page, a previously selected block of text, or specific pages of a document.

The Number of Copies control has a default setting of 1. If you need to print more than one copy select or type the desired number and make sure the Collate box is checked.

The Print What drop-down control allows you to print supplemental document information instead of the document itself. The control has three settings: All Pages, Odd Pages, and Even pages. All Pages is the default.

Odd and Even pages are used when a document (like a thesis or long report) will be printed on both sides of the page and bound. You can print all the odd pages, turn the printed sheets over and put them back in the printer to print the even pages.

Clicking the Print button sends the document to the selected printer and closes the Print dialog box.

■ One-Step Printing in Word

The Print button on the toolbar sends a document to the printer using the current printer settings. No dialog box will be displayed. Once you have established the printer settings, clicking the Print button is the fastest way to print a document. If you share a computer with other users, it is a good idea to check the print settings before printing the first time in a work session.

EXERCISE 4.8   **TO PRINT A DOCUMENT**

Open your *Proposal Letter* if it is not already open.

1. **Choose File ➤ Print to open the Print dialog box.**

2. **Click the down arrow next to the printer name to see the printers available to you.** For now, click again to close the drop-down list without changing the selected printer.

3. **Set the desired Page Range.** Here, select All.

4. **Indicate the number of copies.** Keep this set on 1.

5. **Indicate what part of the document you want to print in the Print What control.** See that Document is selected.

6. **Select what pages you want to print in the Print control: All Pages in Range, Odd Pages, or Even Pages.** Here, select All Pages in Range.

7. **Click OK when all settings are correct to print the document.**

What You Have Learned

You have now learned several ways to move and copy text. Glance back at Tables 4.1 and 4.2 for summaries of the Cut/Copy-and-Paste and drag-and-drop methods. You can also move and copy text between documents by working with several document windows at once. You also know several ways to spell check your documents and are familiar with the ways that Word checks your spelling automatically. Finally you know how to check your print settings and print your document.

Focus Questions

1. What is a context-sensitive menu?

2. When does the drag-and-drop method of moving or copying text work best?

3. When you are viewing two document windows simultaneously, how can you tell which one is the active window?

4. List the steps to copying text between documents using copy and paste.

5. What does the red, wavy line that appears under some text mean?

6. How can you use the book icon on the status bar to check your spelling?

Reinforcement Exercises

Exercise 1   Write a one-page letter to a friend or business associate. Practice using all of the editing methods that you have used so far to improve your letter. Use the Spelling tool to check your letter for misspellings. Save your letter to disk giving it a meaningful name. Preview your letter before printing it.

Exercise 2   If you completed Reinforcement Exercise 2 in Session 3, open the two letters that you wrote to government officials. Check the spelling in each letter and then print them.

Exercise 3   Open the two documents named *Orienteering Trip—Revised* and *Orienteering Instructor*. Copy the contents of *Orienteering Instructor* into *Orienteering Trip*. Edit the new document so that it reads well. You can add or delete text and move sentences around until you like the way it sounds. Use Spelling to correct your misspellings. Save your new document as *Orienteering Trip Information*. Print the document when you are finished. Close *Orienteering Instructor* without saving the changes.

Exercise 4   a) Open a new document. Type the heading **Session 4**. Enter your definitions for the following terms: *context-sensitive, drag-and-drop, pop-up menu, active window, custom dictionary*. Save this document as *Session 4 Definitions*.

b) Open *My Definitions*. Copy all the text in *Session 4 Definitions* to the end of *My Definitions*. Use cut-and-paste to move these new terms into alphabetical order.

c) Correct the spelling. Save and close *My Definitions*. Close *Session 4 Definitions* without saving changes.

PART II

Formatting Documents Using Word

Enhancing Document Text

Vocabulary

- align
- bold
- center
- face (typeface)
- font
- font style
- format
- highlight
- italics
- justify
- point
- printer font
- scalable
- screen font
- serif
- size
- TrueType font
- typeface (face)
- underline

WHILE BEING ABLE to edit documents is an essential word processing skill, learning to enhance documents with special fonts, colors, and graphic lines separates the casual user from the expert. This session focuses on tools to spice up your text. In this session you will learn to:

- Use fonts to format characters
- Change the color of text
- Set the default font
- Highlight text to add emphasis
- Copy formats using the Format Painter
- Align document text
- Add horizontal lines to your document

SECTION 5.1: FORMATTING TEXT

Formatting is changing the appearance of part or all of your document. In this session, you will learn how to format characters and begin formatting lines of text in Word. You will want to have the Formatting toolbar (see Figure 5.1) displayed for your work in this session.

Figure 5.1
the Formatting
toolbar

If the formatting toolbar is not visible, follow these steps to show the toolbar:

1. Point to the standard toolbar and right-click to bring up the list of available toolbars. You can also choose View ➤ Toolbars.

2. Select Formatting from the list to make it visible.

SECTION 5.2: FONT BASICS

A **font** is a specification for how text will appear on the screen and in a printed document. Fonts have three attributes: typeface, also known simply as face; size; and style.

A **face** is a set of characters that share a common design. Although typeface is only one of a font's attributes, the term font is also widely used to refer to typeface alone. Figure 5.2 illustrates various typefaces or fonts.

Figure 5.2
Examples of
commonly used
typefaces

> ALGERIAN
> Arial
> Brush Script MT
> Courier New
> Footlight MT Light
> Times New Roman
> ✢✄■℣♎✄■℣♦ (Wingdings)

■ Typefaces

Typefaces are classified in several ways. The first distinction is between faces that have small, decorative flares, called serifs, and faces without serifs. Courier New, Footlight MT Light, and Times New Roman are <u>serif</u> typefaces. (The serifs are easy to see on the uppercase N.) Arial is a <u>sans-serif</u> (*sans* is French for "without") typeface.

A second classification system separates fonts based on appropriate use. Fonts like Times New Roman and Arial that can be read easily in large blocks are called **text fonts** or **type fonts**. While the serif fonts are, generally, easier to read, there are also many sans-serif text fonts. Fonts that are attention grabbing but hard to read in blocks, like Brush Script MT and Algerian, are called <u>display fonts</u>. Symbol fonts like Wingdings are used to create special characters rather than the letters of the alphabet.

A third distinction is between <u>monospaced and proportionally</u> spaced fonts. In a monospaced font, like Courier New, every character is allocated the same amount of space, whether it needs it or not. Since the letter *w* and the letter *i* are given the same amount of space, a lot of white space separates the letter *i* from the characters before and after it. In proportionally spaced fonts (for example, Times New Roman and the fonts in this book), the characters are given different widths, so that the spacing between them appears to be equal.

Finally, fonts are described as <u>screen fonts, printer fonts, or TrueType fonts</u>, according to how the appearance on screen relates to the appearance when printed. **Printer fonts** (see Figure 5.2) are available on your printer, but no matching font exists for display on your screen. Word will substitute another font for your screen display when you are working in a printer font. This means the printed copy won't necessarily look like the screen display. <u>Screen fonts</u> don't have a corresponding printer font. Again, the hard copy may not resemble the document you see on the screen, since Word has to substitute a printer font for the screen font. **TrueType fonts** are generated for both the printer and the screen, so "what you see (on screen) is what you get (on your printout)." Because of this, TrueType fonts are also known as WYSIWYG (pronounced "wizzy-wig") fonts.

Not all fonts are created equal, and there is nothing that labels a font as "Easy to read: use for text." In general, serif fonts are easier to read than sans serif fonts. The serifs guide the reader's eye along the text. Proportionally spaced fonts are easier to read than monospaced fonts. When in doubt choose the Word default font, Times New Roman, a proportionally spaced serif TrueType font.

When you change any of the font attributes, the new font is applied to future text as you enter it. If you want to change the font for existing text, first select the text.

EXERCISE 5.1   **TO CHANGE A FONT USING THE FORMATTING TOOLBAR**

1. **Select the text whose font you want to change.** In this exercise, open *Proposal Letter* and select the entire document. (Move the pointer to the left margin, press and hold Ctrl, and click; or choose Edit ➤ Select All.)

2. **Choose a new font from the drop-down font list.** Click on the down arrow next to the font name (it probably says New Times Roman) to bring up a list of fonts:

Use the scroll bar to find Arial or Courier New. Click on the font name. The entire document is now using the new font.

Font Sizes

The size of a font is measured in points, the measuring system traditionally used by typesetters. One **point** is 1/72 inch. Most text you read in a newspaper, book, or magazine will be 10 to 12 points in size. That translates to characters that are 1/7 to 1/6 inch high. Headlines range upwards from 14 points. If you want your title to be twice the size of your 12-point text, you would use 24-point type. See Figure 5.3 for examples of font sizes.

Figure 5.3

Font sizes

```
This is 8 point
This is 10 point
This is 12 point
This is 14 point
This is 16 point
This is 18 point
This is 24 point
```

The actual size of an individual character depends on its typeface as well as its point size. If you compare text in one face to text that's the same size in another face, you may find a great deal of variation in size and readability. In some typefaces, a text sized to 10-point is illegible; in others, 10-point is very large and easy to read. As a result, sizes between fonts can't really be compared. You can, however, compare sizes within a font.

Most fonts are fully **scalable**. You can change font sizes by selecting a new size from the drop-down list in the size control on the Formatting toolbar. If the size you want isn't listed, type the size you would like. For example, though 13 point isn't normally listed, you can enter 13 for a 13-point font.

EXERCISE 5.2   **TO CHANGE FONT SIZE**

1. **Select the text you want to resize.** For this example, select all of *Proposal Letter*.

2. **Display the drop-down font size list.** Click on the down arrow next to the font size to bring up a drop-down list of font sizes.

3. **Choose a new size.** Click on 12 (choose 10 if 12 is the current size).

4. **Resave your document.**

■ Font Style

Font Style (see Figure 5.4) refers to the emphasis placed on text. Bold, Underline, and Italics are all styles (as is Normal or unemphasized text). **Bold** text is heavier than normal text. **Italic** characters seem to lean to the right. The Formatting toolbar includes buttons to apply all three font styles individually or in combination.

To turn the styles off, click the buttons on the toolbar again. If these buttons are depressed (pushed in), then that style has been applied to the text where the insertion point is.

Figure 5.4
Examples of
font styles

```
This is normal Courier New text.
This is bold Courier New text.
This is italicized Courier New text.
This is bold, italicized Courier New text.
```

EXERCISE 5.3	TO BOLD, UNDERLINE, AND ITALICIZE TEXT

For this exercise, you first need to create some text to work on. Open a new document (choose File ➢ New ➢ Blank Document ➢ OK), Change the font to Arial 16 pt, and type the following text:

Proposal for Outpatient Database

Executive Summary

Change the font to Times New Roman 14 pt. and click the Bold button on the toolbar. Now, type the following heading:

Database Description

Turn off Bold by clicking it again. Switch to 12 pt and type the following paragraph:

The outpatient database (OPD), written in Microsoft Access for Windows 95, will enable Behavioral Services staff to track, maintain, and report individual and summary information on ambulatory patients. The OPD will provide Behavioral Services with vital information on patients that is currently unobtainable except through labor-intensive manual systems. The OPD will be a well-designed database system that will be easy to use for physicians and support staff alike.

Now you can apply additional font styles to the text you've already entered. Here are the steps:

1. **Select the text whose font style you want to change.** In this example, select the heading "Database Description".

2. **Click the buttons for the style you want to apply.** Here, click the italics button on the toolbar. The following steps provide further practice.

3. Select "Access for Windows 95" in the first sentence.

4. Click the Italics button on the toolbar.

5. Select "easy to use" in the last sentence.

6. Click the Underline button on the toolbar.

7. Save your document as **Executive Summary.** Your document should look like this:

> ## Proposal for Outpatient Database
> ## Executive Summary
>
> ### *Database Description*
> The outpatient database (OPD), written in Microsoft *Access for Windows 95*, will enable Behavioral Services staff to track, maintain, and report individual and summary information on ambulatory patients. The OPD will provide Behavioral Services with vital information on patients that is currently unobtainable except through labor-intensive manual systems. The OPD will be a well-designed database system that will be <u>easy to use</u> for physicians and support staff alike.

■ Font Attributes and the Font Dialog Box

The most accurate description of a font includes all of its attributes. A font's style is assumed to be normal unless otherwise stated. Examples of font descriptions include:

- Times New Roman 12 point Bold

- Arial 14 point

- Courier 36 point Bold Italic

The Font dialog box, shown in Figure 5.5, allows you to change all the attributes of a font at the same time—one-stop font shopping. The Font dialog box provides formatting options that are not available from the toolbar. The dialog box also allows you to view the list of fonts installed on your computer by kind. Printer fonts have a printer icon. Screen fonts have no icon. TrueType fonts—the fonts of choice for all Windows users—have the TrueType icon.

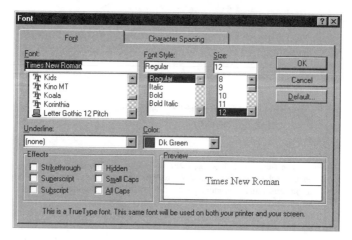

Figure 5.5

The Fonts

dialog box

Clicking once on the name, size, or style of a font displays the font in the Preview control so you can see what it will look like. A description of the font appears at the bottom of the dialog box (see Figure 5.5).

Underline Styles and Special Effects

When you click the Underline button on the toolbar, the default underline style, a single continuous underline, is applied to new or selected text. You can use the Underline drop-down list to select from three other underline styles: *Words Only*, which doesn't underline spaces, *Double*, which applies a double underline to the selected text, or *Dotted*, which underlines each letter and none of the spaces between words. Figure 5.6 contains examples of the four methods of underlining.

Figure 5.6

Examples of

Underlining

Styles

> This is an example of Single underlining.
>
> This is an example of Words Only underlining.
>
> This is an example of Double underlining.
>
> This is an example of Dotted underlining.

The check boxes in the Effects control apply special effects to the fonts. Strikethrough is often used to show proposed deletions to a contract, proposal, or set of bylaws. Superscript and Subscript are used for formulas and notations: $e=mc^2$ or H_2O. Hidden hides the selected text, both on the screen and when it is printed. This can be used to hide notes about a document from other users. Small Caps uses smaller versions of the uppercase letters in place of lower case characters. All Caps converts any lowercase text in the selection to uppercase.

Font Color

The Font dialog box also includes a control for color. The default color is Auto—the default color for text in Windows, usually black. You can specify one of sixteen colors for text (including black). If you have a color printer, the text will be printed as it appears on the screen. If you print to a non-color printer, the text will appear in shades of gray, similar in intensity to the color of your text.

EXERCISE 5.4   **TO CHANGE FONTS USING THE FONT DIALOG BOX**

For this exercise, open *Executive Summary*.

1. **Select the text whose font you want to change.** Select the two lines of the heading.

2. **Choose Format ➢ Font to open the Font dialog box.**

3. **Preview fonts until you find one that meets your needs.** Scroll down the list of fonts and select several to see how they affect the text in the Preview box.

4. **Choose different font styles, font sizes, underlining, colors and effects until you find a combination that appeals to you.**

5. **Click OK to see how your changes affect the document.** Take the following steps for further practice with the Font dialog box.

6. Select "Database Description".

7. Open the Font dialog box (Format ➢ Font).

8. Choose font settings that appeal to you for the subheading.

9. Click OK when you've made your selections.

CONTINUES ON NEXT PAGE

10. Select the paragraph of text.

11. Open the Font dialog box and change the font for the main text.

12. Click OK when you are satisfied with your new settings.

13. Save the changes.

The display on the Formatting toolbar always reflects the settings at the cursor's location. For example, in this toolbar you can see that the insertion point is located in text that is Courier New 14 point, bold and italic:

Anytime you're wondering what font, size, or weight you've used for a block of text, move the insertion point into the text and "read" the information from the toolbar.

EXERCISE 5.5	TO VIEW FONT ATTRIBUTES IN A DOCUMENT

1. **Select the text whose attributes you want to view.** For this exercise, click on the heading in *Executive Summary*.

2. **Notice the font and font size on the Formatting toolbar. Also notice whether Bold, Italics and Underline are turned on or off.**

3. For further practice, click on the subheading and the paragraph text. See how the font settings change.

■ Setting the Default Font

Times New Roman/10 point normal is Word's default font. When you create a new document and begin typing text, the text will appear in this font unless you select a different one. If you find that you are always changing to another font, Word will allow you to change the default font for new documents.

EXERCISE 5.6	**TO CHANGE THE DEFAULT FONT**

1. **Open the Font dialog box (Format ➢ Font).**

2. **Select a font to use as the default.** For this exercise, choose Arial, Regular, 12 point.

3. **Click the Default button. Word will ask you if you want to change the default font to the font that you selected.**

4. **Click Yes.**

5. For practice, open a new document (File ➢ New ➢ OK)

6. Look at the Formatting toolbar to see that your new default font is Arial, Regular, 12 point.

7. Repeat steps 1–4 to change the default font back to the original default font (probably New Times Roman, Regular, 10 point) if you are working on a computer that you share with other people.

SECTION 5.3: USING HIGHLIGHTING TO ADD EMPHASIS

If bold, italics, underline, different typefaces and different sizes don't provide a sufficient toolbox for text emphasis, just wait. There's more. Word for Windows 95 also provides a highlighter. It works just like the highlighter pens they sell in office supply stores, but with a major improvement: one highlighter contains four colors.

To use the Highlight feature, click on the Highlight button. The mouse pointer changes to an I-beam with a pen attached. Highlight will be applied to any text that you select. If you don't like the default yellow highlighting, click the drop-down control attached to the Highlight button. Choose another color (pink, blue, or green) to apply that color to selected text. To remove highlighting from text, select the text and then choose None as the color.

You can also highlight text just as you would add any other enhancement. First, select the text to be highlighted. Then, click on the Highlight button on the toolbar to highlight the text. However, selected text does not stay selected after you highlight it.

EXERCISE 5.7	TO HIGHLIGHT TEXT IN A DOCUMENT

1. Click the Highlight button to turn highlighting on.

2. Select the text you want to highlight. Here, select the first sentence of *Executive Summary.* The text will be automatically highlighted.

3. For further practice, click on the drop-down control attached to the Highlight button and choose another color.

4. Select the first sentence again to change the highlight color.

5. Select all of the highlighted text and choose None from the drop-down list to turn off highlighting.

If you print documents on a color printer, the highlight will appear in the color shown on the screen. If the printer you use does not print in color, the highlight will appear as a gray background.

SECTION 5.4: PAINTING FORMATS ON OTHER TEXT

You may want to apply the same formatting to several blocks of text in a document. For example, you may want all your headings in Courier New 16 point Bold. You could go to each heading, select the text, choose Format ➢ Font from the menu bar, change the font, size, and style and then apply the changes—to ten headings. If you think this is inefficient, you're right. Word provides more efficient ways to format text: one of the simplest is the Format Painter.

Once you have formatted one heading as you want all the headings to appear, move the insertion point into the formatted area. Double-clicking the Format Painter button in the Standard toolbar copies into memory the format in effect at the insertion point. The cursor changes to an I-beam with a paintbrush attached. You can then either drag or click to select the next heading and "paint" the copied format onto the selected heading. When you have painted the format on all the headings, clicking on the Format Painter button turns the Format Painter off. (If you begin painting by single-clicking on the Format Painter button, the Painter will turn off after you have used it once.)

You can also accomplish the reformatting mission in another way. Use the Font dialog box to format one section of text. Once you have formatted your initial selection, select the next section you want formatted the same way.

Choose Edit ➤ Repeat Font Formatting from the menu bar to copy the format to the selected text.

EXERCISE 5.8 **TO PAINT A FORMAT ONTO EXISTING TEXT**

1. **Select a block of text whose formatting you want to copy.** Here, select the first heading in *Executive Summary,* "Proposal for Outpatient Database," and change the font, font style, and font size.

2. **Double-click the Format Painter button on the Standard toolbar.**

3. **Select a block of text where you want to apply the formatting.** Here, select the heading, "Database Description." **The new formatting will be applied to this line.**

4. **Click on the Format Painter button again to turn Format Painter off.**

5. For this exercise, close the document without saving the changes.

SECTION 5.5: ALIGNING TEXT

Fonts are used to format characters. Alignment is used to format paragraphs of text, including single-line paragraphs such as titles. A paragraph can be **aligned** (lined up) with the left, center, or right edge of documents (see Figure 5.7). Text can also be justified. **Justification**, also called full alignment, is the alignment style used in newspaper columns.

Figure 5.7

Examples of text alignment

```
This paragraph of text is left-aligned. Left alignment leaves a
ragged right edge, making it the alignment of choice for text
that has to be read aloud or will be read by people at lower
reading levels. The ragged edge helps the reader keep his or her
place in the text. Book designers sometimes prefer left alignment
over full justification simply because it avoids spacing problems
and reduces the need for hyphenation.

                  Centering is often used for titles.

                       Right-aligned text is also used for titles.

Full justification is used extensively in newspaper or magazine
text that is laid out in columns. The consistent left and right
margins help the reader clearly distinguish where one column ends
and another begins. However, justification sometimes creates
lines with too much or too little space between words.
```

Alignment can easily be applied from the Formatting toolbar. The four alignment buttons are grouped together in the center of the toolbar:

Align left is the default alignment; when you create a new document the text you enter lines up at the left margin. To change the alignment for a block of text, first select the text. Then, click the Center, Align Right, or Justify button to align the text.

EXERCISE 5.9 | **TO ALIGN TEXT IN A DOCUMENT**

1. **Select the text you want to realign.** Here, select the two lines of the main heading of *Executive Summary*.

2. **Click the appropriate alignment button on the formatting toolbar.** Here, click Center.

3. For more practice, select the subheading and the paragraph text.

4. Click on the Justify button to fully align the document.

5. Save the changes.

SECTION 5.6: USING HORIZONTAL LINES FOR ADDED EMPHASIS

Word makes it easy to add horizontal lines to documents. To add a single horizontal line at the insertion point, type the hyphen (-) three times, and then press Enter. Word will convert the three hyphens to a single horizontal line stretching to the right margin. Type three equal signs (=) rather than hyphens to create a double line.

EXERCISE 5.10   **TO ADD A HORIZONTAL LINE**

1. **Place the insertion point where you want the line to appear.** Here, move the insertion point to the beginning of *Executive Summary*.

2. *Type three hyphens (-) for a single line or three equal signs (=) for a double line, and a press Enter.*

3. Move the insertion point to the space between the two heading rows and the subheading.

4. Type three equal signs and press Enter to create a double line below the heading.

5. Save the changes.

What You Have Learned

In this session you have learned to spruce up text using different fonts and font styles. You have also learned how to use Highlight to add emphasis to your text and use the Format Painter to copy text formatting to other text. You are able to right, center, left align or justify text. Finally, you can now add simple horizontal lines to documents with just a couple of keystrokes.

Focus Questions

1. What are the four ways to classify typefaces? Give examples of each.

2. What is a TrueType font?

3. What does it mean to say that a font is scalable?

4. When would it be advantageous to change the default font?

5. What is the purpose of the Format Painter?

6. What are four ways that text can be aligned?

Reinforcement Exercises

Exercise 1   Create a short announcement for an event that you are involved with. Use all of your editing and text enhancement skills to make it attractive and engaging. Don't forget to check the spelling before saving and printing it.

Exercise 2   Make a list of three goals you have for the upcoming year. These can be personal or work/school related. Write a brief paragraph underneath each goal that describes how you plan to accomplish it and why it is important to you. Center a heading that says My Goals for (insert year). Change the font attributes of the three goal statements and the heading to make them stand out from the rest of the text. Check the spelling before saving and printing the document.

Exercise 3   Open the *Orienteering Trip Information* file. Add a centered heading that reads Orienteering Weekend. Choose an exciting display font that catches the eye. Change the font, font size, font attributes and colors in the text so it is easy and fun to read. Emphasize important text with different font attributes. Experiment with different text alignments. Add horizontal lines where appropriate. Save the changes. Print your document if you like.

Exercise 4   a) Open a new document. Type the heading Session 5 and enter your definitions for the following terms: *align, typeface, justify, scalable, format.* Save this as *Session 5 Terms.*

b) Open My *Definitions.* Cut and paste all of the text in *Session 5 Terms* to the end of *My Definitions.* Put the terms in alphabetical order.

c) Insert Word Processing Definitions as a heading at the top of the page. Put your name on a second line of the heading. Center the heading and change its font attributes. Add a horizontal line underneath the heading.

d) Correct the spelling. Save and print *My Definitions.* Close both documents without saving changes to *Session 5 Terms.*

Inserting Dates and Working with Indenting

Vocabulary

- dual indent
- field
- first-line indent
- first-line indent marker
- formats
- hanging indent
- hard return
- indent
- leader
- left indent
- left indent marker
- right indent marker
- right indent
- ruler bar
- paragraph formatting
- spin box
- tab stops

N THIS SESSION, you are going to learn about inserting dates and times into documents and formatting paragraphs through the use of tabs and indents. Tabs and indents allow you to position text so that it is not all lined up against the left margin. Using tabs and indents effectively creates interest for the reader, makes text easier to read, and adds graphic appeal to the documents you create. At the end of this session you will be able to:

- Insert the current date and time in documents
- View the ruler bar
- Use the preset tabs
- Clear and set tabs in Word
- Indent paragraphs of text using the ruler bar
- Use special indents

SECTION 6.1: INSERTING DATES AND TIMES

Word lets you insert dates and times in your document quickly and easily. To insert either date or time, begin by choosing Insert ➤ Date and Time from the menu bar. The Date and Time dialog box (see Figure 6.1) will open.

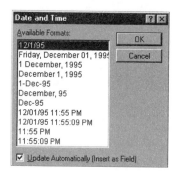

Figure 6.1

The Date and Time dialog box

Eleven date and time **formats** (appearances) are listed in the dialog box, including:

- Short date (8/29/95)

- Day and date (Tuesday, August 29, 1995)

- Long date (August 29, 1995)

- Time (11:51 PM)

- Date and time (08/29/95 11:51 PM)

Word gets the current date and time from your computer's system clock. The date and time will be inserted in your document using the format you select from the list.

Note: If the system clock is wrong, the dates and times that appear in the Date and Time dialog box (and in your document) will also be incorrect. If you need to adjust the system clock, you must do so in Windows. Double-click the time on the Windows taskbar to open the Windows 95 Date/Time Properties dialog box.

Below the list is a check box that allows you to have Word update the date automatically each time the document is opened or printed. Rather than insert the current date in your document, Word will insert a **field** that serves as a placeholder for the date or time. Each time the document is opened, the actual date is substituted for the placeholder.

EXERCISE 6.1   **TO INSERT DATE AND TIME AS UPDATABLE FIELDS**

1. **Place the insertion point where you want the date and time to appear.** For this exercise, open your document named *Proposal Letter*, and press Enter twice to insert two blank lines at the beginning of the document.

2. **Choose Insert ➢ Date and Time from the menu bar to open the Date and Time dialog box.**

3. **Click the Update Automatically (Insert as Field) check box at the bottom of the dialog box.**

4. **Select a date format and click OK.** For this exercise, choose the eighth option (00/00/00 00:00 ?M).

The date displayed in your document is today's date; the time is the current time. If you open *Proposal Letter* again tomorrow, the date field will be updated and tomorrow's date and time will be displayed. Having the date automatically updated works well for documents that are sent on a regular basis—memos, cover letters, or invitations to monthly events. You need to remember, though, that when Update Automatically is selected the date changes each time you open the document. You can't, therefore, return to a document and check the date to see when it was printed or changed.

For many dated documents, you will want a record of the document's actual date, not the current date. To insert the current date and time in a form that won't be updated automatically, click the check box in the Insert Date and Time dialog box to turn off updating before choosing a date format.

EXERCISE 6.2   **TO INSERT A DATE AND TIME AS TEXT**

1. **Place the insertion point where you want the date and time to appear.** For this exercise, press Enter after the time that you entered in Exercise 6.1 to start a new paragraph.

2. **Choose Insert ➢ Date and Time from the menu bar.**

3. **Click the Update Automatically (Insert as Field) check box to turn it off if it is checked.**

CONTINUES ON NEXT PAGE

4. Select a date format and click OK. For this exercise, again choose the eighth option (00/00/00 00:00 ?M) and click OK. The following steps give you further practice working with dates.

5. Note the two times that are indicated.

6. Close the document and save the changes.

7. Reopen *Proposal Letter.*

8. Now notice the times. The time entered as a field is now later than the time entered as text. The first time was updated automatically.

9. Close *Proposal Letter* and save the changes.

SECTION 6.2: USING TABS

Tab stops are locations where the cursor stops when you press the Tab key (to the left of the "Q") on your keyboard. Tab stops are used to line up text vertically within a document. By default, Word has a tab stop every half inch.

Pressing the Tab key moves the cursor a half inch to the next tab stop. To move ½" into the paragraph before entering text, press the Tab key once. (If you already have entered your text and want to tab the first line, move your cursor to the beginning of the paragraph and press the Tab key.)

Many typists learned to create tabs by pressing the space bar five or six times at the beginning of each paragraph. Similarly, text in the middle of a line was often aligned "by eye" using the space bar rather than the Tab key. When a visually spaced document is printed, spaces may be larger or smaller than they appear on screen, giving the text a ragged, misaligned look. Save the space bar for spaces between words and sentences. Unlike spaces, Tab always takes you to a particular location and aligns the text properly. Tabs only affect one line of text at a time. Therefore, we don't recommend using tabs to move an entire paragraph in from the margin. Later in this session, you'll learn how to indent whole paragraphs; in Session 10, you'll learn about tables, which you can use to easily line up blocks of text in columns across a page.

You may also have learned to press the space bar once after a word or comma but twice after a sentence. Proportionally spaced fonts automatically increase the size of the space that follows periods, question marks, or exclamation points. If you type two spaces, the space between sentences will be too large. With Word, one space between words and sentences is best.

■ Viewing the Ruler Bar

The existing tab stops can be seen on the ruler bar, shown in Figure 6.2. The light gray tick marks below the inch numbers and half-inch indicators are the default tab stops.

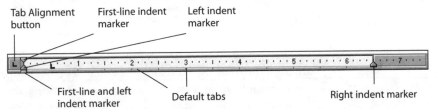

Figure 6.2

The Word ruler bar

You toggle the ruler bar on or off from the View menu. When the ruler bar is visible, a check mark appears in front of the Ruler Bar selection on the View menu:

Choosing View ➤ Ruler Bar will hide the bar if it is displayed, or display the ruler bar if it is currently hidden.

■ Setting and Using Tabs

The preset tab stops work well in many documents. You may, however, wish to set different tab stops for part or all of a document. The document shown in Figure 6.3 is most easily constructed by setting right and center tab stops. The Shift Responsibility information is centered around a tab stop at 2". The start and end times for each employee are lined up on tab stops set on the right (at 4" and 5") rather than on the left.

Figure 6.3
Tuesday's schedule

TUESDAY'S SCHEDULE

Employee	Shift Responsibility	Start Time	End Time
Anna Adams	stock shelves	1:00 p.m.	7:00 p.m.
Barbara Burns	next weeks' schedule	9:30 a.m.	5:30 p.m.
Clyde Clovell	purchasing	7:30 a.m.	2:30 p.m.
Doug Drake	order shipping	5:00 p.m.	10:00 p.m.

To use a custom tab stop you must first define it. Tab stops are a type of **paragraph formatting**. Font and text enhancement changes are tied to individual characters; paragraph formatting is tied to one or more paragraphs.

Paragraph Definition

When we first learned to write, many of us were taught that a paragraph is a collection of sentences all related to single idea or concept. In word processing, paragraphs take on a much broader meaning. In Word for Windows 95, a paragraph is any amount of text that is separated by a hard return. A **hard return** occurs anytime you press the Enter key. That means that in Word, a paragraph can be five sentences, one sentence, one word, or even a blank line. When you set tab stops prior to entering text, pressing the Enter key carries the tab stops forward to the next paragraph.

If you want to change tab stops for existing text, you must first select the paragraphs to be affected. You can then use the ruler or the Tabs dialog box to change the tab settings. If you don't select the paragraph first, the new tab stops will apply only to the paragraph where the insertion point is located at the time you make the changes.

Setting the stops includes choosing the alignment type for each tab stop you want to use. There are four basic types of tab stops—left (the default type), center, right, and decimal:

Left tab   ⌊⌐   Right tab   ⌐⌟
Center tab   ⌐⌐   Decimal tab   ⌐⌐

▧ Setting Tab Stops Using the Ruler Bar

To select a tab alignment type, click the tab alignment tool at the left end of the ruler bar until the type of tab stop you want is displayed. Then, click the ruler bar at the point where you want to place a tab stop of the selected alignment type. All preset tab stops to the left of the new tab stops you place are cleared from the ruler bar.

If you put the tab stop in the wrong location, simply drag it to the correct place on the ruler bar. To move a tab stop, first select all the paragraphs that rely on the tab stop. Dragging the tab stop to a new location on the ruler bar will reposition all selected text.

To clear a tab stop, point to the tab stop and simply drag it off the ruler bar.

EXERCISE 6.3 · **TO SET TABS USING THE RULER BAR**

Create a blank document window if you do not already have one. If the ruler is not visible, click View ➤ Ruler to turn it on. Turn on caps lock and bold. Type TUESDAY'S SCHEDULE. Press Enter twice.

1. **Click the tab alignment tool on the left side of the ruler bar to select the desired type of tab stop: left, center, right or decimal.** Here, click the tab alignment tool once for a center tab.

2. **Point and click the location on the ruler bar where you want to place a tab stop.** Click on the ruler bar at 2 inches to place a center tab.

For more practice:

3. Click the tab alignment tool again for a right tab.

4. Place right tabs at 3.5 inches, 4.5 inches, and 5.0 inches.

5. Turn caps lock off and type Employee.

6. Press the Tab key to move to the center tab and type Shift Responsibility.

7. Press the Tab key to move to the first right tab and type Start Time.

8. Press the Tab key to move to the second right tab and type End Time. Turn off bold and press Enter twice.

9. Type the following information, pressing the Tab key at each point where you see a comma, to enter each column of information.

Anna Adams, stock shelves, 1:00 p.m., 7:00 p.m.

Barbara Burns, next week's schedule, 9:30 P.M., 5:30 p.m.

Clyde Clovell, purchasing, 7:30 a.m., 2:30 p.m.

Doug Drake, order shipping, 5:00 p.m., 10:00 p.m.

10. Select all of the text from "Employee" to the end of the document so that you can adjust the last two tabs stops to allow more room for the text.

CONTINUES ON NEXT PAGE

11. Click on the tab stop in the "End Time" column and drag it off the ruler bar to clear it. The "End Time" column will move to the right to the tab stop at the 5" mark.

12. Click on the tab stop in the "Start Time" column and drag it to the right to approximately 4 inches. (Remember that you have to hold down the left mouse button to drag.)

Your finished document should look like the one in Figure 6.3. Save the document as *Tab Stops*.

■ Setting Tab Stops Using the Tabs Dialog Box

You can also create tab stops using the Tabs dialog box. Make sure the insertion point is located where you want the new tab stops to begin. (If the text you want to format is already entered, select it.) Access the Tabs dialog box, shown in Figure 6.4, by choosing Format ➤ Tabs from the menu bar.

   Note: You can also open the Tabs dialog box from the Paragraph dialog box. Choose Format ➤ Paragraph from the menu bar, or right-click and select Paragraph from the pop-up menu. Then, click the Tabs button in the Paragraph dialog box.

Figure 6.4

The Tabs dialog box

   In the Tab Stop Position text box, type the location for the tab stop you want to create. Use decimal numbers: 2, 2.5, 3.75. In the Alignment control, choose how you want text to align at the tab stop. Here you can also select a bar tab stop, which is used to create a vertical line in your document.

   The Leader control lets you select a **leader** to help the reader follow the text in your document. The leader (see Figure 6.5) will precede the tabbed text.

Figure 6.5

Tab stops and

leaders

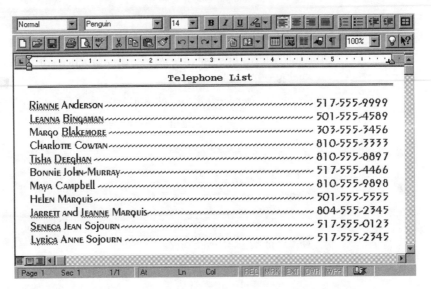

When you have set the position, type, and leader (if you wish) for the tab stop, click the Set button. The new tab stop will be added to the tab stop list. Repeat these steps to set any other tab stops.

You can also use the dialog box to change an existing tab stop. Select the tab stop from the list below the Tab Stop position control. Change the alignment and leader options; then click Set. To remove an existing tab stop, select it from the list and click the Clear button. (Clicking Clear All removes all tab stops, reverting to the default tab settings.) When you are done setting tab stops, click OK to close the Tabs dialog box.

EXERCISE 6.4   **TO SET TAB STOPS USING THE DIALOG BOX**

Begin this exercise by creating a new blank document. Add the centered heading [Your Name]'s Itinerary and apply font attributes to make the heading distinctive. Then press Enter twice and click the Align Left button to return to the left margin. Now take the following steps to set tab stops:

1. **Click Format ➢ Tabs to open the Tabs dialog box.**

2. **Type a decimal value in the Tab Stop Position text box.** For this exercise, type 5.25.

3. **Select an alignment style and, optionally, a leader style.** For this exercise, choose Right alignment and dashes (3) as the leader type.

CONTINUES ON NEXT PAGE

4. Click OK.

The following steps will give you further practice with the Tabs dialog box:

5. Type *October 5-8.* Press Tab and type *San Francisco.* Press Enter.

6. Enter the following information, pressing Tab between each entry:

October 9-12, Las Vegas

October 13, Houston

October 14-19, Denver

October 20-27, Boston

October 27, Return Home

7. Save the document as *Itinerary.*

SECTION 6.3: INDENTING PARAGRAPHS

The left and right margins of a document apply to the entire document. **Indents** are used to change the space between the left and/or right margins and the text of a paragraph, making it look like the margin itself has been changed. The most familiar indent is the **first-line indent** used at the start of a paragraph of text in a book or paper. You can, of course, use the Tab key to advance one tab stop into the paragraph, or you can apply an indent to the paragraph.

A **left indent** sets a paragraph off from the rest of the text by moving it to the right of the left margin. A **right indent** moves text in from the right margin and is typically combined with a left indent to make a **dual indent**. Dual indents are used most commonly to set off quotations from regular text. A **hanging indent** (sometimes called an outdent) "hangs" the first line of a paragraph to the left of the remaining lines. Figure 6.6 illustrates various types of indenting.

Figure 6.6

Indenting
paragraphs

This is a first line indent created using the first line indent marker located on the ruler bar. Although a first line indent can also be created using the tab key, using the first line indent maker at the beginning of the document saves you from having to press tab at the beginning of each new paragraph.

A hanging indent, or outdent, indents all but the first line of a paragraph. A hanging indent would most typically be used for graphic design purposes.

A left indent indents text a designated distance from the left margin. Text in the paragraph continues to flow to the right margin. Left indents can be used to set off quotations or to identify sub points under a major point.

Right indents are seen less often than other types of indents. Right indents are more commonly used in combination with left indents to make a dual indent which is described below.

A dual indent moves text in from both the left and right margins. A dual indent is most typically used to set off quotations or to draw attention to specific parts of the text. This dual indent moves the paragraph in a half inch from the left margin and a half inch from the right margin.

Creating Indents Using the Ruler Bar

The **first-line indent marker** and **left indent marker** are located at the left end of the ruler bar (see Figure 6.2). The rectangular box below the left indent marker moves both the first-line and left indent markers. The right indent marker is located at the right end of the ruler bar.

Indents are also a type of paragraph formatting. If you want to indent existing paragraphs you must first select them. If no text is selected, indents are applied to text entered at or after the current insertion point location.

Moving the first line indent marker indents (or outdents) the first line of each paragraph. Moving the left and or right indent markers indents all lines of each paragraph.

Indenting Using the Toolbar

The Formatting toolbar includes Increase Indent and Decrease Indent buttons. These buttons are used to indent (or "outdent") paragraph text one tab stop at a time. Since they affect all the text in the paragraph, you can't use these buttons to create hanging or first-line indents, but they are a fast, convenient way to reformat paragraphs.

■ Indenting Using the Menu Bar

The Paragraph dialog box, shown in Figure 6.7, can be accessed from the Format menu or the pop-up menu.

Figure 6.7

The Paragraph dialog box

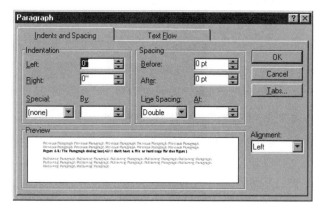

On the Indents and Spacing page, enter decimal numbers to set the left and right indents for text you will enter (or selected paragraphs). In the Special control, you can select First line or Hanging to indent or outdent the first line of the paragraphs by one-half inch. (If you want the indent to be more or less than 0.5", enter the special indent value in the By control.)

EXERCISE 6.5 | **TO INDENT PARAGRAPHS USING THE RULER BAR**

1. **Select the paragraph(s) to be indented.** For this exercise, open the document *Proposal Letter* and select the three paragraphs of the letter.

2. **For a first-line indent, click on the first-line indent marker on the ruler and drag it to the right.** In this exercise, drag the marker to the ½" position.

3. **For a left indent of an entire selected paragraph, drag the left indent marker to the right.** Here, select the middle paragraph and set its left indent at ½".

4. **For a right indent of an entire selected paragraph, drag the right indent marker to the left.** Here, drag the right indent marker an inch to the left to dual indent the middle paragraph.

EXERCISE 6.6	TO INDENT PARAGRAPHS USING THE PARAGRAPH DIALOG BOX

1. Click on Format ➣ Paragraph to open the Paragraph dialog box.

2. Enter the number of inches in the Left Indentation box. Here, enter 0.

3. Tab to the Right Indentation box and enter the desired number of inches there. Here again, enter 0.

4. Click on the drop-down box below Special to select first line or hanging indents. Click OK. Here, choose First Line.

5. Close *Proposal Letter,* saving the changes.

What You Have Learned

In this session, you have learned to insert dates and times into documents both as text and as updatable fields.

You also learned how to use the ruler bar and the Format menu to set tabs and change paragraph indents.

Focus Questions

1. How does Word know the correct date and time to insert into a document? If it is incorrect, where would you change it?

2. Why might you want to insert a date *field* into a document rather than just typing the date?

3. What is the purpose of tab stops?

4. Why is it better to use tabs to line up text than to press the space bar?

5. List the four basic types of tab stops.

6. What is a tab leader?

7. What is a hanging indent?

8. How do you clear a tab stop using the ruler bar?

Reinforcement Exercises

Exercise 1   Create a centered heading that says Holiday Party Plans. Use the ruler bar to set a left tab stop at 2", a decimal tab stop at 3.5", and a right tab stop at 6". Enter the following text, pressing Tab between each piece of information:

ITEM, COST, PURCHASED

Beverages, $28.00, 12/20

Door Prizes, $25.00, 12/15

Invitations, $12.00, 12/08

Decorations, $23.00, 12/15

Cake, $17.50, 12/20

Stamps, $6.40, 12/08

To practice cutting and pasting, use cut-and-paste to reorder the items according to the date they were purchased. (In Session 13, you'll learn a faster way to reorder paragraphs called sorting.)

Exercise 2   Create a telephone list like the one shown in Figure 6.5.

Choose a decorative font and large size for the heading. Center the heading and add horizontal lines below it if you wish. Press Enter twice after the heading section and set the alignment back to left. Select a smaller font for the list itself. Use the Tabs dialog box to set a right-aligned tab stop at approximately 6 inches. Choose #3 as the leader type. Enter the name of a person you know, press Tab and enter their telephone number. Press Enter and continue to enter names until you have completed the list. Enter at least 10 names and numbers before saving the document as *Telephone List.*

Exercise 3   Create a schedule of events for the Orienteering Weekend that you advertised in Session 5. Create about 7–8 events to extend over the course of the weekend. Start with Friday at 7 p.m. and end Sunday afternoon at 5 p.m. Use tabs to show separate columns for the day, start time, end time, and activities.

Exercise 4   Open the My Definitions document. Format the text so that the terms are set off by a hanging indent as in the example below:

Word Processing Definitions

application window - Container that displays a program.
applications (apps) - Programs that allow you to complete specific tasks such as word-processing.
backspace - The key on the keyboard that is often represented by a left arrow. When pressed, it moves the insertion point one space to the left and deletes one character each time it is pressed.
click - To depress the left or right mouse button to select an object after pointing to it.
close - Remove a window and its contents (application or document) from the desktop when you are finished working with it. Closing does not remove programs or documents from your disks or hard drive.

You need to select the text from the first term through to the end of the document before dragging the left indent marker to approximately the half inch mark on the ruler. Save the document before closing.

Lists, Lines, Numbers, and Symbols

THIS SESSION gives you more tools for paragraph formatting. You can change the vertical spacing between lines of document text. Word can be required to keep two or more lines of text together on a single page. Bullets and numbers make lists stand out from regular text. You can add emphasis to sections of text with borders and shading.

At the end of this session you will be able to:

- Create numbered or bulleted lists
- Use symbols and special characters
- Change line spacing
- Keep text together on a page
- Place a border around text
- Add shading to parts of your document

■ Vocabulary

- border
- bullet character
- character map
- line spacing
- orphan
- page break
- shading
- soft page break
- symbol
- widow

SECTION 7.1: NUMBERED AND BULLETED LISTS

Word contains two formatting tools you can use to draw attention to items in a list: numbering and bullets. Numbered lists are useful when you need to describe a sequence (such as a series of steps to be completed), points in order of importance, or topics that users will refer to verbally ("I'd like to discuss topic 2 . . ."). **Bullets** can be used to separate equally important points or components from each other and the surrounding text. Figure 7.1 illustrates bulleted and numbered lists.

Figure 7.1

Bullets and

numbers

Rules for Public Speaking:
1. Be getting up.
2. Be brief.
3. Be sitting back down again.

Several departments have requested help with e-mail:
- Language and Literature
- Sociology
- Education

If you are the last person to leave the building, please remember to:
♦ Turn OFF all office lights.
♦ Turn OFF the copy machine.
♦ Turn ON the alarm.
Thank you!

■ Creating a Numbered List

To number list items automatically as you enter them, begin by typing the number 1 and a period. Space once, then begin entering your text for item 1. When you press Enter, Word will automatically number the next item 2 and depress the Numbering button on the toolbar.

Continue entering text and pressing the Enter key to create numbered points. When you are finished creating the numbered list, press Enter twice to turn automatic numbering off. If the text you want to number is already entered, highlight the paragraphs to be numbered and click the Numbering button to number each paragraph. (You can also begin numbering by clicking the Numbering button before you type your first paragraph.)

If you want to use letters rather than numbers in automatic numbering, type A. rather than 1. to begin. Word will number the second and succeeding paragraphs B, C, D, and so on. If you number your first paragraph I., Word will use Roman numerals when numbering your paragraphs.

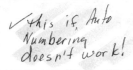
✓ this if Auto
Numbering
doesn't work!

Note: If numbering does not work when you follow the steps in Exercise 7.1, the AutoFormat As You Type option for numbered and bulleted lists is turned off. Go to Tools ➤ Options ➤ AutoFormat and make sure that Automatic Bulleted Lists and Automatic Numbered Lists are checked under AutoFormat As You Type.

EXERCISE 7.1   **TO NUMBER PARAGRAPHS AUTOMATICALLY**

To begin this exercise, create a new blank document and enter a left-aligned heading that says: The Ten Nicest People I Know.

1. **Type 1. and press the space bar once before typing the first list item. Press Enter. Word will automatically enter "2" and will tab both lines over .25 inches.** In this case, type the name of a person on your list before pressing Enter.

2. **Type the second item and press Enter.** Continue entering names until you have completed the list.

3. **After the last item, press Enter twice to turn automatic paragraph numbering off.**

4. Save the list as *People I Know*.

Creating a List with Bullets

Bulleting works just like numbering. To add bullets automatically as you type text, type an asterisk (*) before the first paragraph. When you press Enter to begin the second paragraph, Word will change the asterisk to a round bullet symbol, add a bullet for the second paragraph, and depress the Bullets button on the Formatting toolbar. When you are done typing the list, press Enter twice or click the Bullets button to turn off automatic bullets.

EXERCISE 7.2   **TO CREATE A BULLETED LIST**

In *People I Know*, enter another left-aligned heading: The Five Most Successful People I Know.

1. **Type an asterisk (Shift + 8), press the space bar once and enter the first item. Press Enter. Word will automatically change the asterisk to a bullet and insert a new bullet on the next line, tabbing over 0.25 inches.** Type the first name on your list, press Enter, and continue entering names until you have completed the list.

CONTINUES ON NEXT PAGE

2. **Press Enter twice at the end of the list to turn off bulleting.**

3. Save again.

■ Modifying the Bullet or Number Format

Word automatically uses a round symbol as a **bullet character.** You can choose a different bullet character or numbering format before entering your list, or you can modify the format of an existing list. (If the bulleted or numbered list has already been entered, select the paragraphs you want to change.) To change formats, choose Format ➢ Bullets and Numbering to open the Bullets and Numbering dialog box, shown in Figure 7.2.

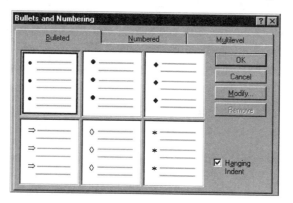

Figure 7.2
The Bullets
and Numbering
dialog box

Click the tab for Bullets. The dialog box displays sample formatting styles for bulleted text. By default, numbered and bulleted lists include a hanging indent, so the bullet is to the left of all the text in the list. If you want the bullet imbedded in the text, click the Hanging Indent check box to remove the hanging indent. The samples for the formatting styles change to reflect the change in hanging indent.

You aren't limited to the six types of bullet characters and layouts shown in the samples. Clicking the Modify button opens the Modify Bulleted List dialog box, shown in Figure 7.3. You can change bullet size, using the Point Size spin box, or the color, using the drop-down color list.

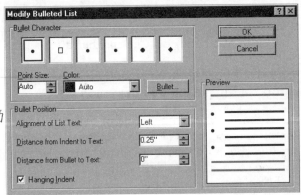

Figure 7.3
The Modify Bulleted
List dialog box

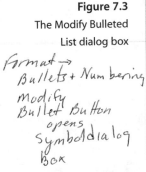

The Bullet Position controls let you change the position of the bullet relative to the text. As you modify the Bullet Position settings, the Bullet List Preview will change to reflect your modifications. A selection of Bullet Characters appears at the top of the dialog box. You can replace any of the bullet characters that appear here. Clicking on one of the bullet characters you don't want to use at this time will select it for replacement. Clicking the Bullet button opens the Symbol dialog box, shown in Figure 7.4.

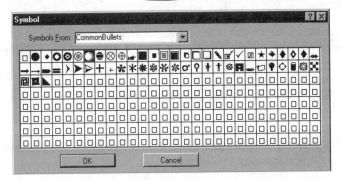

Figure 7.4
The Symbol
dialog box

The Symbols From drop-down list contains symbol and display fonts. Choose a font (symbol set) from the list, and the characters in the symbol set will be displayed in the **character map** below the drop-down. Any of the individual characters shown can be used as a bullet character. Click on any character and then click OK to replace the selected bullet character with the symbol you've chosen. You will then be able to select the new symbol from the Bullet Character samples.

To remove numbers and bullets from text, you must first select the bulleted or numbered list. Click the Bullets or Numbering button on the toolbar to turn bullets or numbering off. Clicking the button again will turn the feature back on.

EXERCISE 7.3	TO MODIFY A NUMBERED OR BULLETED LIST

1. **Select the list whose numbering or bullet style you want to change.** For this exercise, select all ten paragraphs of the first list in *People I Know*. (If you move the mouse pointer to the left margin, you'll get a right-pointing arrow. Hold down the mouse button and drag down to get all ten items. The numbers themselves will not appear selected.)

2. **Choose Format ➢ Bullets and Numbering from the menu bar.**

3. **Make sure the tab you want (Numbers or Bullets) is displayed.** Here, click the Numbers tab at the top of the box to make sure that number formats are visible.

4. **Click a number or letter format and click OK to return to the list.** Notice how the list numbering has changed.

5. Save the changed document.

EXERCISE 7.4	FURTHER PRACTICE WITH NUMBER AND BULLET FORMATS

You will still be working with *People I Know* for this exercise.

1. Select the first list and choose Format ➢ Bullets and Numbering.

2. Choose the first format option, *1.* and click Modify.

3. In the Text Before box, type A-. Notice how the picture changes in the preview box.

4. Double-click in the Start At box and enter *50*.

5. Use the Distance from Number to Text spin box to increase the distance from 0 to 2. Click OK. The list numbering should now begin at 50 and the list should be indented farther from the numbers.

6. Select the second list that contains bullets.

7. Choose Format ➢ Bullets and Numbering and click on the Bulleted tab.

8. Select the bullet that looks like an asterisk in the bottom right corner. Click Modify.

9. Double-click the Point Size box and type in 25.

10. Choose a color by clicking on the drop-down list and scrolling through the choices. Click the color you want. Click OK to return to the list. Notice that the spacing between the lines of text appears to have changed. This is because of the point size of the bullet that you selected in step 10.

11. Save the changes.

SECTION 7.2: USING SYMBOLS IN YOUR DOCUMENTS

Word includes a list of commonly used symbols that you can use in your documents. When you type a specific combination of keystrokes, Word automatically converts the keystrokes to a special symbol. Table 7.1 lists the keystroke combinations that are automatically converted to symbols.

Table 7.1:
Special Characters and Their Keystroke Combinations

Keystrokes	Symbol	Description
(tm)	™	trademark symbol
(c)	©	copyright mark
(r)	®	registered trademark symbol
:)	☺	happy
:|	☺	less than happy
:(	☹	unhappy
—>	→	thin right arrow
==>	➔	thick right arrow
<—	←	thin left arrow
<==	⬅	thick left arrow

Many fractions are also automatically converted to symbols. If you enter 3/4, Word will convert it to a single character: ¾

SECTION 7.3: CHANGING LINE SPACING

Line spacing refers to the vertical distance between lines of document text. Several types of line spacing are shown in Figure 7.5. Single spacing leaves enough room to display the largest character on a line (with a bit of extra space thrown in). Double spacing leaves twice as much room as single spacing.

Figure 7.5

Examples of
line spacing

> This is single spaced text. The line is vertically sized to leave adequate space for the largest character in the line.
>
> Line and a half spacing (1.5) is 50% larger than single spacing. Not as space consuming as double spacing, 1.5 line spacing is useful when more white space is needed and double spacing leaves too much.
>
> The text in this paragraph is double spaced, twice the height of single spaced text. Double spacing is often used in term papers, reports, or draft copies of documents that will be edited.

Line spacing is another type of paragraph formatting. It applies to all new text you enter. To change the line spacing for existing text, you must first select the paragraphs you want to change. Choosing Format ➢ Paragraph from the menu bar (or selecting Paragraph from the pop-up menu) opens the Paragraph dialog box.

Figure 7.6

The Paragraph
dialog box

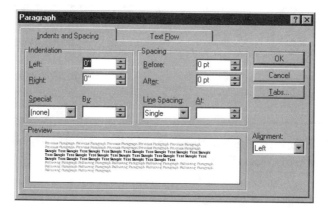

There are four controls in the Spacing section of the Indents and Spacing page, shown in Figure 7.6. Use the Line Spacing control to specify the amount of vertical space between lines. You can select Single, 1.5 Lines, or Double spacing from the Line Spacing drop-down list:

To choose any other line spacing, first select Multiple from the drop-down list, then enter a value in the At control by using the spin arrows or typing in a decimal number. For example, you can triple-space selected paragraphs by choosing Multiple, then entering 3 in the At control. The At Least and Exactly choices and the Before and After controls are used in desktop publishing; you will learn about them in later sessions.

EXERCISE 7.5   **TO CHANGE LINE SPACING**

Open *People I Know* if it is not still open.

1. **Move the insertion point to the position for the new line spacing to begin. If the text is already entered, select the text.** For this exercise, select the first list of ten items.

2. **Choose Format ➤ Paragraph from the menu bar to open the Paragraph dialog box. Click the Indents and Spacing tab.**

3. **Click the Line Spacing drop-down list to select the desired line spacing. If Multiple is selected, enter the number of lines in the At: box. Click OK.** Here, select Double and click OK.

For more practice:

4. Open the Paragraph dialog box a second time.

5. Click the drop-down arrow under Line-Spacing and select Multiple.

6. Use the spin box below At: to enter 3. Click OK. Notice that the list is now triple-spaced.

7. Save the changes.

SECTION 7.4: MANAGING TEXT FLOW

For documents longer than one page, you may want to exert some control over where the beginning of a new page (a **page break**) occurs. **Text flow** is controlled in the Text Flow page (see Figure 7.7) of the familiar Paragraph dialog box.

Figure 7.7

The Text Flow page
of the Paragraph
dialog box

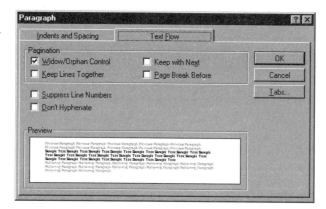

The Pagination section of the page includes four check boxes: Widow/Orphan Control manages text flow throughout the document; Keep Lines Together, Keep with Next, and Page Break Before are used to dictate text flow for a specific part of a document.

A **widow** is a single line that appears by itself at the top of a page, and an **orphan** is a single line at the bottom of a page. (Our apologies to anyone offended by this unfortunate, but standard, terminology. If we could avoid using it, we certainly would.) Word's default setting is to prevent widows and orphans, breaking pages so that at least two lines of a paragraph appear at the top or bottom. Use the Widow/Orphan Control if you need to turn off (or restore) this setting.

You may have text you want to keep together: a title and a paragraph, several lines within a paragraph, or a name and complete address that span several lines. Select the text, then choose Keep Lines Together. Keep with Next keeps the selected text with the next paragraph.

Page Break Before inserts a user-created or "hard" page break prior to the insertion point. (A page break created by Word is a **soft** page break.) You can also hold Ctrl and press Enter to create a hard page break at the insertion point.

| EXERCISE 7.6 | TO MANAGE TEXT FLOW BETWEEN PAGES |

Although this is not a specific exercise, here are the steps for managing text flow in case you need them.

1. **Select the text that should remain together on one page.**

2. **Choose Format ➢ Paragraph. Click on the Text Flow tab and on Keep Lines Together.**

3. **Choose Keep with Next to tie the selected text to the same page as the paragraph that follows it.**

4. **Choose Page Break Before to insert a hard page break prior to the insertion point.**

SECTION 7.5: ADDING BORDERS AND SHADING TO A DOCUMENT

Borders are lines above, below, around, or to the left or right of a section of text. You can also use **shading**, to add a background behind the text. Both borders and shading are tools to emphasize or separate a section of text within a document. See Figure 7.8 for examples of shading and borders.

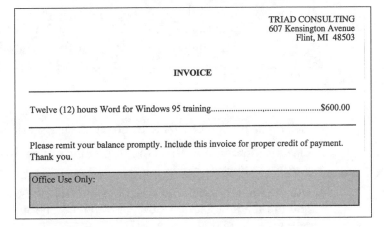

Figure 7.8
A document
with shading
and borders

 Clicking the Borders button on the Formatting toolbar displays the Borders toolbar:

The drop-down list at the left end of the toolbar is used to set the thickness of the border line. The seven buttons on the toolbar are used to add a border of the specified thickness at the insertion point (or around selected text):

- Border Above
- Border Below
- Left Border
- Right Border
- Inside Border
- Outside Border
- No Border

To draw a border around a paragraph, begin by selecting the paragraph text. Then, click the Outside Border button. To draw a border under the current line of text, click the Border Below button. To remove an existing border, select the bordered text and then click the No Border button.

The other drop-down box on the Borders toolbar controls shading (illustrated in Figure 7.8's "Office Use Only" box). The default shading is Clear (no shading). Clicking the drop-down arrow opens a scroll list of shading percentages and types. Select a shading type from the list to apply it to selected text. Of course, shading that is too dark will make the text difficult to read. To remove shading, choose Clear from the shading list.

EXERCISE 7.7	TO ADD A BORDER TO TEXT

Open *People I Know* if it is not still open.

1. **Select the paragraph text to be affected.** Here, select the first list.

2. **Click the Borders button on the Formatting toolbar to turn on the Borders toolbar.**

3. **Use the Borders toolbar to select the line style, the border position, and the shading.** Click the down arrow in the Line Style box and select the 1½ pt double line.

4. **Click the Outside Border button.**

5. **Click the down arrow in the Shading box and select 5%.**

6. **Click the Borders toolbar button a second time to close the toolbar.**
   (For this exercise, skip this step until you've completed Steps 7–11.)

   Try the following steps for practice:

7. Select the second list.

8. Change the line style to 2¼ pt single line.

9. Click the top border and the bottom border buttons.

10. Click the Borders button on the Formatting toolbar to close the Borders toolbar.

11. Save the changes.

Like any other formatting technique, borders and shading can be overdone. Too many borders crowd a document; overuse of shading decreases the readability of the text. Used sparingly, borders and shading can direct the reader to important parts of a document.

What You Have Learned

In this session, you have learned ways to create automatically numbered and bulleted lists and to select different symbols to serve as bullets.

You have also learned several keystroke combinations that will produce commonly used symbols like the symbol for copyright ©. You can now change line spacing between lines in the document and manage text flow between pages. You can also add borders and shading to selected paragraphs.

Focus Questions

1. When are bulleted lists more appropriate than numbered lists?

2. Outline the steps for replacing the standard round bullet character with a character from a symbol font character map.

3. How do you create fractions like ½?

4. List the steps for spacing lines in a document so that they are four lines apart.

5. What is the purpose of widow/orphan control?

6. What is shading and how do you use it?

Reinforcement Exercises

Exercise 1   Create a bulleted or numbered list of things you have to do this week.

Exercise 2   Open the list of goals for the year that you created in Reinforcement Exercise 2 in Session 5. Select the three goal paragraphs and apply bullets or numbering to them. Modify the design of the bullets/numbering until you are satisfied with their appearance.

Exercise 3   Open the *Orienteering Weekend* file. Turn the "things to bring" list into a bulleted list like the example shown in Figure 7.9. You may need to rearrange some text so that it still fits on one page. Remember to save the document when you are finished.

Figure 7.9
Orienteering
Weekend with
bulleted list

ORIENTEERING WEEKEND

Remember to put the weekend of **July 14-16** on your calendar for an exciting Orienteering Weekend sponsored by the Grand Traverse Wilderness Conservancy. We will spend Friday evening and Saturday morning learning all about orienteering. Saturday afternoon we will head into the woods for some real life experience finding our way with map and compass. Food will be provided. You will need to bring:

- ✓ a tent,
- ✓ sleeping bag,
- ✓ rain gear,
- ✓ compass,
- ✓ water bottle and
- ✓ good hiking shoes.

Instruction in orienteering will be provided by *Charlotte Cowtan, renowned wilderness explorer and orienteering expert.* Ms. Cowtan will set up both a beginner and an intermediate course.

So whether you are brand new to the sport or already have some experience, you are invited to join us on this exciting weekend. The fee is $35 for the entire weekend. Invite your friends to come with you.

To register call 616-555-5555

Exercise 4   Open your *My Definitions* list. Add definitions for the following terms: *hanging indent, tab stops, border, bullet character,* and *line spacing.* When you are finished defining the new terms, add bullets to the entire list.

Document Formatting

YOU CAN CHANGE the layout for pages in a document just as you can format characters and paragraphs. For example, you can increase or decrease page margins and you can center text vertically and horizontally on a cover page. By changing paper orientation, you can print with the long edge of the paper at the top. Additionally, Word will automatically number pages and repeat page headers and footers, which can contain information such as the report or section title and the author's name. At the end of this session you will be able to:

- Change the way you view a document
- Alter document margins
- Change paper orientation
- Add page numbering
- Create headers and footers
- Center text vertically on a page

Vocabulary

- footer
- gutter margin
- header
- landscape
- margin
- mirror margins
- normal view
- orientation
- outline view
- page layout view
- portrait
- vertical centering
- zoom

SECTION 8.1: VIEWING DOCUMENTS IN WORD

Word gives you four ways to view your document. In the default **normal view**, the text between the margins occupies the full width of the screen for ease in entering and editing text. **Page layout view** shows the entire page, including the margins; it's useful when you want to work with page numbers and other page features covered in this session. Page layout view is similar to Print Preview (see Session 3) which displays the document as it will appear when printed. **Outline view** shows the structure (headings and titles) of the document. In Session 15 you'll learn about working with a document in outline view. Changing views doesn't change your document, but does allow you to see it from another perspective.

Master document view, accessible only from the View menu on the menu bar, is used to tie many separate documents together (like documents that contain chapters in a book). Unless you are working with long, multiple-file documents, you won't be using master document view.

You can switch to Outline or Page Layout view from the View menu, or by clicking the Outline View or Page Layout View buttons to the left of the horizontal scroll bar:

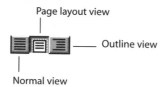

Page layout view

Outline view

Normal view

Click the Normal View button to return to normal view.

■ Zooming In on a Document

You use the Zoom control on the Standard toolbar to increase or decrease the size of the document display in any view—as if you were using a camera's zoom lens. "Zooming in" makes the text on the page appears larger, and less text fits within the document window. Decreasing the display size fits more text in the document window.

Clicking the drop-down arrow in the Zoom control opens a list of zoom ratios:

Select a zoom ratio from the list to zoom in or out on your document.

■ Displaying Nonprinting Characters

When you press a letter, number, or symbol on the keyboard, the character you entered appears on the screen. Tabs, spaces, and the Enter key also place characters in your document. These are **nonprinting characters** (not included in the printed copy of a document) and are normally hidden from view on screen. You can change Word's settings to display nonprinting characters. Viewing all characters (printing and nonprinting) provides a "nuts and bolts" perspective that can be helpful if you need to diagnose problems in your document layout.

 To display nonprinting characters, click the Show/Hide button on the Standard toolbar. Click the button again to hide nonprinting characters.

Since you will be working with page layout during this session, this is a good time to change to Page Layout view and explore zooming and showing/hiding nonprinting characters.

EXERCISE 8.1   **CHANGING DOCUMENT VIEWS**

To begin this exercise, open *Proposal Letter,* which you last saved in Exercise 5.2.

1. **Choose View ➤ Page Layout to change to page layout view.** Scroll up, down, left, and right to see the various margins.

2. **Click on the Show/Hide button on the tool bar to show nonprinting characters.** Examine the document carefully to see if there are extra spaces. Notice where the paragraphs start and end.

3. **Click the Show/Hide button a second time to hide the nonprinting characters again.**

CONTINUES ON NEXT PAGE

> **4.** Click on the Zoom control on the toolbar.
>
> **5.** Select a zoom option. Here, choose Page Width to see both sides of the document page.
>
> **6.** Click the Zoom control again and select Whole Page to see what the document looks like on the entire page.
>
> **7.** Experiment with different zooms until you find one that you like.

SECTION 8.2: CHANGING MARGINS

A **margin** is white space between text and the edge of the paper the text will be printed on. Word's default margins are 1", the top and bottom of the page, and 1.25" on the sides. Many situations require that you change the margins:

- Preprinted letterhead may have text on the top two inches of the sheet. If you leave the top margin at one inch, some of your text will print on top of the preprinted text.

- The left margin may be too narrow for pages that will be placed in a binder or notebook, making text near the bound edge difficult to read.

- You may need to fit, say, three and a quarter pages of text into three pages. Decreasing the margins is one way to leave more room for text.

You change margins using the Margins page of the Page Setup dialog box, shown in Figure 8.1. The Page Setup dialog box can be opened in two different ways: by selecting File ➤ Page Setup from the menu bar, or by double-clicking on the gray frame at the top of the ruler bar.

Figure 8.1
The Page Setup
dialog box

You use the Top, Bottom, Left, and Right spin box controls to set the amount of white space on the four edges of the document. The margins will change by 0.1" increments. If you want a 1.5" margin, type the decimal value in the appropriate control. As you change the values for the margin settings, the Preview reflects your changes.

The **gutter margin** is used to add additional space to a document that will be bound. If the binding material takes up a half inch, adding a 0.5" gutter will maintain equal white space on the portion of the document that extends past the binding. (You could, of course, set the left margin to 1.5 instead.)

Documents that will be printed or duplicated back to back before binding present some unique challenges. The left margin of the even pages is on the outside (away from the binding), but the left margin of odd pages is toward the binding. The mirror margin feature helps you format margins for back-to-back printing. Clicking the **mirror margin** check box changes the Preview model to a two-page document and replaces the Left and Right controls with Inside and Outside margin controls. Setting the outside margin changes the two margins that will be back to back: the left margin of the left page, and the right margin of the right page in the preview.

The default for the Apply To control is Whole Document. You can, however, change margins from the insertion point forward for the rest of a document by choosing This Point Forward from the Apply To drop-down list.

EXERCISE 8.2 | **TO CHANGE DOCUMENT MARGINS**

1. **Move the insertion point to the point where you want the margin changes to take effect.** Here, move to the top of *Proposal Letter* (pressing Ctrl+Home moves it there quickly).

2. **Choose File ➤ Page Setup to open the Page Setup dialog box, and click the Margins tab.**

3. **Use the spin arrows or type in the text boxes to increase or decrease the margins.** Here, enter 1.5 for the each of the margins, Top, Bottom, Right and Left.

4. **Click OK to return to the document.** The following steps provide further practice with margins.

5. View the full page again to see how the document has changed.

6. Double-click the top of the ruler to open the Page Setup dialog box again.

CONTINUES ON NEXT PAGE

7. Change the top margin to 2.5" to allow room for the letter to be printed on company letterhead.

8. Click OK to return to the document.

9. Save the changes.

SECTION 8.3: CHANGING PAPER ORIENTATION

Orientation refers to the direction of the paper in a printed document. Most documents are printed in **portrait** orientation, with the short edge of the paper at the top. You can turn the paper sideways to **landscape** orientation with the long edge up. (These terms refer to the orientation of the canvas in portrait and landscape paintings.)

Figure 8.2

The Paper Size tab of the Page Setup dialog box

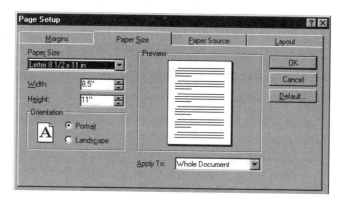

To change paper orientation, open the Page Setup dialog box and click the Paper Size tab, shown in Figure 8.2. In the Orientation control, choose Portrait or Landscape. The Preview will change to reflect your choice. By default, the entire document will be changed to the selected orientation. With the Apply to control, you can choose to change the paper orientation only from the insertion point forward.

EXERCISE 8.3   **TO CHANGE PAPER ORIENTATION**

1. Choose File ➢ Page Setup to open the Page Setup dialog box.

2. Click the Paper Size tab.

3. **Click Portrait or Landscape to change the Orientation.** Here, choose Landscape.

4. **Click the Apply To: Drop-down to choose if you want the change to apply to the whole document or from this point forward.** Select Whole Document.

5. **Click OK to return to the editing screen.** View the changes by switching to Whole Page view.

6. Close *Proposal Letter* without saving changes.

When you choose landscape orientation, Word instructs the printer to print "sideways" on the page. If you are using an impact printer (with a ribbon), printing in landscape orientation will be much slower than portrait orientation. Laser and ink jet printers have no problems printing in landscape.

SECTION 8.4: ADDING PAGE NUMBERS

To add page numbers to a document, choose Insert ➢ Page Numbers from the menu bar to open the Page Numbers dialog box, shown in Figure 8.3.

Figure 8.3
The Page Numbers
dialog box

Page numbers can be positioned at either the top or the bottom of the page. Use the Alignment control to place the number at the left, center, or right of a single page, or at the outside or inside of pages that will be printed for back-to-back duplication. If you don't want a page number on the first page, clear the Show Number on First Page check box.

No 1st pg # wanted?

The default numbering format is Arabic numerals: 1, 2, 3, and so on. Clicking the Format button opens the Page Number Format dialog box, shown in Figure 8.4, where you can drop down the Number Format list to select uppercase or lowercase letters or Roman numerals.

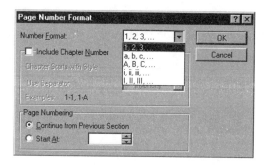

Figure 8.4

The Page Number
Format dialog box

EXERCISE 8.4   **TO NUMBER PAGES**

To begin this exercise, open *Executive Summary,* which you created in Exercise 5.3, and make sure you are in Page Layout view.

1. **Choose Insert ➢ Page Numbers from the menu bar to open the Page Number dialog box.**

2. **Select a position and an alignment.** Here, select Bottom of Page (Footer) as the position and center alignment. Check to see that Show Number on First Page is checked.

3. **Click OK to return to the document.**

4. Scroll to the bottom of the page to see the page number. (It will show in gray since it appears in the footer.)

5. Press Ctrl+End to move the insertion point to the end of the document.

6. Press Ctrl+Enter to insert a hard page break. Press Ctrl+Enter a second time to create a third page. You should be able to see the page number on the bottom of page 2.

7. Save the changes.

SECTION 8.5: CREATING HEADERS AND FOOTERS

Header - typical

A **header** contains information that will be printed in the top margin of each page of a document. **Footers** are printed at the bottom of the page. A typical header or footer may include the author's name or the document's title and a page number. (Headers and footers appear as gray text and are only visible on screen in Page Layout and Print Preview views.) Page numbering makes use of the space reserved for headers and footers. The page numbers you added earlier were placed in the document footer.

Choosing View ➢ Headers and Footers from the menu bar opens the header view and the Header and Footer toolbar, shown in Figure 8.5.

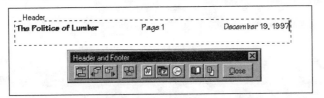

Figure 8.5
The Header and
Footer toolbar

You can enter text in the header. To include your name at the top of every page, simply type your name. The header (or footer) can be formatted as you format any other text. It can be left-, center-, or right-aligned.

The three buttons at the left end of the Header and Footer toolbar are navigation buttons. The first button switches between the document header and footer. Since you can create more than one header or footer in a document, you may want to view other headers or footers. The second and third buttons are used to move from the current header/footer to the previous or next header/footer. The fourth button, Same as Previous, makes the current header/footer the same as the previous header/footer created in this document.

The three buttons in the center of the toolbar are used to add fields to the header.

To add the page number to the header, put the insertion point where you will want the page number to appear and click the Page Number button. The correct page number will be placed on each page.

The Date button places the current date in the header.

The Time button prints the current time in the header. (Both Date and Time are fields, so they are updated and change each time you open the document.)

The Page Setup button opens the Page Setup dialog box, shown in Figure 8.6, where you can change margins or other settings for the header or footer. When you open this dialog box, you'll see the Layout page. In the Headers and Footers section here, you can tell Word that you will have a different header/footer on even and odd pages, or a different first page. If your document will be printed double-sided and bound, you might place the document's title on odd page headers and the title of each chapter on even pages. To omit a header/footer from a document's first page, choose Different First Page and simply leave the header/footer area blank.

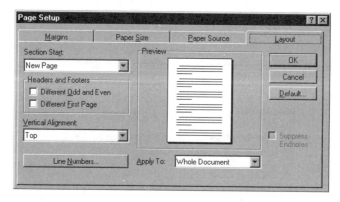

Figure 8.6

Page Setup

Layout page

The Margins page also has settings that affect headers and footers. Below the settings for the page margins are controls for header and footer margins.

The default margin settings leave one inch at the top and bottom of the document and place the header and footer in the middle of the white space at 0.5". Clicking OK closes the Page Setup dialog box and returns you to the header.

If you find that you are distracted by your document text while working with headers or footers, there is a solution. Use the Show/Hide Document Text button to turn the display of everything except the header and footer on and off.

EXERCISE 8.5   **TO CREATE A DOCUMENT HEADER**

Open *Executive Summary* for this exercise.

1. Choose **View ➢ Header and Footer** to open the Header and Footer toolbar and to move the insertion point into the header/footer area of the document.

2. **Enter the header/footer information by typing text and optionally using toolbar buttons to add fields.** Here, type the following text:

   Proposal for Outpatient Database

3. **Press Enter and click the date code on the Header and Footer toolbar to insert an updatable date field.**

4. Select the two lines and turn on bold. Change the font size to 12 pt.

5. **Click the Page Setup button on the Header and Footer toolbar to change margins and other settings.** Click the Different First Page option. **Click OK.** When you return to the document, you see the area for the First Page Header. Since you won't typically want a header on the first page, leave this area blank.

6. **Click the Close button on the header and footer toolbar.**

7. **Click the Next Page button on the bottom of the scroll bar to see the** header on pages 2 and 3.

8. **Save the changes.**

■ Editing or Deleting Headers and Footers

Headers and footers must be <u>activated</u> before you can edit them. To activate a header or footer, choose View ➢ Headers and Footers or, if you are in page layout view, double-click on the header or footer you want to edit. Make any changes you desire before clicking the Close button to inactivate the header/footer and return to the document text.

EXERCISE 8.6   **TO EDIT A HEADER**

1. **Double-click on the header or choose View ➢ Header and Footer.** Here, you'll return to the header that you created in the previous exercise.

2. **If necessary, use toolbar buttons to display the header/footer you want to edit.** Click the Show Next button on the Header and Footer toolbar to move to the header on page 2 and beyond.

3. **Make your changes.** Move the insertion point to the end of the date field, press Enter to create a new line, and type DRAFT.

4. **Click Close on the toolbar to return to the document.**

SECTION 8.6: VERTICAL CENTERING

Vertical centering centers text between the top and bottom page margins. It is often used in combination with horizontal centering for cover pages for reports or term papers. To center text vertically on a page, first select that text and open the Layout page of the Page Setup dialog box. Here, change the setting in the Vertical Alignment drop-down control to Center. Make sure the Apply to drop-down is set for Selected Text (if Whole Document is selected, all the text in your document will be vertically centered), and choose OK.

EXERCISE 8.7   CREATING A COVER PAGE

1. Create a new, blank document. Change the font to a large sans-serif font like Arial, 48 point, bold.

2. Click the center align button on the toolbar to align the text between the left and right margins. Type *Proposal for Outpatient Database*.

3. Press Enter twice and click the Right Align button on the toolbar. Change the font size to 18 point. Turn off bold.

4. Insert an automatically updatable date code. Press Enter.

5. Type DRAFT and press Enter. Type your name.

6. Click the Zoom control and select Whole Page to see the cover page at this point. You must be in Page Layout view to have the Whole Page option.

7. Return to normal zoom.

8. Select the title and click the Borders button on the toolbar.

9. Choose a line style, click outside the border, and turn on 5% shading. Click the Borders button to close the Borders toolbar.

10. Select all of the text on the page. Choose File ➢ Page Setup to open the Page Setup dialog box. (Yes, we're finally going to center the page!)

11. Click the Layout tab and select "Center" from the Vertical Alignment drop-down list. Click OK. Go to Zoom Whole Page again and the cover page should be centered on the page.

12. Save the document as *Proposal Cover Page*.

What You Have Learned

In this session, you learned to see the document in different ways by changing the view and controlling how much of the document is visible. You also learned about how to change the margins and paper orientation. One of the most valuable skills that you learned this session was how to instruct Word to automatically number the document's pages and repeat a header or a footer on every page. In the session, you also learned how to vertically center text on a page as in the case of a cover page.

Focus Questions

1. Name an advantage of Normal view over Page Layout view.

2. When is Page Layout view most useful?

3. What are nonprinting characters and why might you want to view them?

4. What is the purpose of a header?

5. How do you indicate that you do not want a header to show on the first page?

6. List the steps for vertically centering text on a page.

7. What is portrait orientation? Landscape orientation?

Reinforcement Exercises

Exercise 1   Create a new blank document with a header that contains your name, address, and telephone number, as in a letterhead. Remember that you can use all the editing and text enhancement techniques that you already know while working in a header. Save the document as *My Letterhead.*

Exercise 2   Write at least a two-page letter to a friend or business associate using the letterhead that you created. To do this, open *My Letterhead* and resave it immediately as *Letter to* [insert name]. Adjust the margins to 1.5 inches all around. Create a footer for the second page that includes the page number. Set it off with a horizontal line. Preview the letter before printing it.

Exercise 3   Open the *Orienteering Weekend* document. Change the left and right margins to 1.25 inches. Center the page vertically. View the whole page to see how it looks. Adjust the margins if it does not still fit on one page.

Exercise 4   Open *My Definitions*. Change the left and right margins to 1.5 inches and the top and bottom margins to 1.25 inches. Add a header that starts on the second page and includes the following:

Word Processing Definitions

[Your Name]

Make the header bold and include a horizontal line (bottom border) underneath it to separate from the rest of the text. Create a footer that includes the page number.

PART III

Word Tables and Tools

Polishing the Writing in Your Document

WRITING AND THEN EDITING a document to be sure it says exactly what you want it to say can be a painstaking task. Word takes much of the guesswork out this process by providing comprehensive spelling and style checking tools. An online Thesaurus helps you improve your writing by providing synonyms and antonyms for words. Word makes it very easy to find specific words or phrases and, if you want, will replace them with other words automatically. In this session you will learn to:

- set options for document spell checking
- find synonyms and antonyms with the Thesaurus
- use Find and Replace

Vocabulary

- find
- replace
- text string
- Thesaurus
- wildcards

SECTION 9.1: CHANGING SPELLING OPTIONS

As you learned in Session 4, Word gives you two ways to check document spelling. You can leave the automatic spell-checking (Spell It) turned on, or you can turn it off and use the Spelling tool from the Tools menu or the Spelling button on the Standard toolbar. Automatic spell-checking checks a document for misspelled words as you type. It is useful for a short document where you want to stop and correct words as you type. Manually running the Spelling checker is useful with a longer document where you want to write a complete first draft, and then go back through to check for spelling and other errors.

You enable(or disable) automatic spell-checking from the menu bar. Selecting Tools ➤ Options opens the Options dialog box, shown in Figure 9.1. There are many user-modifiable options in Word, so this dialog box has multiple tabs, including a tab for the Spelling page.

Note: When you change settings in Tools ➤ Options, the new settings remain in effect until changed again. For example, if you turn off automatic spell-checking it will remain disabled until someone enables it again.

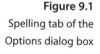

Figure 9.1

Spelling tab of the
Options dialog box

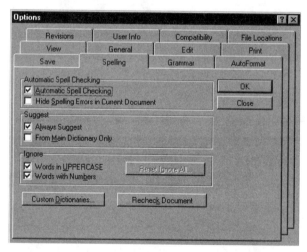

In Figure 9.1, we've accepted all of the Spelling tab's default settings. Automatic Spell Checking is enabled. Word will generate a list of suggested words for any error it encounters. The suggested words will be taken from all dictionaries accessible to Word, including the Custom dictionaries. (There is one custom dictionary created by default. Users can create other custom dictionaries if they produce two types of documents that use different jargon—for example, transcribers who work on both medical and legal documents.) Finally, Word won't bother checking any word that is completely uppercase—these words are likely to be acronyms or abbreviations—or any words that include numbers.

EXERCISE 9.1	TO CHANGE SPELL-CHECKING OPTIONS

1. Select Tools ➢ Options ➢ Spelling from the menu bar.

2. Click an option to turn it on or off. A check mark will appear next to an option that is on.

3. Click on Custom Dictionaries to review and edit the Custom Dictionaries.

4. Click Edit on the Custom Dictionaries dialog box. (Custom.dic should be selected, with a check next to it.)

5. Click OK after reading the Warning message box.

6. Scroll down the list of words in the custom dictionary. Select any word that you would like to edit.

7. Choose File ➢ Close when you finish editing.

8. Click on Yes to save changes.

9. Select Tools ➢ Options from the menu bar.

10. Click on Automatic Spell Checking to turn the option back on.

11. Click OK.

No matter how nifty it is, spell-checking is not a replacement for proofing a document. Remember that no spelling program corrects misused words or typos that create other words. If you mean to type *from* and type *form*, for example, Word won't flag it as a problem. *Their, there* and *they're* are all spelled correctly, but often used incorrectly. After checking the spelling, you still need to proofread your document for other possible errors. Word includes a Grammar checking program to help you search for grammatical errors.

SECTION 9.2: USING THE THESAURUS

In your writing, you may find yourself looking for a replacement word: a stronger word than *angry*, a less bland word than *happy*, a larger word than *big*. A **thesaurus** provides lists of synonyms (words with a similar meaning) and antonyms (words with an opposite meaning) so you can spice up your document or choose exactly the right word in a specific situation. There are synonyms listed for nouns, verbs, adjectives and adverbs.

The Thesaurus applies to one word at a time rather than the whole document. Begin by moving the insertion point anywhere within the word you want to find a synonym or antonym for. (You may select the word if you wish.) Choose Tools ➤ Thesaurus from the menu bar to open the Thesaurus dialog box, shown in Figure 9.2. The selected word is displayed in the Looked Up control. The Meanings control lists various meanings, different ways a word can be used. *Opposite* can be used as an adjective to mean *facing* ("the opposite wall," for example), *contrary* ("the opposite opinion"), or *adverse* ("an opposite effect"). It can also be used as a noun. Choose a word from the Meanings control, and the synonyms listed as possible replacements changes.

Figure 9.2

The Thesaurus

dialog box

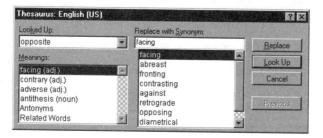

Instead of a meaning, you can choose Antonyms (for "opposite" words) or Related Words. Related words are "root words"; the related word listed for *opposite* is *oppose*. Both antonyms and related words can help you get a better sense of a word's meaning.

To replace the word in your document, choose any word from the Replace with Synonyms list and click the Replace button. Or, you can continue to browse for the perfect word. Find the suggested word that comes closest to your desired meaning. Double-click the word to move it to the Looked Up control and have the Thesaurus generate a list of synonyms. (You may, of course, decide that your original word really was the perfect word and click the Cancel button.)

TO USE THE THESAURUS

To practice using the Thesaurus, type the following paragraph:

The sunset is pretty today. The sky looks like it is burning. The colors are bright red and orange. The moon is rising in the East.

1. **Click on the word you want to look up.** Here, click on "pretty."

2. **Choose Tools ➤ Thesaurus.**

3. **Click on Meanings to select a context for the word.** Click on "Attractive" under Meanings.

4. **Click on the synonym in the right column that best describes your meaning.**

5. **Click on Look Up to look up synonyms for the words listed.** For this exercise, click on "beautiful" and then click on Look Up to see synonyms for it.

6. **Click Replace when you have found the best word or Cancel if there is no better word listed.** Click on "Dazzling" and click OK.

7. For more practice, replace "burning," "bright" and "rising" with words in the Thesaurus to make the paragraph more alive and interesting.

SECTION 9.3: SEARCHING FOR TEXT USING FIND AND REPLACE

While editing a document, you may need to locate a specific group of words or make a correction repeatedly. Find and Replace are among Word's most useful tools for advanced editing. You use **Find** to locate a **text string** (one or more side-by-side characters), format or feature in a document. **Replace** finds your text or formatting and then lets you choose whether to replace it with something else. Both Find and Replace can be used for all or part of a document. To use these tools in only part of a document, begin by selecting the appropriate text. (To use Find or Replace from a specific point to the end or beginning, place the insertion point where you want to begin.)

Finding Text

Choose Edit ➤ Find from the menu bar to open the Find dialog box, shown in Figure 9.3. Type the word or words you want to find in the Find What text box control. Select a search direction from the Search drop-down list. All will search the entire document or selection. Up searches from the insertion point to the beginning of the document or selection; Down, from the insertion point to the end.

Figure 9.3

The Find dialog box

You use the check boxes to provide specific information to guide the search. For example, if you enter *Base* as the Find What text:

- Match Case will limit the search to text whose capitalization exactly matches the text you entered. *Base* will be found, but not *base*.

- Find Whole Words Only eliminates plurals, possessives, and other extended forms of the word. *Base* will be found, but not *bases*.

- Use Pattern Matching allows you to use substitute characters called **wildcards** in a search. A question mark (?) stands for any single character; the asterisk (*) stands for any number of characters. (If you wanted to find all words that begin with the letter *Z*, you could search for the string Z*. Searching for Z??? would find all four-letter words beginning with the letter Z.)

- Sounds Like will find homonyms—words that are pronounced the same, like *bass*.

- Find All Word Forms will find *base, baseless, bases,* and all other words that are forms of the Find What text.

The Format and Special drop-down lists are used to search for non-text attributes. If you know a particular format was used in the text you are searching for (for example, **base** in bold or Courier New), use the Format drop-down list to specify a format. To find underlined text in a document, leave the Find What box blank and set the Font format to underline. You can also select the format that you want to search for by clicking the appropriate buttons on the toolbar; in this case, click the Underline button.

GREAT

The Special button opens a drop-down list of special codes (like a tab or page break) you can Find instead of or as part of a text string (see Figure 9.4).

Tip: If you are going to search for special codes, it's helpful to display them with the Show Codes button, so you know when you have successfully found them.

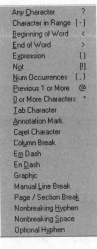

Each time you open the Find dialog box, the last text and formatting you searched for will be displayed in the Find What control. The No Formatting button is used to remove previously chosen formats so you can search for unformatted text. If the last text you searched for was formatted, you need to click the No Formatting button to search for new text that is not formatted.

After you have entered a text string and any formatting information, click the Find Next button to search in the specified direction. Word will stop and select the first occurrence of the text string. To find the next string that meets your criteria, click the Find Next button again. When you have found the text string(s) you are looking for, click the Cancel button to close the Find dialog box.

Figure 9.4
Finding special codes

EXERCISE 9.3 | **TO FIND TEXT IN A DOCUMENT**

For this exercise, open *Executive Summary.*

1. **Choose Edit ➢ Find.**

2. **Enter the text or string that you want to find.** Type *OPD.*

3. **Select the search Direction: All, Up, or Down.** Here, accept All.

4. **Mark appropriate search options.** Select Match Case and Find Whole Words Only.

5. **Click Find Next.**

6. **Continue clicking Find Next until all occurrences have been found.**

7. **Click OK to acknowledge the end of the document search.**

8. **Click Cancel to close the Find dialog box.**

▧ Replacing Text

The Replace tool allows you to substitute a text string for some or all occurrences of another text string. You can use it to save time keyboarding longer documents with frequently repeated text strings. For example, when entering a report to the Office Automation Committee, you could type *OAC* each time the name occurred and then replace them all with the full name. (AutoCorrect provides another way to do this, as you'll learn in Session 11.) Or, if the committee later changed its name to the Networking Committee, you could make that substitution with Replace.

Open the Replace dialog box (see Figure 9.5) by selecting Edit ➤ Replace from the menu bar. (If you are using the Find dialog box and have already entered a text string to find, clicking the Replace button opens the Replace dialog box and keeps the Find What text string and formatting in place. Your Find What and Replace With strings also stay in place the next time you open either the Find or Replace dialog box.)

Figure 9.5
The Replace
dialog box

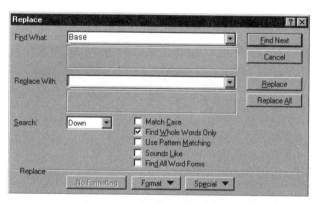

Enter the replacement text string in the Replace With text box. If you want to format the replacement text or include special characters, use the Format and Special buttons. When both the text to find and the replacement text have been entered, click the Find Next button to find the first instance of the Find What text string. Word will search in the specified direction and locate the string. Check to make certain you want to replace the text. Then, click the Replace button to substitute the Replace With text for the Find What text. To move to the next occurrence of the Find What text, click the Find Next button again.

If there are multiple replacements to be made, you can click the Replace All button. All occurrences of the Find What text will be replaced. Word will not stop to ask you about each replacement, so use Replace All with great care. The key is to define both the Find What and Replace With strings as precisely as possible. Check your document immediately after a Replace All operation, and use Edit ➤ Undo Replace All if you see unintended replacements.

EXERCISE 9.4 **TO CHANGE DOCUMENT TEXT USING REPLACE**

1. **Choose Edit ➤ Replace.**

2. **Type the text you want to replace in the Find What text box.** In this instance, Word remembers the last word you searched for in *Executive Summary* and places OPD in the text box for you.

3. **Type the text you want to use as a substitute in the Replace With text box.** Type *OPDB*.

4. **Use the drop-down control next under Search to indicate what part of the document you want to search.** Click the drop-down box and select All.

5. **Click Replace to replace each occurrence one at a time. Click Replace All to replace all occurrences of the text.** Choose Replace All.

6. **Click OK to acknowledge the replacements made.**

7. **Click Close to close the Replace dialog box.**

8. For more practice, replace all occurrences of "Behavioral Services" with "Henry Ford Behavioral Services."

9. Save *Executive Summary* before closing it.

Altering Formats Using Replace

Since Find and Replace can be used to search for formatting features, they can also be used to replace one format with another. For example, you can search for all text with an Arial Bold 14 point font and replace it with the same text in a New Courier 12 point italics. You can search for all tabs and replace it with no tab to remove tabs from a document.

| EXERCISE 9.5 | USING REPLACE TO CHANGE FORMATTING |

For this exercise, open *People I Know,* which you created in Session 7. You are going to use Replace to change the line spacing from 3 to 1.5 lines.

1. **Choose Edit ➢ Replace.**

2. **Click on Format and then choose the type of format that you want to replace. The format options you selected appear underneath the Find What text box.** Here, choose Paragraph. Choose Indents and Spacing ➢ Line Spacing ➢ Multiple At 3.

3. **Click on Replace With ➢ Format. Choose the type of format you want to replace the previous formatting with.** Here, choose Paragraph ➢ Indents and Spacing ➢ Line Spacing ➢ 1.5 lines.

4. **Choose Replace or Replace All.** The first list should now be spaced at 1.5 lines.

5. **Save the changes before closing the document.**

What You Have Learned

In this session, you have learned how to enhance your writing by using Word's writing tools. You have also learned to set personal options for document spell checking and to edit the custom spelling dictionary. You now know how to use Find and Replace to locate or change multiple occurrences of the same text or formatting codes in one easy step. You've seen how these features not only improve your writing but make it easier and faster to accomplish writing projects.

Focus Questions

1. Give two examples of spelling errors that Word's Spelling feature will not identify. Why will it not identify these errors?

2. List the steps to turning off automatic spell-checking.

3. What Word feature do you use to find a more descriptive or interesting word or phrase to replace one in your document?

4. Give an example where using Replace might help you work more efficiently.

5. What is a wildcard and how would you use one with the Find feature?

Reinforcement Exercises

Exercise 1   Enter the following paragraph exactly as it appears:

On Monday, February 4, at 7 PM there will be a meetings of the CANA to *talk* about the goals for the year. Ms. Evelyn Neumann will *talk* about the *good* things that CANA plans to do. It's a *good* idea for everyone to come. *Food and drinks* will be served. You're *help* is appreciated by CANA.

a) Use the Spelling tool to fix the spelling. Look up the italicized words in the Thesaurus and replace them with more interesting words. Feel free to make your own editing changes in addition.

b) Use Replace to replace all occurrences of CANA with College Area Neighborhood Association.

c) Save the document as CANA Meeting.

Exercise 2   Open the letter that you wrote in Session 8 and saved as *Letter to [Name]*. Identify at least eight words to look up in the Thesaurus and replace with more interesting words. After you have replaced a word, highlight the new word using the highlight button on the toolbar. Save the changes to the letter when you are completed.

Exercise 3   Open the *Orienteering Weekend* document.

a) Use Replace to replace every occurrence of "orienteering" with "bird-watching."

b) Use Replace to change "our way with map and compass" in the third sentence to "and identifying various birds and their habitats."

c) Use the Thesaurus to find a better word for "exciting" in the first sentence and one for "good" to describe "hiking shoes."

d) Save your revised document as "Bird-watching Weekend."

Exercise 4 a) Add the following terms and their definitions to My Definitions: *text string, find, replace, Thesaurus, wildcard.*

b) Use Find to locate the definition for *custom dictionary.*

c) Using wildcards, find all occurrences of words that begin with the letter *c.*

d) Using Find and Replace, change all bolded words to bold and italics.

e) Use Find and Replace to replace the hyphen after each term with a colon. If you pressed the space bar before and after typing the hyphen in the document (-), you will have to enter a space, then the hyphen, and then another space in the Find What box.

Constructing High-Quality Tables

N SESSION 6 you learned to set tab stops and use tabs to format text into columns of information. Word provides several other options that make it even easier to construct crisply formatted columns. Many Word users use tables to present information that would have previously been entered using tabs.

In this session you will learn to:

- Create a table using the toolbar or Table menu
- Enter text in a table
- Format a table using AutoFormat
- Select parts or all of a table
- Format and align table text
- Insert and delete columns and rows in a table
- Merge and split table cells
- Use SUM to calculate totals

Vocabulary

- AutoFormat
- cell
- column
- dynamic
- gridlines
- merge
- row
- split
- static
- table
- Table Wizard

SECTION 10.1: CREATING A TABLE IN WORD

Tables are one of most powerful tools available to Word users. There is no better method for organizing and presenting columns of information ranging from agendas to class lists to conference or room schedules (see Figure 10.1).

Figure 10.1
Training Room
Schedule table

TRAINING ROOM SCHEDULE
Week of April 12

Time	Room 100 Windows 95 Lab	Room 101 Windows 95 Lab	Room 102 Windows NT Lab
8 a.m. to 10 a.m.	Beginning Word	Beginning Excel	PageMaker
10 a.m. to noon	Beginning Excel	PowerPoint	
noon to 2 p.m.	Windows 95	Beginning Access	Works
2 p.m. to 4 p.m.	Access Programming	WordPerfect	NT Networking
4 p.m. to 6 p.m.	Beginning Word	Advanced Word	Intro to Computers
6 p.m. to 8 p.m.		Beginning Excel	
8 p.m. to 10 p.m.	Beginning Word		

Tables consist of horizontal **rows** and vertical **columns**. The intersection of a column and row is called a **cell** (see Figure 10.2). If you can visualize your information in columns and rows, consider creating a table to present it. Borders can be added to make the table more attractive and easier to read.

Figure 10.2
Parts of a Table

	January	February	March
	23,283	12,124	89,992
	112,123	139,983	

Column ↓
Row →
↑ Cell

Creating a Table Using the Table Wizard

There are two basic ways to create a table: using the Table Wizard, or choosing settings "from scratch" using either the Table menu or toolbar. Wizards walk you through a Word task step by step. The Table Wizard is not installed when you install Word unless you specifically select it. If you want to create a table in one of Word's standard formats, installing and using the Table Wizard makes good sense. Most tables, however, don't fit into one of the Wizard's formats.

Creating a Table Using the Table Menu

Begin by approximating the number of rows and columns you will need in your table. (You don't need to be exact, as you can always insert or delete rows and columns later.) Make sure the insertion point is located where you want the new table to appear. Before creating a table, it is best to determine whether you want the table to appear in portrait or landscape and set the page orientation accordingly. See Exercise 8.3 if you need a reminder about doing this.

Choose Table ➤ Insert Table to open the Insert Table dialog box. You'll see spin boxes for the number of rows and columns required for the table (see Figure 10.3). Set the rows and columns; then click the OK button to close the dialog box and create a simple table at the insertion point in your document.

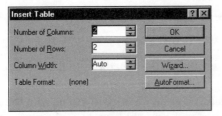

Figure 10.3
Insert Table
dialog box

Creating a Table Using the Toolbar

If you prefer a visual approach, you can specify the number of columns and rows from the toolbar. Point to the Insert Table button on the Standard toolbar. Press and hold the mouse button to open the table sizing box. Drag the pointer into the sizing box until you have selected the correct number of columns and rows. If you select too many or too few, don't worry—just don't release the mouse button until the correct dimensions have been selected. In Figure 10.4, we are asking for a table of three columns and three rows.

Figure 10.4
Creating a table
from the toolbar

When you release the mouse button, Word creates a table of the specified dimensions at the insertion point.

Note: If you need a table that is more than nine columns wide, it is best to use the Insert Table menu option rather than the toolbar button. It is easy to add rows but can be more challenging to add columns to a large table.

EXERCISE 10.1 **TO CREATE A TABLE FROM THE TOOLBAR**

Open a new blank document.

1. **Point to the Insert Table button on the standard toolbar.**

2. **Press and hold the mouse button to open the table sizing box.**

3. **Drag the pointer until you have selected the correct number of rows and columns.** For this exercise, select 5 columns and 6 rows.

4. Save this table as *Actual Sales Figures.*

■ Entering Text in the Table

Entering text in a table is the same whether you use the Table Wizard, the Table menu, or the toolbar to create a table. **Gridlines** are dotted lines that create the cell borders in a table. It is easier to work in a table with the gridlines on. Before you begin entering text, open the Table menu and make certain that Gridlines is selected. (If it isn't, click on Gridlines to turn the feature on.)

The insertion point should be located in the first cell of the new table. Start typing the contents of the first cell. If the contents exceed the width of the cell, they will automatically wrap to the next line of the cell. To move to the next cell, press the Tab key. (If you press Enter, you will move to the next line of the current cell.) Type the contents of the next cell; then press Tab again. (Use Shift+Tab to back up a cell.) When you reach the last cell in the first row, your natural tendency will be to press the Enter key. This will insert a hard return and create a new paragraph within the same cell. To move to the first cell of the next row, simply press Tab.

When you reach the final cell of the table (the far right column and last row), pressing Tab creates a new, blank row in the table. This is a convenient feature, as it allows you to add rows to a table easily. To leave the table, use the mouse and click below the table or press the down-arrow key on the keyboard.

| EXERCISE 10.2 | TO ENTER TEXT IN A TABLE |

1. Move the insertion point to the first cell of the table if it is not already there.

2. Choose Table on the menu bar and make sure that Table Gridlines has a check mark.

3. Enter data in the table. Use Tab to move between columns and Up and Down arrow keys to move between rows. For this exercise, enter the following information:

	1st Q	2nd Q	3rd Q	4th Q
Apple	20	45	60	10
Blue Spruce	15	37	45	17
Cherry	22	39	57	11
Pin Oak	12	32	40	9
Pear	20	38	52	8

4. Save the document when you have finished entering the data.

SECTION 10.2: FORMATTING A TABLE

Once you've created a table you can format it easily using AutoFormat or by selecting and formatting text within the table.

Using AutoFormat

Make sure the insertion point is somewhere in the table and choose Table ➤ Table AutoFormat to open the dialog box shown in Figure 10.5. The Table AutoFormat dialog box contains a number of predesigned table formats. To preview a format, select it from the Formats list. The format will be applied to the sample data in the Preview pane.

Figure 10.5

The Table

AutoFormat

dialog box

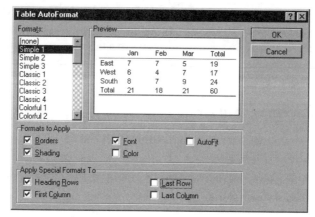

A format has many components. You may decide that you like the borders used in a format, but don't like the shading or colors included with the borders. In the Formats to Apply section, select or deselect the portions of the format you want applied to your table. The Heading Rows, First Column, Last Row, and Last Column of your table may contain summary or special information. You may want these cells to look different from the data in the other cells. Use the Apply Special Formats To controls to turn on or off AutoFormat's distinctive treatment of these rows and columns; you'll see the effect in the Preview. When you are satisfied with the formatting selections you have established, click the OK button to apply the format(s) to your table. Remember that you can always click the Undo button if you decide you don't like the format you selected.

EXERCISE 10.3	TO AUTOFORMAT A TABLE

1. Move the insertion point inside of the table that you want to format. In this case, move the insertion point inside the table in *Actual Sales Figures.*

2. Choose Table ➢ Table AutoFormat.

3. Choose the format that you want to apply to the table. A preview of each format is displayed in the preview window as it is selected. For this exercise, choose Simple 1.

4. Choose which formats you want to apply: Shading, Fonts or Color. Leave Borders, Shading, and Font selected.

5. **Indicate if you would like a special format applied to the Heading Rows, First Column, Last Row or Last Column.** Leave Heading Rows and First column selected.

6. **Click OK when you have finished selecting format options.**

7. **To see how the table looks with the AutoFormat you have selected, turn off Table Gridlines.** Choose Table ➢ Gridlines.

8. **Save the document.**

■ Selecting and Formatting Table Cells

Columns, rows, cells, and the entire table can be selected for formatting, deletion, cutting, or copying. Select text in cells using the same methods as in any part of a document. Drag across text to select a word or group of words. To select a row, move the pointer to the left of the row and click the mouse button. Hold and drag to select multiple rows.

To select a column, position the pointer just above the column you wish to select. The pointer will change shape to a dark, downward pointing arrow. Click to select a single column, or drag to select multiple columns. To select the entire table, select all table rows beginning with the top row, select all table columns beginning with the left column, or choose Table ➢ Select Table.

To select a cell, point to the cell with the mouse pointer. (If the pointer is an insertion point, move it so it turns back into a pointer.) Click once to select the cell. Hold and drag to select multiple cells.

After you have selected the cell, row, or column you want to format, you can change fonts, alignment, font attributes, borders, and other formatting features as you would regular document text. Selected cells can be cut, copied, and pasted using the Edit menu or toolbar; cell contents can be moved or copied using drag-and-drop.

Highlight to change Format fonts etc.

EXERCISE 10.4 | **TO FORMAT SELECTED AREAS OF A TABLE**

For this exercise, you will want to turn table gridlines back on. Choose Table ➢ Gridlines.

1. **Point to a cell and click to select it. Hold the mouse button down and drag to select multiple cells.** Select the column headings in *Actual Sales Figures.*

CONTINUES ON NEXT PAGE

2. **Apply formatting and editing to selected text.** Click the Bold button on the toolbar.

3. **Click anywhere else in the table or the document to de-select the cells.**

4. To finish formatting this table, select the column with the row headings, turn on bold, and give it a right border.

5. Select the 2nd Q column and turn on a right border.

6. Select the four quarter columns and click the Center align button on the toolbar.

7. Save the changes.

■ Inserting and Deleting Rows and Columns

We often need to change the contents of a table. A student moves, for example, and the row containing the student's information needs to be deleted from the Class List table. A new employee joins the staff, and you need to insert a row to place the new hire in alphabetical order in the list. An extra review stage is added to a project, and you need to insert a column for it in the project schedule.

To add a row to the end of the table, move the insertion point to the last cell in the table. Press the Tab key, and a new blank row is inserted below the last row of the table. To insert a row in the middle or at the beginning of a table, select the row that should follow the new row. (To insert multiple rows, begin by selecting the number of rows you want to insert.) Choose Table ➢ Insert Rows to insert a new row and shift all existing rows down. With a column selected, choosing Table ➢ Insert Columns inserts a new column and shifts the current column (and those that follow) to the right. (As you may have already guessed, this means you can't easily add a column at the far right.)

EXERCISE 10.5   **TO INSERT ROWS AND COLUMNS**

1. **Place the insertion point in the row or select the column that you want to follow the new row or column.** In this case, place the insertion point in the Cherry row of *Actual Sales Figures*.

2. **Choose Table ➢ Insert Rows or Table ➢ Insert Columns.** In this case, your option is to insert a row.

3. To practice inserting a column, select the 4th Q column.

4. Choose Table ➤ Insert Columns.

5. Repeat steps 1–4 to insert another row and another column.

6. Enter the following information in the empty row below "Blue Spruce":

   Flowering Crab 1st Q - 15; 2nd Q - 23; 3rd Q - 37; 4th Q - 8

7. You will learn how to widen columns later in this session. For now, save the changes.

To delete a row, begin by selecting the row. (You can, of course, select multiple rows.) If you want to delete the text in the row but leave the empty row, press the Delete key on the keyboard. To delete the text *and* the row, choose Table ➤ Delete Rows.

EXERCISE 10.6 **TO DELETE ROWS AND COLUMNS**

1. **Select the column or row that you want to delete.** In this exercise, select the blank row that you created in Exercise 10.5.

2. **Choose Table ➤ Delete Column or Table ➤ Delete Rows.**

3. For more practice, select one of the blank columns that you created in Exercise 10.5.

4. Choose Table ➤ Delete Columns.

5. Save the changes.

■ Changing the Width of Columns

After you've entered text in a table, you may find that the columns are not wide enough to accommodate the text adequately. There are several ways you can adjust the column widths. The easiest way is with AutoFit. To use this feature, first select the column that needs to be adjusted. Then choose Table ➤ Cell Height and Width to open the Cell Height and Width dialog box.

Be sure that the Column tab is selected and choose AutoFit. Word will automatically widen the column to conform to the widest text and still keep within the left and right page margins.

Manual adjustment

You can also adjust the margins manually—for example, when you need to leave room for handwritten comments in a column. Select the column you want to adjust. Move the mouse pointer to the border of the column. The pointer will turn into a resize tool with left and right arrows. Hold down the mouse button and drag the column border to the desired width.

To reset multiple columns to the same width, first select the columns you want to adjust. Choose Table ➢ Cell Height and Width. Use the Width of Columns spin box to enter the appropriate width.

EXERCISE 10.7   **TO ADJUST COLUMN WIDTH**

1. **Select the column or columns that you want to adjust.** In this case, select the first column in *Actual Sales Figures.*

2. **Choose Table ➢ Cell Height and Width Columns.**

3. **Select AutoFit or enter a number in the Width of Columns spin box.** Here, select AutoFit.

4. For additional practice, select the Totals column.

5. Choose Table ➢ Cell Height and Width ➢ Column ➢ AutoFit.

6. Although the text now fits in the Totals column, it might look better if it were wider still. Select the column. Move the pointer to the right border until it turns into the resize tool. Drag the border to the right to widen the column.

7. Select all four Quarter columns.

8. Choose Table ➢ Cell Height and Width.

9. Enter .7 in the Width of Column spin box. Click OK.

10. Save the changes.

■ Merging and Splitting Table Cells

To present your information as clearly as possible, you may sometimes need to combine or split the cells of a table. For example, the Employee Schedule shown in Figure 10.6 has column headings that span two columns. The cell containing "Monday" was formerly two cells that were **merged**—combined into one cell. Otto is working a split shift on Tuesday, and the cells in the table were **split** to accommodate his hours. The four cells with Otto's hours were formerly two cells.

Figure 10.6
Merging and
splitting cells

Please examine the schedule and notify me of any problems or concerns. Thank you!

	Monday		Tuesday		Wednesday	
	Start	End	Start	End	Start	End
Matt	7	11			7	11
Nora	10	3	7	2	10	3
Otto	2	6	10 | 2	4 | 6	2	6

To merge cells, first make sure that Gridlines are on. Then begin by selecting the cells that will be merged into one cell. Choose Table ➢ Merge Cells. To split a cell into two side-by-side cells, select the cell or cells to be split. Choose Table ➢ Split Cells; then choose the number of columns each cell should be split into from the Split Cells dialog box.

CAUTION

Word has difficulty discerning columns that contain split or merged cells. If you try to select a column that contains a merged or split cell, not all cells in the column may be selected. And because table formulas rely on columns, it is best not to split or merge columns that contain numbers you intend to perform math functions with.

EXERCISE 10.8   **TO MERGE OR SPLIT CELLS**

For this exercise, you want to add two rows to the top of the table. Select the first two rows of the table. Choose Table ➢ Insert Cells ➢ Insert Entire Rows ➢ OK.

1. **Select the cells you want to merge or split.** Select the first empty row of Actual Sales Figures.

2. **Choose Table ➢ Merge Cells to merge the cells into one, or choose Table ➢ Split cells to separate the cells into columns. When splitting cells, you will be prompted for a column number.** Here, choose Table ➢ Merge Cells.

3. To continue designing the table, select the cells in the second empty row above the four Quarter columns. Choose Table ➢ Merge Cells.

4. Move the insertion point to the first row. Type THE GRAWN GREENERY.

5. Move the insertion point to the cell above the four Quarter columns and type 1996 Actual Tree Sales.

6. Save the changes.

SECTION 10.3: SIMPLE MATH IN TABLES

Word tables are no substitute for spreadsheets like Excel, which allow you to perform hundreds of mathematical operations. But if you just need to total the numbers in a table, you can add row and column totals simply. If no blank row exists for totals, move to the last cell in the table and tab to create a new row. (If there is no empty column, you will need to insert one.) Place your insertion point in the first cell that should contain a total, and select Table ➤ Formula to open the Formula dialog box, shown in Figure 10.7.

Figure 10.7

The Formula dialog box

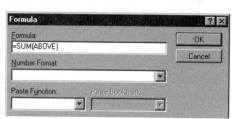

If there is an empty cell in the bottom row of the table and any cells in the column above it contain numbers, Word assumes you want to add the numbers in the column above the current cell. If you place the insertion point in the empty cell, Word provides a formula to total the column: =SUM(ABOVE). If the empty cell is in the last column of the table and any cells in the row to the left have numbers, the formula will read =SUM(LEFT). Click OK to calculate the column or row total.

(linked) - will recalculate w/ changed numbers in cells

CAUTION

Spreadsheet programs like Excel are **dynamic:** as numbers in a spreadsheet change, the results of formulas that rely on those numbers reflect the changes. Word table formulas, by contrast, are **static:** once a formula has been entered, the result does not change, even if the contents of the cells in the column or row change. If you change the numbers in a table, you must delete any affected totals and create them again using Table ➤ Formula. If you do not, the totals will be incorrect.

EXERCISE 10.9   **TO ADD TOTALS TO A TABLE**

- To add columns and rows to the table to accommodate totals, place the insertion point in the last cell (Pear 4th Q).

- Press Tab to insert a row at the end of the table.

- Click on the empty cell below "Pear" and type "TOTALS."

- Select "Totals" and click the Align Right button on the toolbar.

- Select the 4th Q column and drag the contents one column to the left into the empty column you created in Exercise 10.6.

- Click on the empty cell to the right of 4th Q and type TOTALS.

- Select the Totals column and turn on a 2¼ pt left border.

- Select the Totals row and turn on a 2¼ pt top border. Click the bottom border button to remove the bottom border.

You are now ready to add totals.

1. **Position the insertion point in the cell where you want the answer to appear.** In this case, place the insertion point in the empty cell in the Total column across from "Apple."

2. **Choose Table ➢ Formula to open the formula dialog box.**

3. **Enter the desired formula in the Formula text box.** Since there are no numbers above this cell, Word assumes that you want to total from the left and enters =SUM(LEFT).

4. **Select a number format if a specific format is desired.** Leave this blank to accept the default format.

5. **Click OK.**

6. **Repeat Steps 1–5 above for the remaining totals.** Because Word always looks above first, now that there is a total for Apples, the suggested formula will be incorrect. Replace "Above" with "Left" for each of the remaining totals in the right hand column. The correct formula for each of these should be =SUM(LEFT).

7. Before saving the table as *The Grawn Greenery*, experiment with different borders, shading, alignment and fonts to make the table look attractive.

What You Have Learned

In this session, you have learned to create a variety of exciting tables to present information. You have learned how to use AutoFormat to format attractive tables with minimal effort. You have also learned how to create and format tables that incorporate your own designs. Finally, you have learned how to include simple formulas in your tables to save time and effort when creating tables of numbers.

Focus Questions

1. What is a cell?

2. What happens when you press the Enter key in a table?

3. How do you move from one cell to another?

4. How do you select an entire column?

5. Give three reasons why you might want to select a column.

6. List the steps to merging cells.

Reinforcement Exercises

Exercise 1   Create a table that tracks the things you have to do this week. Include columns for task, due date, date completed, priority, and comments.

Exercise 2   Create and AutoFormat a table that shows your typical weekly schedule (Monday through Sunday or Sunday through Saturday) from 8 AM to 9 PM in one hour increments. You will have to add a column on the left side to show the times.

Exercise 3   Create a table to show the numbers of employees hired by various departments in each quarter of last year. Provide totals for all departments and quarters. Include the following information:

	1st	2nd	3rd	4th
Finance	9	4	8	0
Human Resources	4	5	4	2
Administration	2	4	2	2
Marketing	5	6	3	4

Exercise 4

a) Add the following terms and their definitions to *My Definitions: row, column, cell, merging cells, splitting cells, gridlines.*

b) Select all of the terms and definitions. Use Table ➢ Convert Text to Table to convert the document into a two-column table. For the text separator, indicate Other and enter a colon.

c) Change the width of the columns so that the text fits better in each of the two columns.

d) Save the document as *My Definitions—Table.*

PROJECT A: PAINT THE TOWN REPORT

Overview

This exercise will allow you to create a document that encompasses the word processing skills you have learned in the first ten sessions. If you need a refresher on how to do something, refer to the Guide to Quick Steps following the Table of Contents.

Description

Create a report for a community involvement project sponsored by the (fictitious) computer technology firm you work for. The report will include a cover page, the body of the report, and an announcement about how to get involved with next year's project. Use all the formatting features that you know, and do not hesitate to use the Thesaurus and Grammar tools to improve the content of the report. Use borders, tables, and bulleted lists to present information clearly and concisely. Suggested information is provided in the paragraphs below. Add to or change the information as you desire.

1. Create a cover page with the following text:

Report on 1996-97 *Paint the Town* Activities

Sponsored by Marcotan Technology Enterprises

[Your Name]

2. On a new page, create the body of the report that includes:

Description of project—*Paint the Town* was conceived in 1993 by Mary Smith and Bill Piper in Development as a way for Marcotan to show support for the community and get employees involved in community events. Each year, a committee of four people raises funds to buy paint and supplies and arranges for employee volunteers to paint the exterior of houses and do clean up in various parts of the city.

Goals—Goals for the project include: raise enough money within the company to paint a minimum of five houses each year; recruit at least five committed volunteers per house; formalize an agreement with a different neighborhood association each year; publicize the event in the local newspaper and assist other companies in developing similar programs.

Generating Interest—This year's *Paint the Town Committee* began work on this year's event within a week of last year's event. They went to department meetings, held informal brown bag lunches to discuss the program, sent out promotional materials to each employee's home, and printed progress reports in the company's monthly newsletter.

Organization—The *Paint the Town* Committee for this year consisted of Mary Smith, Bill Piper, Amy Courter, and John Robinson.

This Year's Results—79 people from six departments participated in painting nine houses in the east side neighborhood of Canton Heights. We raised over $2,600. Costs came to just over $2,400. The additional money was donated to the Canton Heights soup kitchen.

Plans for Next Year—Next year, we plan to paint 12 houses. To be successful, we need to raise $3,300 and sign up 100 volunteers. The *Paint the Town Committee* has decided to expand its membership from four to six members. Recruitment is underway to fill the additional two slots and to replace committee members, Bill and Amy, who will be stepping down this year.

3. Use different fonts for headings and subheadings.

4. Create a header with the name of the report and the page number.

5. Create a footer with the company name.

6. Design a table that includes the following information:

   Cost of Materials—Paint $1857.64; Brushes $47.37; Rollers $97.69; Tape $62.25; Drop Cloths $88.32; Beverages $37.54; Food $245.73; Total Cost of Materials

7. Design a table that shows how many people were involved from each department, how much money each department raised, and how many houses they painted. The table should also show the total number of people, the total money raised, and the total number of houses painted.

   Administration—12 people, $347, 1 house; Human Resources—10 people, $345, 1 house; Marketing—14 people, $635, 1.5 houses; Tech Support—13 people, $390, 1.5 houses; Development—19 people, $532, 2 houses; Maintenance—11 people, $352, 2 houses

8. Create an announcement that invites employees to become involved in working on next year's event. They could donate work on the organizing committee; raise money; donate money; donate materials; sign-up workers; become a worker; publicize the events. An open meeting will be held September 2 at 1 PM to enlist support.

Customizing the Word Environment

MANY OF THE FEATURES of Word for Windows 95 can be changed to keep the tools you use frequently close at hand. You can select the toolbars you wish to display or create custom toolbars with buttons for functions you use frequently. Custom AutoCorrect entries instruct Word to correct words you often miskey as you type. You can customize other features in the various pages of the Options dialog box. At the end of this session you will be able to:

- Show or hide toolbars
- Customize toolbars
- Create personal toolbars
- Add entries to the AutoCorrect list
- Change options using the Options dialog box

■ Vocabulary

- AutoCorrect
- automatic save
- convert
- customize
- embed
- link
- password
- repagination

SECTION 11.1: DISPLAYING TOOLBARS

Word includes predesigned toolbars, the sets of buttons grouped by function. In previous sessions, you have used four: the Standard, Formatting, Tool Wizard, and Borders toolbars. To access all the toolbars available in Word, choose View ➤ Toolbars to open the Toolbars dialog box, shown in Figure 11.1.

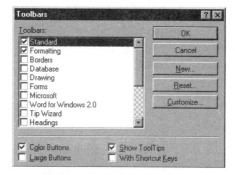

Figure 11.1

The Toolbars dialog box

Toolbars currently displayed have a check mark; to turn a toolbar off, click to remove its mark. To display a different toolbar, click on its check box. Below the toolbar list are four display options, which affect all toolbars.

- Color buttons: The use of color always takes a bit of computer memory, but it makes buttons easier to look at.

- Large buttons: Fewer large buttons fit on a toolbar, but large buttons are useful if you have difficulty seeing the buttons as normally displayed.

- Show ToolTips: When you point to a button, the ToolTip shows the name of the button.

- With Shortcut Keys: If there is a keyboard shortcut associated with a button, it will be included in the ToolTip.

When the toolbars you want to display are selected and you have chosen the display options, clicking the OK button closes the dialog box and displays the toolbars you have selected. Word places no limit on the number of toolbars you can display at one time. There is, of course, a practical limit.

Each additional toolbar you display reduces the amount of space available for the document window (see Figure 11.2). Too many toolbars, and you have no space left to enter text!

Figure 11.2

Too many toolbars!

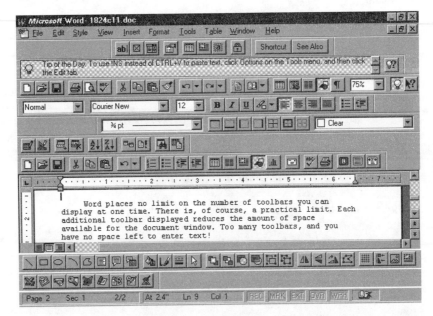

Each toolbar can be displayed in a strip at the top or bottom of the window, or as a floating palette in the document window. You move a toolbar by dragging it from one location to another. To begin, point to the gray area of the toolbar that frames the buttons and hold the mouse button. As you move the mouse, the outline of the toolbar will move. It will also change shape. In the document window, the outline will change to a narrower, taller rectangle. At the top or bottom of the screen, the toolbar outline will change to a long strip. Drop the outline in the new location to move the toolbar.

You can quickly move any toolbar to the document window by double-clicking on the gray frame. To restore the toolbar to its prior location above or below the document window, double-click on the toolbar title bar. Clicking the toolbar's Close button closes the toolbar.

You can also display or hide any toolbar by using a context-sensitive menu. Point to any toolbar and right-click to open the Toolbar pop-up menu (see Figure 11.3). Click on any toolbar listed to display or hide it.

Figure 11.3

The Toolbar

pop-up menu

If you use the same toolbars repeatedly, you may want to instruct Word to display these toolbars by default each time you start Word. Selecting Toolbar Preferences from the pop-up menu opens the dialog box shown in Figure 11.4.

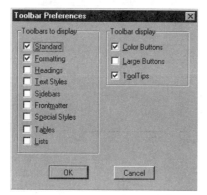

Figure 11.4

The Toolbar

Preferences

dialog box

The Standard and Formatting toolbars are displayed by default. If you never use the Formatting toolbar, you could turn it off here. In the future, Word won't display the Formatting toolbar unless you ask to have it displayed. You can also set toolbar display options in this dialog box.

Note: If you share your computer with other users, always display the default toolbars even if you don't personally use them, so other users don't have to search for them.

EXERCISE 11.1   **TO DISPLAY TOOLBARS**

1. Choose View ➤ Toolbars.

2. Select the toolbars that you want to display by clicking them so that a check mark appears in front of them. For this exercise, turn on the Drawing and Forms toolbars.

3. **Turn off toolbars by clicking toolbars that are checked.** Turn off the Formatting and Tip Wizard toolbars.

4. **Click the display options that you want on: Color Buttons, Large Buttons, Show ToolTips, With Shortcut Keys.** Here, turn Color off. Turn on the other three options on.

5. **Click OK.**

6. Point to a gray area of a toolbar and hold down the mouse button to drag it to another location on the screen. Drag the Drawing toolbar to the left side of the screen. Drag the Forms toolbar to just above the Ruler.

7. Look at each of the tool tips for the buttons displayed to give you an idea of what these toolbars do. Notice the shortcut keys displayed on the tooltips on the Standard toolbar.

8. Choose View ➤ Toolbars to turn the Formatting toolbar back on and the Drawing and Forms toolbars off. Turn on the options that you most like.

SECTION 11.2: CUSTOMIZING TOOLBARS

Over time you will discover that there are Word features you wish were available as toolbar buttons. If you create lots of short documents, for example, you might want a button to close the current document. Perhaps there will be other buttons you rarely use. Word allows you to **customize** (modify) toolbars, adding and deleting buttons to create one or more personalized toolbars.

Adding or Deleting Toolbar Buttons

The changes you make when customizing toolbars are implemented at the application (Word) level, not the document level. When you remove a button from a Word toolbar, it is removed for all documents until you or another user restores the button.

CAUTION

It is considered bad manners (at least) to remove buttons on toolbars that other users need. If you share a computer with other users, you will need to restore the default toolbars, menu bar, and shortcut keys before ending this session.

First, display the toolbar you want to customize. Then open the Customize dialog box (see Figure 11.5) by choosing Customize from the toolbar pop-up menu; or by choosing View ➤ Toolbars and then clicking the Customize button in the Toolbars dialog box; or by selecting Tools ➤ Customize.

Figure 11.5

The Customize
dialog box

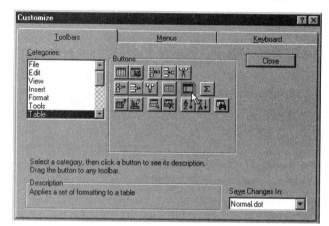

The Customize dialog box contains sets of buttons organized in the same categories as the menu bar. If, for example, you want to add a button to AutoFormat a table, you would select Table from the Categories list. The buttons then displayed in the Buttons control are related to the options on the Table menu. The meaning of some buttons is obvious; others require some explanation. Click on any button in the Buttons section, and a description of the button appears at the bottom of the dialog box, as shown in Figure 11.5.

To add a button to a toolbar, drag the outline of the button from the Buttons section to the toolbar and drop it in place. You can also drag a button from one toolbar to another, or to another location on the same toolbar. To delete a button from a toolbar, drag the button off the toolbar and drop it in the document window.

Note: The Customize dialog box must be open before you can remove buttons from the toolbar.) When you have finished customizing the open toolbars, click OK to close the Customize dialog box.

Use the Toolbars dialog box to restore the default settings for a toolbar. Choose Toolbars from the toolbar pop-up menu, or View ➤ Toolbars from the menu bar. Click the name of the toolbar you want to restore; then click the Reset button. The Reset Toolbar dialog box will appear, indicating the name of the selected toolbar. Click the OK button to reset the selected toolbar to its original form.

ADD /Delete buttons to/from present toolbars Drag & Drop

EXERCISE 11.2 | **TO ADD OR DELETE TOOLBAR BUTTONS**

To make restoring the defaults easier, make sure that just the Standard and Formatting toolbars are open.

1. **Point to a toolbar and right-click to open the pop-up menu.**

2. **Choose Customize to open the Customize dialog box.**

3. **Drag buttons off the toolbar to delete them.** Drag Insert Address and Insert Microsoft Excel Worksheet off the Standard toolbar. Drag Highlight off the Formatting toolbar.

4. **To add buttons, select a category from the category list and click on a button to see a description of the button at the bottom of the dialog box.** Select Format and click on several buttons to see what they do.

5. **Drag the buttons you want to add to the open toolbars.** Select one button from the Format category and drag it to the Formatting toolbar. Select two buttons from Tables and drag them to the Standard toolbar.

6. **Click Close when you are finished editing the toolbars.**

7. **To reset the toolbars to the default, Choose View ➢ Toolbars, select the toolbar you want to reset, and click the Reset button.** Reset the Standard toolbar. Select the Formatting toolbar and click Reset again to reset it. Make sure the Standard and Formatting toolbars are left on.

■ Creating a New Toolbar

Many people using this book share a computer with other users, but would still like to have custom toolbars of their own. Word lets you create new toolbars which you can then customize, leaving the predesigned toolbars intact for others to use.

To create a new toolbar, open the Toolbars dialog box. Click the New button to open the New Toolbar dialog box. Enter a name for your new toolbar (your name will be just fine), as shown in Figure 11.6. You can dedicate a toolbar to certain types of documents, or make it available for all documents by simply clicking the OK button.

Figure 11.6
The New Toolbar
dialog box

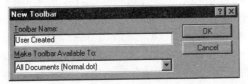

Word will create a new square little toolbar and open the Customize dialog box. Select the buttons you want and drag each onto your new toolbar. (**Tip:** Keep buttons that fall into the same category next to each other; this makes it easier to remember their locations.) When you are done, click the OK button to close the Customize dialog box. The new toolbar can be placed above or below the document window with the other toolbars. When you select toolbars from the list in the Toolbar dialog box, your new toolbar will appear on the list.

EXERCISE 11.3 **TO CREATE A NEW TOOLBAR**

1. **Choose View ➢ Toolbars to open the Toolbars dialog box.**

2. **Select New.**

3. **Enter a name for the toolbar. Click OK.** Enter your first or last name as the toolbar name.

4. **Drag the buttons you want to the toolbar.** Select five buttons to place on the toolbar, keeping related buttons together.

5. **Click Close when you have finished creating the new toolbar.**

6. **Choose View ➢ Toolbars to turn the new toolbar on or off.**

SECTION 11.3: CUSTOMIZING AUTOCORRECT

In Session 7, you learned shortcuts to create symbols in Word. Replacing keystrokes with symbols is just one example of Word's **AutoCorrect** feature. You can customize AutoCorrect so it handles your common typos. Choose Tools ➢ AutoCorrect to open the AutoCorrect dialog box, shown in Figure 11.7.

The first option, Correct Two Initial Capitals, fixes typos created when you don't release the Shift key quickly enough. When you enter two capital letters in a row (CAlifornia), AutoCorrect changes the capital A to a lowercase A. (It won't, however, change a word that is all caps, so you can still enter state or province abbreviations and acronyms like HUD or HEW.) The Capitalize First Letter of Sentences option will capitalize the first letter of a sentence if you forget to. You can enable or disable either of these features. You can also provide Word with a list of exceptions to either of these automatic corrections.

Capitalize Names of Days will automatically capitalize Monday, Tuesday, and other days of the week. With Correct Accidental Usage of CAPS LOCK

Key enabled, <u>Word will sense that the uppercase and lowercase letters you</u> have entered <u>are reversed and replace them</u>.

Figure 11.7
the AutoCorrect
dialog box

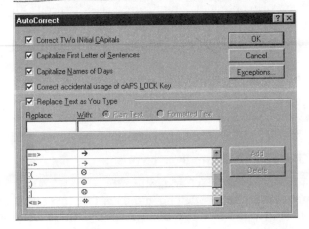

Tip: Having Word automatically replace a second uppercase letter in a word is convenient—but there are exceptions. Rather than disable checking for two initial capitals, <u>create an exceptions list</u>—words that Word knows begin with two capital <u>letters. Click the Exceptions button to add frequently</u> used words that begin with two capital letters to the exceptions list.

The final option, <u>Replace Text as You Type</u>, is the heart of AutoCorrect. You can turn this feature off or on by clicking on the check box. (Don't turn it off yet—used properly, AutoCorrect is a great time saver.) Skillful use of the replacements list can make real improvements in your efficiency. For example, you may often type *dailu* when you mean to type *daily*. By including the mistake and the correction in the list, you can have Word fix this error on the fly. <u>To enter an automatic correction</u>, enter the misspelling in the Replace control and the corrected word in the With control. <u>Click the Add button to add</u> the replacement to the AutoCorrect list. If you <u>make a mistake</u> creating an AutoCorrect entry, just select it from the list and <u>click the Delete button</u>.

Some errors aren't good candidates for AutoCorrect. If you type *form* instead of *from*, you may be tempted to create an AutoCorrect entry. If you do, when you really want the word *form*, you'll have to turn AutoCorrect off.

You can also use AutoCorrect to <u>expand unique phrases and names you</u> enter frequently. In the Replace control, enter a short string that stands for the phrase you want to expand; then enter the complete phrase in the With control:

Click the Add button. Now, the user can type *OAC* and have it automatically replaced with *Office Automation Committee*, saving lots of keystrokes. It's also worth noting that AutoCorrect is a Microsoft Office feature accessed by other Office products like Excel, Access, and PowerPoint. Entries you add to AutoCorrect in Word also work in other Office applications on your system. AutoCorrect can help anyone who wants to increase her or his keyboarding efficiency.

EXERCISE 11.4   **TO SET AUTOCORRECT OPTIONS**

1. **Choose Tools ➢ AutoCorrect to open the AutoCorrect dialog box.**

2. **Click options to turn them on or off.**

3. **Add words that you frequently misspell to the AutoCorrect dictionary. Enter the misspelling in the Replace text box. Enter the correct spelling in the With text box.** Review the list for words already included. For this example, enter *slect* in the Replace box and *select* in the With box. Also, enter *TV* in the Replace box and *television* in the With box.

4. **Click OK to close the dialog box.**

5. To test the AutoCorrect entries that you made, open a new blank document. Type *slect* and press the space bar. The word *slect* should be replaced with *select*.

6. Type *TV* and press the space bar. It should be replaced with *television*.

SECTION 11.4: SETTING OPTIONS IN WORD

Options provide another method of customizing Word. Choosing Tools ➢ Options opens the Options dialog box, shown in Figure 11.8. You have used the Print, AutoFormat, and Spelling pages of this dialog box in previous sessions, so you have a good idea how to work with it. This section covers some of the options that determine how Word responds to user instructions. You may want to change these options, or know where they are located in case another user changes their settings.

Figure 11.8
The General page
of the Options
dialog box

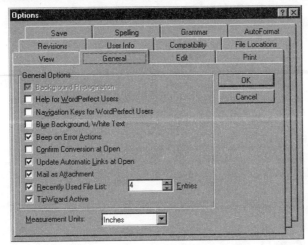

Tip: If you don't know what an option means, click on the Help question mark in the top-right corner of the dialog box and then click on any of the options to get a description of it.

The General Options

The General options page contains miscellaneous settings that affect the user interface. The General options and the most important default settings are:

- Background Repagination (on): When text is inserted or deleted, Word automatically adjusts document page breaks.

- Blue Background, White Text (off): Changes the screen display to white print on a dark blue background, making text more visible on some monitors. This can also provide a good change of pace and reduce eyestrain when you are working in Word for extended periods of time.

- Beep on Error Actions (on): When you make a mistake (like trying to resume working in a document without closing an open dialog box), Word warns you audibly.

- Update Automatic Links at Open (on): Documents can contain information created in another application (for example, part of an Excel worksheet or a sound clip). When you open a document that contains information **linked** to another application, Word updates the linked portions of the document to provide the most current information.

(You might choose to turn this off if the files linked to a document aren't present on the computer. See Session 18 for more information on linking.)

■ Recently Used File List (on, 4 entries): Allows you to specify the number of recently used files that appear at the bottom of the File menu.

■ TipWizard Active (on): With the TipWizard on, Word monitors the way you complete tasks and provides help on streamlining your Word work in the TipWizard toolbar.

■ Measurement Units (inches): You can change this to centimeters if you prefer. The ruler bar and status bar information will change to reflect the change in measurement unit.

■ The Edit Options

Editing options (see Figure 11.9) affect the way Word responds when you cut and paste, move, or edit text. If someone changes one of the editing options, you might try to do something simple (like drag-and-drop to move text) only to find that it doesn't work. It's useful to know how to turn these options on and off so you can go back to editing as you normally have.

Figure 11.9

Editing options

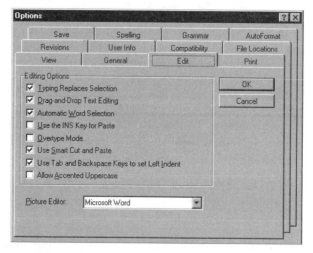

The most important editing options and their default settings are:

■ Typing Replaces Selection (on): If you have text selected and begin typing, the selected text is deleted and the newly entered text is inserted in its place.

- Drag-and-Drop Text Editing (on): Lets you use drag-and-drop to move text in a table or document.

- Automatic Word Selection (on): Allows you to select only whole words with the I-beam. If this option is off, you can select parts of a word.

- Use the INS Key for Paste (off): With this option enabled, pressing the Insert key pastes the contents of the clipboard at the insertion point as if you had clicked the Paste button.

- Overtype Mode (off): When this option is off, text you enter is automatically inserted at the insertion point rather than typing over existing text.

- Use Smart Cut and Paste (on): Automatically deletes or adds required spaces when you cut or paste text.

- Use Tab and Backspace Keys to Set Left Indent (on): simultaneously pressing the Tab and Backspace keys indents the current paragraph to the next tab stop. (This doesn't work on all keyboards, even if it is on.)

File Location Options

The File Locations options set the default locations for documents opened or saved in Word as well as for dictionary files, templates, and pictures. The file locations are established by Word during installation. Unless you have an excellent understanding of the Windows 95 folder structure, don't change any of the file locations. If you do, Word may be unable to locate required files to check spelling or open specific documents.

Compatibility Options

These options determine how a document created in another application or an earlier version of Word will be converted when you open it in Word. If you regularly work with such documents and notice that they contain extra spaces, extra blank lines at the top of the document, or other strange features, look at the compatibility options for the word processing program used to create the original document.

User Info Options

User information is entered when Word is installed. (If you work on a computer owned by a school or company, the name listed may be "Employee" or

"Guest User.") If you entered the information on your computer incorrectly, you can fix it here.

■ View Options

There are three View Options pages. The page displayed when you open the Options dialog box depends on the current document view: normal, page layout, or outline. To change the options for normal view, the active document must be in normal view. The options are similar for all three views, but are set separately. Figure 11.10 shows the options for Page Layout view.

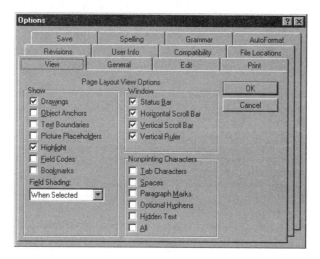

Figure 11.10
Page Layout view options

The view options are grouped into three areas:

- ■ Show: Determines what objects will be displayed within the document window.

- ■ Window: Use to set the features you want to have displayed outside the document window.

- ■ Nonprinting characters: Use this section to have nonprinting characters such as tabs and paragraph marks displayed even when the Show/Hide Nonprinting Characters button is not depressed. Clicking that button has the same result as selecting All in this section.

■ Revisions Options

You use revision options when more than one person is working on a document. The original author's work appears as black text; subsequent editors or author's additions show up in color. These options allow you to choose colors and methods for indicating text that has been added or removed by different users.

■ Save Options

Save options (see Figure 11.11) determine how a document will be saved and whether the user will need to supply additional information when a document is initially saved.

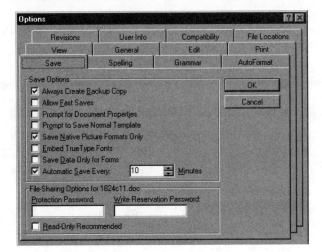

Figure 11.11

The Save options

The most important Save options are:

- Always Create Backup Copy (off): When an existing file is saved again, the original, unedited file is saved with the name *Backup of FILENAME*. If you don't like the changes you made while editing, you can open the Backup file.

- Embed TrueType Fonts (off): Normally, Word uses the fonts on your computer each time a document is opened. If you need to open a document on a computer that doesn't have the same fonts as your computer, **embedding** (saving a copy of the font with the document) is a good idea. Otherwise, leave this option off, as embedded fonts take up additional disk space.

- **Automatic Save:** Word saves your document at the intervals designated to protect your document in case of power loss. When the power comes back on and you launch Word, the last Automatic Save of your document will be recovered. A basic rule of thumb to set the number of minutes is to decide how much work you are willing to lose. Most users set the interval between 5 and 15 minutes.

- **File Sharing Options:** used to prevent other users from viewing your document or altering your document. The protection **password** can be up to 15 characters. It is case sensitive: *OOPS* is not the same as *oops.* Each time the protected document is opened, you will be asked to enter the correct password.

CAUTION

If you enter and then forget the password, you will not be able to open your document ever again. Ever.

Word contains literally hundreds of customizable settings and options. You don't need to set them all at once. In fact, many users never change most of the defaults. As you learn more about Word, return periodically to tweak settings or change options to make Word work most efficiently for you.

EXERCISE 11.5 **TO SET OPTIONS**

1. Choose Tools ➢ Options from the menu bar.

2. **Click on the tab that contains the option you want to change.** For this exercise, click on each tab and look at the options available. If you do not understand an option, click on the Help question mark and then on the option to get a definition. Do not make any changes at this time.

3. **Click the option to turn it on or off.** For now, click on the View tab. Click on Horizontal and Vertical Scroll Bars to turn them off.

4. **Click OK when you have finished setting the options.** Notice that the scroll bars are missing when you return to the document window.

5. To set a few more options, open Options again. Turn Horizontal and Vertical Scroll bars back on.

6. Click on the Save tab. Change the Automatic Save Option to 8 minutes.

7. Click on the Grammar tab. Change the Rules setting to Strictly (All Rules). Click OK.

What You Have Learned

In this session, you have learned how to customize the Word environment to fit your style of working. You have learned how to add and delete buttons from the Word toolbars and how to create custom toolbars to meet your needs. You now know how to set options for the AutoCorrect features of Word, including how to add words to the AutoCorrect dictionary that may include abbreviations and other typing shortcuts. Finally, you have learned about the many options available to make working with Word easier and more convenient for you as a user.

Focus Questions

1. How do you move a toolbar to a different part of the screen?

2. List the steps to adding a button to the Standard toolbar.

3. How do you reset a toolbar to the default if it has been customized?

4. What steps would you take to customize Word so that when you typed "USA" it automatically changed the abbreviation to "the United States of America"?

5. What option would you set to change the Ruler bar to centimeters instead of inches? Where is the option located?

6. List the steps to turning off Automatic Word Selection. How would Word work differently with this option turned off?

Reinforcement Exercises

Exercise 1   Create a custom toolbar that you can use when you work in tables. Name it *[Your Initials] Tables*. Add the following buttons: Insert Table, Table Gridlines, Table AutoFormat, Insert Rows, Delete Rows, Insert Cells, Delete Cells, Insert Columns, Delete Columns, AutoSum, Sort Ascending, Sort Descending. Your toolbar should look like this when completed:

Exercise 2   Edit the toolbar you created earlier in this session in Exercise 11.3. Add additional buttons to it so that you can use it in place of the standard toolbar. Only include buttons for features that you use regularly.

Exercise 3   Add at least five words to the AutoCorrect dictionary that you commonly misspell. Add at least five abbreviations for phrases or names that you use regularly so that when you type them they are replaced with the full text.

Exercise 4   Add the following terms and their definitions to My Definitions: *options, automatic save, convert, embed, link, repagination.*

PART IV

Greater Efficiency for Repetitive Tasks

Working Efficiently in Word

THIS SESSION introduces Word's most important tools for streamlining and automating your work. Wizards guide you through the process of creating quality, preformatted documents. AutoFormat formats text as you type, like AutoCorrect. Text that you type repeatedly can be saved as AutoText. Styles provide ease and consistency in formatting sections of text. You will learn to:

- Use a document Wizard
- Construct a document using a special template
- Set and use AutoFormat
- Create and apply styles
- Save an AutoText entry
- Place AutoText in a document
- Work in Outline view

■ Vocabulary

- AutoFormat
- AutoText
- style
- template
- Wizard

177

SECTION 12.1: WIZARDS AND TEMPLATES

Wizards are programs that ask you a series of questions and then create all or part of a document based on your answers. When you are finished answering the questions, the Wizard completes the task for you.

A **template** is a document "skeleton" that contains settings and tools used to create a complete document. Templates can include special toolbars, text, and formats that appear in every document created with the template. Templates may also include macros, styles, and AutoText entries. (You'll learn about macros in Session 15. Styles and AutoText are included in this session.)

Up to this point, you have used the Normal template to create documents. Word includes additional templates for letters, faxes, memos, reports, newsletters, calendars, and other documents. The templates are optional when Word is installed; not all the templates may be installed on the computer you are working on.

Using a Wizard to Create a Document

When you use the New button on the toolbar to create a document, Word opens a blank document based on the Normal template. To access the Wizards and other templates, choose File ➤ New from the menu bar instead of using the toolbar. The New dialog box is shown in Figure 12.1.

Figure 12.1

The New dialog box

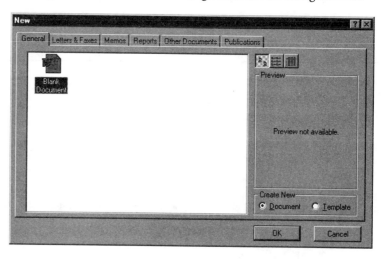

Wizards and templates are separated into six categories (pages) in the New dialog box:

- General: a blank document based on the Normal template

- Letters and Faxes: Fax Wizard, Letter Wizard; fax and letter templates

- Memos: Memo Wizard; memo templates

- Reports: report templates

- Other Documents: Agenda, Award, Calendar, legal Pleading, Resume and Table Wizards; templates for invoices, resumes, time sheets

- Publications: Newsletter Wizard; templates for newsletters, brochures, manuals, directories

Each Wizard clearly includes the word "wizard" as part of its name, like *Newsletter Wizard.wiz*. Click once to select a Wizard's icon, and a preview of the document created by the Wizard will be displayed in the Preview pane (see Figure 12.2). Click the OK button to start the selected Wizard.

Figure 12.2
Previewing a Wizard

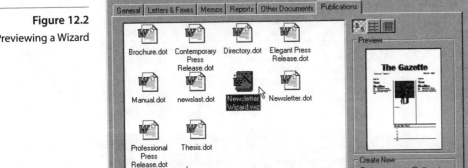

The first page of the Newsletter Wizard asks you to choose a style for your newsletter: Classic or Modern. The selected style appears in the sample, allowing you to preview both styles. Choose a style and click Next (see Figure 12.3). You set the number of newsletter columns in the next step. Again, you can preview the effect of your choice before clicking Next.

Figure 12.3

Choosing a

newsletter style

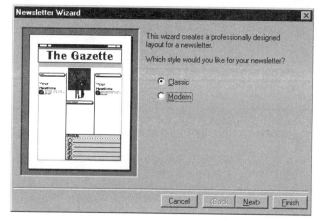

Enter the name of your newsletter in the text box on the next page (see Figure 12.4). If you make a mistake, you can edit the name after you leave the Wizard, but you may as well enter it correctly now before clicking OK. Select the number of pages you think you need for your newsletter. Click OK.

Figure 12.4

Entering a

newsletter

name

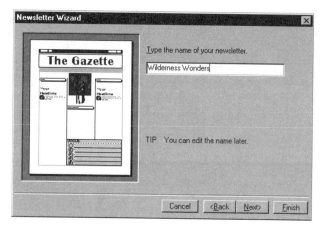

The last step asks you to determine which design elements (see Figure 12.5) you want to include in the newsletter. As you turn elements on or off, the preview changes to reflect your choices. Click OK to proceed to the Finish page. This is a good time to review the choices you have made in the Wizard; you can click the Back button to change choices made on prior pages. When you are ready to exit the Newsletter Wizard, click the Finish button.

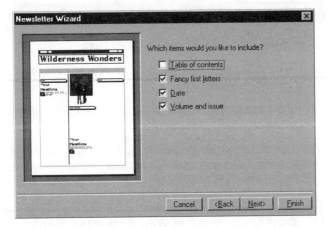

Figure 12.5
Choosing design
elements

The Newsletter Wizard will process your choices and create a newsletter document, as shown in Figure 12.6. Click on any element (headings, pictures, text areas) to enter text or edit the placeholders left by the Newsletter Wizard. The newsletter you create will need to be saved, just like any document created with the normal template.

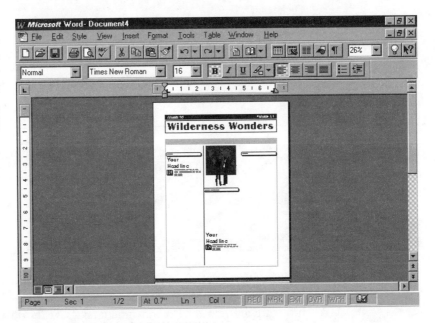

Figure 12.6
A Newsletter
document, ready
for text to be
entered

EXERCISE 12.1	TO CREATE A DOCUMENT USING A WIZARD

1. **Choose File ➤ New from the menu bar.**

2. **Click the tab to select the desired Wizard category.** For this exercise, choose *Letters and Faxes*.

3. **Select a document with "Wizard" as part of its name. Click OK.** Select *Letter Wizard.wiz*.

4. **Answer the questions posed by the Wizard to create your document. Click the Next and Back buttons to move forward and backward through the Wizard.** To continue with the Letter Wizard, choose *Select a Pre-written Business Letter*. Click Next.

5. **Review the list of pre-written letters available and for the fun of it,** select *Letter to Mom*. Click Next.

6. **Choose Plain paper as the type of paper the letter will be printed on.** Click Next.

7. **Enter your mother's or another significant person's name and address as the recipient. Enter your name and address for the return address.** Click Next.

8. **Choose a style that you like.** Click Next.

9. **Click "Just display the letter."** Click Finish.

10. **Now that the Wizard has created the letter, feel free to edit it just as you would any other document.**

The Wizards use templates to create documents. You can access the templates directly if you don't want to use a Wizard. (Some templates, like the report templates, don't have Wizards.) To create a new document based on a template, just select the template from the New dialog box.

SECTION 12.2: DOCUMENT FORMATTING WITH AUTOFORMAT

AutoFormat offers another way to give groups of documents a consistent look, by applying simple formats based on a document's underlying template. When you are finished entering document text, save the document and select AutoFormat from the Format menu.

The AutoFormat dialog box will open. To begin formatting, click the OK button. Word will analyze and format the document, applying the Body Text style to anything that looks like body text, the Heading 1 style to whatever looks like a main heading, and so on. When formatting is complete, the AutoFormat dialog box (see Figure 12.7) gives you an opportunity to:

■ Review the formatting changes one at a time

■ Accept all the changes without looking at them

■ Reject all changes (this is the same as canceling changes)

■ Choose a different formatting style from the Style Gallery.

Figure 12.7
The AutoFormat
dialog box

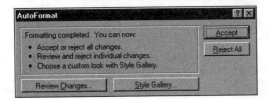

Take advantage of this opportunity to see how minor changes can improve the appearance of a document. Click the Review Changes button to proceed to the Review AutoFormat Changes dialog box, shown in Figure 12.8.

Figure 12.8
Reviewing changes

Click the Find button to move to the first formatting change. The change is selected in the document text, and a description of the formatting change is provided in the dialog box.

Non-printing characters are displayed while reviewing changes. If you don't like viewing them, click the Hide Marks button. You can choose to Reject any change at any time. However, when you initially use AutoFormat, don't spend time deciding whether to reject individual changes. Instead, click the Find → button to move through the changes, noting the overall look of the document. You can reject some or all changes later if you desire.

When you have reviewed the changes, click the Cancel button to return to the AutoFormat dialog box. Click the Style Gallery button to open the Style Gallery dialog box, shown in Figure 12.9. Your document is previewed on the right; the templates you can use to AutoFormat the document are shown on the left. The template initially used by AutoFormat is selected.

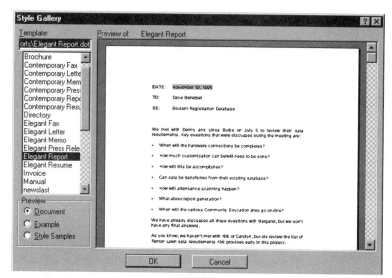

Figure 12.9

The Style Gallery dialog box

Below the template list, you can choose the contents of the preview window. You can preview an Example for the selected template rather than your document, to see the type of document a particular template was designed for. Each template consists of placeholders for text you enter and styles to format that text. The Style Sample will display a list of styles used in the template. A **style** is made up of one or more formatting choices:

- bold 14 point New Courier right aligned

- 28 point Arial centered

- left aligned 72 point Bold Timpani

Choose a different template, and the preview document will be AutoFormatted in the styles included in the selected template. At this point you have a number of options: choose a template from the list and click OK, or Cancel and return to the AutoFormat dialog box where you can reject or accept some or all of the auto-formatting. (If you accept Auto Formatting, you can still change your mind and Undo the formatting!)

EXERCISE 12.2   **TO AUTOFORMAT A DOCUMENT**

1. **Create a document and save it.** For the purposes of this exercise, open a new blank document and enter the following text without any formatting except centering the title:

   Results of the *We Do It Best* Marketing Campaign

   Description of Campaign

   The *We Do It Best* campaign was conceived by the Technical Support department as a way to bolster consumer confidence in our products. Through ads in national newspapers, computer magazines, and several national news magazines, the campaign focused on making consumers aware of our excellent reputation for technical support and customer service.

   Highlights of Campaign

   A series of six ads appeared over a six week period, each ad building on the ad from the previous week. The first two ads educated consumers about who we are as a company and what we stand for. The second two ads focused on the studies that were conducted by *PC Update* and *Technology Today* showing our company as the leader in customer responsiveness. The final two ads outlined what our customers can expect from us and why they should join the group of satisfied consumers.

   Save the document as *We Do It Best*.

2. **Choose Format ➤ AutoFormat.**

3. **Click OK to start auto-formatting your document.**

4. **Click Review Changes and then click Find to review each change that AutoFormat made to the document. Be sure to read the description of the AutoFormat change in the dialog box.**

5. **Click Reject if you want to reject an individual change.**

6. **Click Cancel when you have reached the end of the document or OK if you want to review the changes again.**

7. **Click Cancel to close the Review Changes dialog box.**

8. **Click Accept to accept all the changes or Reject All to revert back to the original document. If you want more styling options, click Style Gallery.** Here, click Style Gallery.

CONTINUES ON NEXT PAGE

9. **Click each of the templates to see how it affects your document.** Because this is a report, be sure to look at the Contemporary, Elegant and Professional Report styles.

10. **Click OK when you find a style you want to apply or click Cancel to revert back to the AutoFormat dialog box.** You now have another chance to accept or reject all changes. Click Accept.

11. Save the formatted document as *We Do It Best—Formatted*.

SECTION 12.3: CREATING AND APPLYING STYLES

Styles like those used in templates and AutoFormat are easy to create and apply. There are two types of styles: **character styles,** which include settings from the Fonts dialog box; and **paragraph styles**, character styles that can also include paragraph formatting. Paragraph styles are applied to all the text in a paragraph, including single-line paragraphs like titles and headings.

Built-in styles are available from the Style drop-down list on the Formatting toolbar:

Paragraph styles are indicated by a paragraph code; character styles are preceded by a lowercase A. To apply a style, select the text to be formatted, then select the style. To apply a style before entering text, select the style and then enter the text you want the style to apply to.

To view more details about styles, choose Format ➤ Style from the menu bar to open the Style dialog box, shown in Figure 12.10. The List control in the lower-left corner of the dialog box determines which set of styles will appear in the Styles list. You can view Styles in Use in the current document, All Styles, or User Defined Styles. Click on a style in the Styles list to see a description and previews of its paragraph and character formatting.

The style shown in Figure 12.10 is the character style for the Normal template. Your Normal template may use a different font or font size, and may not include Widow/Orphan control. When this style is changed, all existing documents based on the Normal template will change the next time they are opened. You can apply a style to selected characters or paragraphs by clicking the Apply button. If you choose Apply without any text selected, the style will apply to the next text you enter.

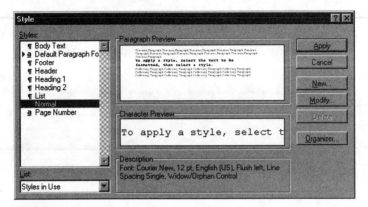

Figure 12.10

The Style dialog box

EXERCISE 12.3 **TO APPLY A STYLE**

For this exercise, open *We Do It Best* (the unformatted version).

For existing text:

1. **Select that text you want to apply the style to.** Select "Results of the *We Do It Better* Marketing Campaign."

2. **Click the drop-down style list to select the desired style.** Select Heading 1. For more practice, apply Heading 2 to "Description of Campaign" and "Highlights of Campaign."

For new text:

1. **Select the style you want to apply.** Move the insertion point to the end of the document (Press Ctrl+End). Press Enter to start a new paragraph. Select Heading 3.

2. **Enter the new text.** Type

   Why We Do It Better

Notice that a blank line is inserted and the new text appears in Arial 12 pt. (The fonts assigned to particular styles may differ on your computer. Other users may have changed the styles.)

3. Close the document without saving the changes.

■ Creating a New Style

There are two ways to create a new style: from the dialog box, or using preformatted text. From the Format menu, choose Style. In the Style dialog box, click the New button to open the New Style dialog box, shown in Figure 12.11. In the Name control, enter a name for the new style. (The name should reflect the contents or function of the style so you don't have to guess: Large Heading, Signature, Bold Arial 14).

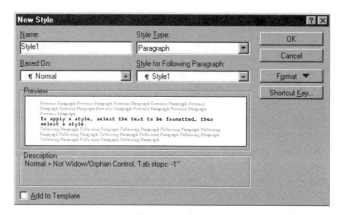

Figure 12.11

The New Style

dialog box

Choose a Style Type (choose Paragraph if you want to format entire paragraphs with the style, Character for text formatting). If you want to use some of the attributes of an existing style, select that style in the Based On drop-down list. (The default setting is the style applied to the current paragraph.)

If you choose a Paragraph style type, the Style for Following Paragraphs control allows you to turn a style off by specifying the style that the *next* paragraph should use. For example, if you're defining a heading style, you probably want the paragraphs following the heading to revert to a body text style.

Styles are saved with the current document. To have a style saved with the active template (and available each time you create a document using the active template,) click the Add to Template check box in the lower-left corner of the dialog box.

Now, click the Format button and choose the formatting elements you want to include in your style. Character styles can include font and language attributes. Paragraph styles can include character formatting, paragraph formatting, tabs, borders, and numbering and bullets. When you have selected all the formatting elements you wish to include, click the OK button. To apply your newly created style, select it from the Formatting toolbar or Style dialog box.

EXERCISE 12.4	TO CREATE A STYLE USING THE STYLE DIALOG BOX

For this exercise, open *We Do It Better*. Move the insertion point into "Results of the *We Do It Best* Marketing Campaign."

1. **Choose Format ➢ Style.**

2. **Click New.**

3. **Enter a name for the style.** Enter *Title 1*.

4. **Choose a style type.** Here, choose Paragraph.

5. **If you choose Paragraph, indicate what style should be used in the following paragraphs by selecting from the drop-down list.** Choose Body Text.

6. **Indicate if you want the style saved with the current template so that it is available in any document you create with that template.** Choose Add to Template.

7. **Click the Format button and choose the formatting elements that you want to include in this style.** Choose Font and select Arial 18 pt Bold. Select Borders and choose Box ¾ pt.

8. **Click OK to close the New Style dialog box and return to Style.**

9. **Click Apply to apply the new style.** The style now appears in the Style drop-down list.

■ Viewing a Paragraph's Style

The Formatting toolbar's Styles control displays the name of the current style—the style of the paragraph where the insertion point is located. To get detailed information about that style, use the Help system. Click the Help button on the standard toolbar. The pointer changes to the help pointer. Click on a paragraph, and Word supplies paragraph and font formatting information as shown in Figure 12.12. The Help tool stays on until you click the Help button again to turn it off, allowing you to check more than one paragraph.

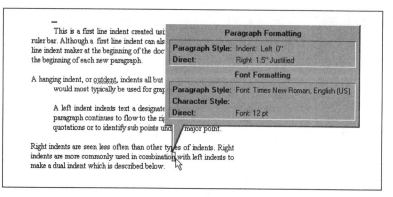

Figure 12.12

Using Help to

get formatting

information

Creating a Style from Formatted Text

You can also create a paragraph style "on the fly" from text that already includes the formatting characteristics you desire. (Use the Help button to view the formatting that will be included in the new style.) Place the insertion point within a text string that includes the formatting elements you want to save as a style. Select the current style name from the Style list in the Formatting toolbar and type a name for the new style. Press the Enter key, and your new style will be included in the style list for the current document.

To add a new document style to the current template as well as the current document, open the Style dialog box by choosing Format ➤ Style. Select the style from the Style list; then click the Modify button to open the Modify Style dialog box. Click the Add to Template check box; then choose OK.

EXERCISE 12.5   **TO CREATE A STYLE FROM FORMATTED TEXT**

You will continue to use *We Do It Better* for this exercise. First, format the heading "Description of the Campaign" to Arial 14 pt Bold Italics.

1. **Position the insertion point in the text that contains the formatting features you want to define as a new style.** For this exercise, place the insertion point in the first paragraph.

2. **Use the Help tool to view the formatting for the paragraph.**

3. **Click on the Styles drop-down list and type the name of the new style in the text box. Press Enter.** Type Arial 14 Bold Italics and press Enter.

4. To apply the new style to existing text, move the insertion point to "Highlights of the Campaign" and click the drop-down list of styles. Select Arial 14 Bold Italics (you may have to scroll up the list to find it.) Save the document.

SECTION 12.4: USING AUTOTEXT

AutoText is text you save to use again in the current document or other documents based on the current template. AutoText is a more comprehensive version of AutoCorrect. While AutoCorrect substitutes one text string for another, AutoText can include multiple formatted lines of text. This makes AutoText ideal for signature lines or return addresses. AutoText is saved with the active template.

Creating an AutoText Entry

Type, format, and then select the text you want to save as AutoText. Choose Edit ➤ AutoText to open the AutoText dialog box, shown in Figure 12.13. Word suggests a name for the AutoText entry; you will often want to change this to a shorter name that you will easily remember and can type quickly. Enter the name in the text box; then click the Add button to store the AutoText and close the dialog box.

Figure 12.13
The AutoText
dialog box

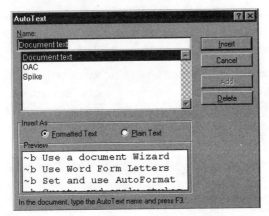

Pasting AutoText in a Document

Make sure the insertion point is located where you want the AutoText to appear. If you're not at the beginning of a line, make certain there is a space in front of the insertion point. Type the name of the AutoText; then press F3 to paste the complete AutoText entry.

If you use AutoText extensively, you might want to add an AutoText button to one of your toolbars. You can select text and click the button to create

AutoText, or type an AutoText name and click the button to paste AutoText. See Session 11 for instructions on customizing toolbars.

EXERCISE 12.6	TO CREATE AND USE AUTOTEXT

You will continue to use *We Do It Best* for this exercise.

1. **Enter, format, and select the text that you want to save as AutoText.** For this exercise, select the text string "We Do It Best."

2. **Choose Edit ➤ AutoText to open the AutoText dialog box. Your selection should appear in the Name and Selection boxes.**

3. **Enter a short, easy-to-remember name for the selection and click Add.** In this case, enter *wdib*.

4. **To use the AutoText entry, type the name that you gave it.** Move to a new line at the end of the document and type wdib.

5. **Press F3 to paste the expanded AutoText entry into the document.**

6. Close *We Do It Best* without saving the changes.

What You Have Learned

In this session you learned how to automate your work in Word. You can use AutoFormats to standardize the look of documents automatically. Creating and using AutoText entries can help you construct documents faster. You can use styles to format sections of text easily and consistently

Focus Questions

1. What is the advantage of using a Wizard?

2. What is the difference between a Wizard and a template?

3. Once you've AutoFormatted a document, how do you indicate that you don't want to accept one of the formatting changes that Word made to the document?

4. What is the difference between a character style and a paragraph style?

5. List the steps to creating a new style from formatted text.

6. Why might you want to use AutoText?

Reinforcement Exercises

Exercise 1   Use a document template to create a memo to your instructor. In your memo, tell your instructor what you like about the class so far. Include a list of three word-processing skills that you feel comfortable with and three skills that you would like more practice with. Save your memo as *Memo To [Instructor's Name]*.

Exercise 2   Use the Style Gallery to apply a different style to the memo you created in Reinforcement Exercise 1.

Exercise 3   a) Use the Resume Wizard to create a resume for yourself. Save it as *My Resume*.

b) When you have finished, use the style Gallery to examine different style options. Select a style that appeals to you.

c) Select one of the section headings and edit the style. Reapply that style to the document.

Exercise 4   a) Open *My Definitions*. Create a character style for the terms, including font, point size, font style, and color. Name it *Terms*.

b) Create a paragraph style for the definitions. Name it *Definitions*.

c) Apply the new styles to the existing text. You will have to select each term to apply the term style to it and then select each definition to apply the definition style.

d) Enter the following terms and their definitions using the new styles: *style*, *template*, and *Wizard*.

e) Edit the Terms style by selecting an already formatted term and changing the font or its characteristics. Re-apply the edited style using the selected text as an example.

Managing Data in Word

WORD IS MORE than just a word processor: it is a tool for managing information. In this session, you will learn to create and sort lists and find specific records in those lists. You'll learn how to produce form letters, labels, and other merged documents in Session 14. At the end of this session you will be able to:

- Define basic merge terminology
- Create a data source
- Sort your data

■ Vocabulary

- database
- data source
- field
- field names
- merge
- record
- sort
- source document

195

The ability to store lists of personal or business contacts, members of groups or clubs, or videotapes, CDs, or books puts extra power in your hands. Using Word, you can access data stored in any of three ways:

1. in a file created using Word;

2. in an external file created using other Windows software;

3. in a file that can be shared by Word and other Microsoft Office products.

If you are using another Office or Windows application to create databases, Word Help provides useful information on importing databases into Word.

The file that contains a list of information is called a **data source** (or **database**). You can easily sort the information in the data source, or use it to create labels or envelopes. Once you have a data source, you can create a main document that refers to the information in the data source. **Merging** the main document with the data source creates letters, labels, or other documents that have been personalized by the inclusion of the data source information.

■ Creating a Table Data Source in Word

Word data sources can be stored in tables. Figure 13.1 shows a typical Word data source table.

FirstName	LastName	CurrentAssignment	HireDate
Robert	Johnson		12/12/93
Ruth	Martin	Sales	5/4/83
Janice	Reams	Marketing	6/8/95
Allen	Thompson	Finance	8/12/91
Mary	Struthers	Production	

Figure 13.1

The Employee table

Each row of the table includes information on one employee. Each employee's information constitutes a **record**. Every record contains an individual employee's data in four categories: first name, last name, current assignment, and hire date. A data source category is a **field**. The column headings in the first row of the data source are **field names**. A field name can be up to 40 characters long, but shorter names are easier to use in the main document. (In Session 14, you'll create main documents using fields you create in this session.) Within a data source, each field name must be **unique**—no two fields can have the same name. Field names can't contain spaces (you can use the underline character instead) and must begin with a letter rather than a number. Field names cannot contain any characters that you can't put in file names, such as periods, commas, colons, semicolons, slashes, and backslashes.

You can create a data source just as you would any other Word table if you follow these additional rules:

- Make sure column headings follow the guidelines for field names given above.

- Limit your table to no more than 31 columns; there is no limit on the number of rows.

- Don't leave blank rows in the table, even directly below the row of field names.

An existing Word table can be converted for use as a data source by removing blank rows or changing column headings to fit the data source rules.

Tip: Save your data source files with names that reflect their purpose. You may want to begin all of your data source file names with *Data*. Since Word alphabetizes document names, the data source files will appear consecutively in your document list.

EXERCISE 13.1 | **TO CREATE A TABULAR DATA SOURCE**

1. Choose Table ➢ Insert Table or click the Insert Table button.

2. Create a table with a column for each field in the data source you want to create. (See Session 10 to review creating tables.) For this exercise, create a table in a blank document with six columns and six rows.

3. Enter the field names as the column headings. Make sure the names are short, unique, contain no spaces, and begin with a letter. Enter the following field names:

   LNAME, FNAME, DEPARTMENT, JOBTITLE, EXT, EMAIL

4. Enter data in the table. Enter the following data:

   Beelar, Barbara, Marketing, Sales Manager, 213, bbeelar@triad.com

   Quick, Stephan, Finance, Director, 456, squick@triad.com

CONTINUES ON NEXT PAGE

Kenkel, Sue, Director, Director, 567, skenkel@bendle.com

Davis, Doreen, Reception, Office Manager, 135, ddavis@traid.com

Popovski, Jenny, MIS, Office Manager, 487, jpopovski@triad.com

Kokoska, Mary Jean, Marketing, Business Manager, 343, mkokoska@triad.com

5. Close the document and save it as *Data—Management Staff.*

■ Creating a Delimited Data Source

Table data sources are easy to work with. All the skills you use to work with regular tables can be brought to bear on them. But if you have more than 31 fields of information, Word doesn't allow you to use a table. Instead, create **delimited data files**, where fields are separated by a tab or comma, and the end of each record is marked by a hard return. Figure 13.2 contains the same data as Figure 13.1, but in a comma-delimited format. Since Johnson has no current assignment, there are two commas after LastName; one marks the end of the LastName field; the other marks the empty Assignment field.

Figure 13.2

A comma-delimited data source

> **FirstName, LastName, CurrentAssignment, HireDate**
> Robert, Johnson, ,12/12/93
> Ruth, Martin, Sales, 5/4/83
> Janice, Reams, Marketing, 6/8/95
> Allen, Thompson, Finance, 8/12/91
> Mary, Struthers, Production,

Commas can be problematic as delimiters. If the information in the data source might contain commas (like 1401 Wood St., Apt. 13), you need to enclose any field that contains a comma in quotes ("1401 Wood St., Apt. 13"), or Word assumes that 1401 Wood St. is one field and Apt. 13 is another. This is easy to forget and grows tiresome even when you remember. You may choose, instead, to create a tab-delimited data source.

Better Method →

If you use tabs to delimit a data source, change the tab stop settings to make sure your data lines up. (With the preset tab stops you may have to press Tab twice after a short entry. While this visually lines up the data, the two tabs signify the end of two different fields, just as the two commas do in Johnson' record; so the data will be misaligned with the field names.) In Figure 13.3, the user has created a data source after first changing the tab stop settings.

Figure 13.3

A tab-delimited
data source

When you have a choice, tables are the easiest way to create a data source with fewer than about seven or eight fields. You should, however, know how to create a delimited data source for longer records. Also, many of the external files you might use as data sources will open in Word in a comma-delimited format, so it's important to be familiar with delimited data. If you prefer to view delimited data in a table, you can convert the data using the Convert Text to Table option on the Table menu.

Note: You may ultimately choose to create your source data files in another program. Word is fine if you are creating relatively small data sources: fewer than 500 records with less than a dozen fields. If you need to track forty fields of information on thousands of individuals, Word is not a good choice. Database programs like Microsoft Access are designed to manage larger quantities of data.

EXERCISE 13.2 | **TO CREATE A COMMA-DELIMITED DATA SOURCE**

1. **Type the field names separated by commas. Press Enter at the end of the list of field names.** For this exercise, open a new blank document and type:

   DESCRIPTION, DEPARTMENT, DATE_PURCHASED, VENDOR, COST

2. **Enter the data in the fields separated by commas. Enter a comma if the data is missing for a field.** Here, enter:

   486DX 75mhz 8 MB, Admin, 12/12/94, PC Warehouse, $2200

   Pentium 90 16 MB, Finance, 5/6/95, Computers Unlimited, $2695

   386SX 16mhz 2 MB,, 6/7/91, Computers Unlimited, $1995

   Pentium 90 8 MB, Admin, 7/12/95, PC Warehouse, $2625

   Pentium 120 16 MB, Marketing, 12/15/95, Computers Unlimited, $3200

CONTINUES ON NEXT PAGE

Pentium 120 20 MB, Finance,, Computers Unlimited, $3300

Pentium 90 16 MB, Staff Development, Better Buy, $2300

486DX2 75mhz 8MB Laptop, Admin,, Better Buy, $2900

3. Save the document as *Data—Computer Inventory* and close it.

■ Using the Mail Merge Helper

The Mail Merge Helper (which works like a Wizard) helps you create data sources and produce merged documents, including lists, catalogs, and directories, to name a few. To create a new data source using the Mail Merge Helper, choose Tools ➤ Mail Merge. Click the Create button (see Figure 13.4) under Main Document and select the type of document you will create using your data source. For now, choose Form Letters. Don't worry if you don't know yet how you will use the data source you are creating. Although Word asks you to specify a type of document, your choice at this point doesn't preclude creating any of the other types of main documents later, as the needs arise.

Figure 13.4

Opening screen of the Mail Merge Helper

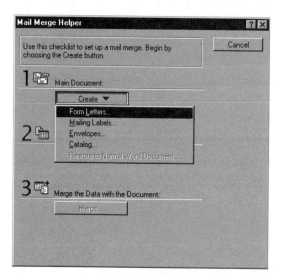

This is a good time to think about how you will use your data source. When you create a main document, you will be able to include entire fields from the data source. If, for example, you separate names into FirstName and LastName fields, you can begin a letter with *Dear FirstName (Dear Joe,*

Dear Sally). If you use one Name field for both first and last names, you can't include just a first name in a letter using this data source. And if you might want *Dear Mr. Chen* as the salutation, you will want to include the field Title for Mr., Mrs., Ms., and Dr.

Addresses should be separated into StreetAddress or Address, City, State (or Province), and ZipCode or PostalCode fields. Later, you can choose to print labels that are sorted by zip code, or only print envelopes and letters for clients in Arkansas. If you enter city, state, and zip code as one long field, you rule out some future possibilities.

Remember that your data source can be used over and over again. Don't turn what should be separate fields into one field to save a few minutes. You may end up going back and separating the data into two fields for another project later on—a very inefficient use of your time.

Note: If you are creating several data source files, it's helpful to repeat as many of the field names as you can between data sources. For example, if you use "FirstName" in one data source, avoid using "FNAME" or "First" in other source files. That way, you'll often be able to use the same main documents with different data source files rather than recreating them each time.

After you select the type of main document you want to create, previously dimmed buttons are available. Click the Get Data button under Data Source; then choose Create Data Source from the drop-down list. The Create Data Source dialog box (Figure 13.5) comes with a list of field names commonly used in mail merges. Scroll the list to see if any of the field names you want to use in your data source are included. You must remove names you do not want included.

Figure 13.5

The Create Data Source dialog box

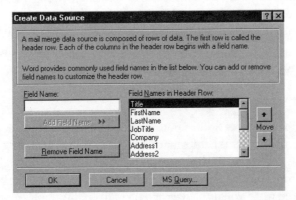

To remove a field name from the list, select the field name and click the Remove Field Name button. To add a field name to the list, type the name in the Field Name control and click the Add Field Name button. If you enter an illegal field name (for example, a name that contains a space or that already appears on the list), the Add Field Name button will be disabled.

If you will be entering records from a membership form or handwritten list, it's convenient if the field names appear in the same order as they do on the **source document**—the form or list. You can enter data more efficiently if you don't have to skip around on a page. For the same reason, you may be better off to include some fields that you don't really need now. If you originally set up the Access database illustrated in Figure 13.6 as a data source for creating mailing labels, you wouldn't need to include the birthday field. However, there may be a good reason to include it anyway. When your boss asks for a list of all the employee birthdays that month, you won't have to create the list from scratch or go back and hurriedly add the information to your data source.

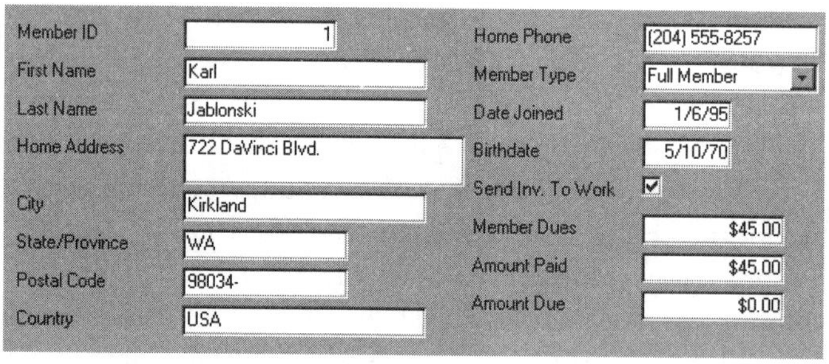

Figure 13.6
A source document

When you have entered and arranged the field names to your satisfaction, click OK. You will be prompted to save the data source file. When you save the file, Word will remind you that the file contains no records and ask whether you want to edit the data source or edit the main document. At this point, you can begin entering information in the data source file by choosing Edit the Data Source.

■ Entering Records

Click the Edit Data Source button to open the Data Form dialog box, shown in Figure 13.7. Enter the information for each field in your first record. When you are ready to enter another record, click the Add New button. Continue entering records until all records are entered. (You can add other records any time you need to, so you don't have to enter all ten thousand employees at one time.) When you are finished, click the View Data Source button. If you have 31 or fewer field names, Word places your document in a table.

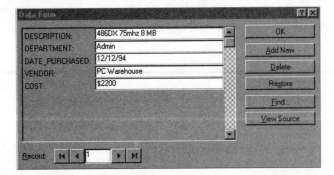

Figure 13.7
The Data Form
dialog box

TO CREATE AND ENTER RECORDS IN A DATA SOURCE FILE

1. Choose Tools ➢ Mail Merge.

2. Choose Create and select a type of Main Document. Unless you plan to merge the data source at this time, the type of Main document you create is irrelevant. For this exercise, choose Form Letters.

3. Indicate if you want to use the active window as the Main Document or create a new document. Here, choose New Main Document.

4. Choose Get Data Source and then choose Create New Data Source.

5. Review the list of suggested field names in the Create Data Source dialog box and delete field names that you don't want. Delete Title, JobTitle, Company, Address 1, Address 2, City, State, PostalCode, and Country.

6. Add new field names by entering them in the Field Name text box and clicking Add Field Name. Add "Birthday" and "Supervisor" fields.

7. Use the Move arrows to put your fields into the desired order. Put the fields in this order: LastName, FirstName, Department, Supervisor, Birthday, HomePhone, WorkPhone.

8. Click OK when you are finished entering field names and are ready to save the file.

9. Enter a file name for the data source file in the Save dialog box. Click Save. For this exercise, enter *Data—Employee List* as the file name.

10. To begin entering data, choose Edit Data Source when the option dialog box is presented.

CONTINUES ON NEXT PAGE

11. Enter records in the data form, pressing Tab between each field and Enter at the end of a record. Enter the following data:

Robert, Mitchell, Janitor, Maintenance, Rally, 5/6/55, 810-555-9999, 2345

Mary, Richardson, Secretary, Admin, Marsted, 4/21/64, 810-555-8980, 4345

Bobby, Rogers, Cook, Food Services, Dart, 3/4/76, 810-555-8980, 4567

Mary, Smith, Janitor, Maintenance, Rally, 6/16/73, 810-555-3456, 2345

John, Ford, Cook, Food Services, Dart, 11/30/73, 810-555-9099, 4567

Helen, Davids, Secretary, Admin, Marsted, 9/17/65, 810-555-9456, 4343

12. Use the record navigation buttons at the bottom of the window to view previous records.

13. Click View Data as Source when you are finished entering records. This takes you to the table that Word creates with your data.

14. Review your data and click Save on the toolbar to save your records before proceeding.

▨ Using the Database Toolbar

When the active file is a data source file, Word automatically displays a Database toolbar:

From the toolbar, you can conveniently access tools you will use to manage the data source. You can enter new records, edit, or delete records in the data source just as you would in any table. To add a new record to the end of your data source, click the Add New Record button on the Database toolbar. To delete a record, move the insertion point within the record you want to delete; then click the Delete Record button on the Database toolbar.

Be careful not to delete the first row, which contains the field names. If you do, you will have to recreate it to use this file as a data source. Save the data source file again to save the records.

If you prefer to enter or view records using the data form, clicking the Data Form button on the toolbar reopens the Data Form dialog box.

SECTION 13.2: SORTING A DATA SOURCE

You can organize your data source by sorting it on any field. You can sort by last name, zip code, or any other field that you find useful. Records can be sorted in **ascending order** (A to Z, or 0 to 9) or **descending order** (Z to A or 9 to 0).

To sort the records in the data source, place the insertion point anywhere in the column you want to sort by. Click the Sort Ascending button or Sort Descending button on the Database toolbar to sort the records in the order your specified.

Tip: You can sort any list, whether or not it's a data source. A list of employees, students, or friends can be sorted by last name to make it easy to find someone on a printed list. Labels can be printed in zip code order, which earns a discount from the Post Office for bulk mailings.

The Database toolbar's Find tool lets you quickly locate a particular record, based on the information in one field, so you can edit or delete the record to keep your data store up to date. The "Finding Records" Help topic shows how to find a specific record.

EXERCISE 13.4	TO SORT A DATA SOURCE

1. **Open a data source document in data source view.** For this exercise, you should still have Data—Employee List open. If you closed it, reopen it and display the Database toolbar. (Select View ➤ Toolbars ➤ Database ➤ OK.)

2. **Move the insertion point to the column that you want to sort.** Here, move to LASTNAME.

3. **Click the Sort Ascending or Sort Descending button on the Database toolbar.** Click Sort Ascending to sort by last name.

4. For more practice, sort by Department.

CONTINUES ON NEXT PAGE

5. Sort by birthday. Notice that the birthdays sort by year and then by month and day.

6. Sort by last name again before saving the document.

What You Have Learned

In this session, you have learned the essential first steps to creating merged documents. You now know three ways to create a data source: by creating a table, creating a comma- or tab-delimited data file, or using the Mail Merge Helper. You know how to define fields so that you can access the data in a number of ways. You also know how to sort data and add and delete records.

Focus Questions

1. What are the requirements of a field name?

2. Why is it useful to know about delimited data source files? What does *delimited* mean?

3. What is the easiest type of data source file to use when you are creating a database with 10 or fewer fields, and why?

4. List the steps to adding a record to a data source file.

5. List three examples of data that you might want to collect in a data source file.

6. Why is it important to be able to sort records in a data source? List three ways that you might want to sort the data source file in Figure 13.3.

Reinforcement Exercises

Exercise 1   a) Open *To Do List,* which you created as a table in Session 10. Convert this table to a data source table by deleting blank rows and using the data source rules outlined in Section 1.

b) Switch to the data form and enter at least five things that you have to do this week.

c) Save the data source file as *Data—To Do List.*

Exercise 2 a) Using any one of the methods described in this session, create a data source file that contains information about your friends and family. Decide what the field names should be to give you maximum flexibility for retrieving the data later. The file should contain the following information: name, address information, phone numbers, birth date, spouse/significant other's name, other.

b) Enter at least 10 records. Leave fields blank if you do not have the information.

c) Sort alphabetically by last name.

d) Save the document as *Data—Friends and Family.*

Exercise 3 a) Create a data source file using the Mail Merge Helper to create a media catalog of tapes, CDs, videotapes, and/or books that you own. Use the following fields: "Title," "Artist/Author," "MediaType," "DatePurchased," "PricePaid," and "Comments."

b) Enter at least 10 records. Leave fields blank if you don't have the information available.

c) Sort the records by title and then by artist/author. **d)** Save the document as *Data—Media List.*

Exercise 4 a) Add the following terms and their definitions to *My Definitions: data source, record, field, field names, delimited data file, source document.*

b) Select all of the terms and definitions and choose Table ➤ Sort Text to put the terms in alphabetical order.

c) Close and save the changes.

Creating Customized Merge Documents using Word

N THIS SESSION, you will merge the data source file created in Session 13 with main documents to create form letters, lists, and labels. Anyone who works with groups of people or collections of objects finds a use for merging sooner or later. At the end of this session you will be able to:

- Create a main document for a form letter
- Insert merge fields in a main document
- Merge a main document and data source
- Select records to be merged
- Print labels and envelopes
- Troubleshoot problems with merged documents

Vocabulary

- document incompatibility
- main document
- merge field code
- navigation buttons
- query
- string

SECTION 14.1: CREATING A MAIN DOCUMENT

Now that you have data sources, you can merge the data source records to create personalized form letters, labels, or envelopes. You need two documents to complete a merge: a data source with field names and a main document that uses the field names. Always construct your data source before creating the main document, since you will need to use the data source field names in the main document.

Creating a Main Document from Scratch

Open the Mail Merge Helper (Tools ➤ Mail Merge) to create a main document. Choose Form Letter as the document type. Word will ask if you want to use the current document or begin in a new document window. If the current window is empty, you can choose either. Otherwise, you should begin in a new window.

Word again displays the Mail Merge Helper. Click the Get Data button, and choose Open Data Source. In the dialog box, select the data source file to use with the main document you are creating. Word confirms that the file meets the rules listed in Session 13 and can be used as a data source. This is an important step; you cannot create a main document without choosing a data source. After the data source is confirmed, Word will return to the main document and open a dialog box to remind you that the main document has no merge fields, so you cannot merge the main document and data source yet. Choose Edit Main Document to begin creating the main document. The Mail Merge toolbar will be displayed:

There are two types of text in a main document: "regular" text, and variable text. Regular text is the same in each copy of the document, like the body text in a letter. Variable text is anything that will change from copy to copy—names, addresses, and so on. In a Mail Merge main document, merge fields take the place of variable text.

In the main document, enter and edit regular text as you would in any other Word document. Where you want text from the data source to appear in your final, merged document, enter a merge field code. A **merge field code** provides a link to the field name used in the data source that contains the variable data for the finished letters.

To enter a merge field code in the main document, place the insertion point where you want the merge field to appear; then click the Insert Merge Field button on the Database toolbar to display the list of field names from the data source. Choose the field name from the list, and Word inserts it as a merge code:

> **TO:**   «FirstName» «LastName», «JobTitle» «Department»

When you save a main document, indicate in the filename that it is a main document, just as you did by putting "Data" at the start of data source files. If you begin each filename with the word Main (for example, *Main—Holiday Letter to Employees*), you can find your main documents easily. It's also a good idea to give the main document a name that indicates its data source. This way, you can tell by looking at the names which main documents and data sources go together. For example, if your data source is named *Data—Management Staff*, your main document could be *Main—Management Staff Meeting Notice*.

EXERCISE 14.1   **TO CREATE A MAIN DOCUMENT**

1. **Choose Tools ➢ Mail Merge from the menu bar.**

2. **Choose Create and then select the type of main document that you want to create.** In this case, choose Form Letters.

3. **Indicate whether you want to use the document in the active window or create a new main document.** Here, choose New Main Document.

4. **Choose Get Data under Data Source to open an existing data source file or create a new data source.** Open *Data—Employee List*.

CONTINUES ON NEXT PAGE

5. Click Edit Main Document to enter the regular text that you want to appear in the Main Document. For this exercise, create the following memo:

MEMORANDUM

[Insert Date]

TO:

FROM: Elaine Helms, Administrative Director

RE: Staff Meeting

This is a reminder that there will be a staff meeting to develop goals and objectives for next year and prepare a calendar to track our accomplishments. Please make every effort to attend.

Thanks for your continued hard work.

6. Place the insertion point where you want merge data to appear. Move the insertion point one tab position from "To:"

7. Click Insert Merge Field to insert fields at the desired positions in the main document. Here, click Insert Merge Field and select First Name. Press the space bar once and select Last Name. Type a comma, press the space bar, and insert the Job Title field. Press Enter, tab once and insert Department.

8. Save the Main Document. Save this document as *Main - Employee Meeting*.

Your memo should look like this:

MEMORANDUM

[Insert date]

TO: «FirstName» «LastName», «JobTitle»
            «Department»

FROM: Elaine Helms, Administrative Director

RE: Staff Meeting

This is a reminder that there will be a staff meeting to develop goals and objectives for next year and prepare a calendar to track our accomplishments. Please make every effort to attend.

■ Previewing the Merged Document

When the main document and data source are merged, Word will generate a separate letter for each record in the data source, based on the main document. To see what the first document will look like when the merge is completed, click the View Merged Data button on the Mail Merge toolbar. The toolbar includes a set of **navigation buttons** that you can use to move to the first record, back a record, forward a record, or to the last record:

Click again on the View Merged Data button to return to the main document.

EXERCISE 14.2	TO PREVIEW THE MERGED DOCUMENT

1. **Click the View Merged Data button on the Mail Merge toolbar.**

2. **Use the navigation buttons to view each of the merge records.**

3. **Click again on the View Merged Data button to return to the main document.**

SECTION 14.2: CONVERTING AN EXISTING DOCUMENT TO A MAIN DOCUMENT

You can also create a main document by adding merge field codes to an existing document. The document shown in Figure 14.1 is a plain vanilla letter addressed to one person only. What if you wanted to send the same letter to a number of people? Create a data source that lists all recipients; then you can modify *Safety Inspection Letter* to create a main document.

Figure 14.1

The safety inspection letter

Interdepartmental Communication
May 31, 1996

TO: Janice Jacobs, Supervisor
FROM: Sandy Mertz, Manager
RE: Safety Inspection

Congratulations! I'm pleased to inform you that your division passed the most recent safety inspection with flying colors. You are a model for the company. I hope that you will make the time to share your expertise with other divisions so they can do as well in the future

In thanks, please arrange to take your staff out to lunch on the company.

To convert an ordinary document to a merge main document, open the document and then open the Mail Merge Helper (Tools ➤ Mail Merge) to create the main document. Click the Create button under Main Document and choose the type of main document you want to create. The dialog box appears, asking whether you want to convert the active document to a main document or start in a new document window; choose Active Window. In the Mail Merge Helper, click the Get Data button and open the data source so the data source field names will show up in the list of Merge Field Codes.

Word will return to the main document and inform you that it doesn't have any merge field codes. Click Edit Main Document. Delete each piece of variable information and replace it with the appropriate merge field code by clicking the Insert Merge Field button and selecting the field from the list of data source field names. (You must enter merge field codes from the toolbar; you cannot simply type "<<" before the field name and ">>" after.) When you are finished, click View Merged Data and make sure the results are as you anticipated. Use Save As to save the changed main document using a filename beginning with Main.

EXERCISE 14.3 **TO CONVERT AN EXISTING DOCUMENT TO A MAIN DOCUMENT**

For this exercise, you need to produce a memo that you will then convert to a main merge document. Create the following memo and save it as *Safety Inspection Memo*.

Interdepartmental Communication

May 31, 1996

TO: Janice Jacobs, Supervisor

FROM: Sandy Mertz, Manager

RE: Safety Inspection

Congratulations! I'm pleased to inform you that your division passed the most recent safety inspection with flying colors. You are a model for the company. I hope that you will make the time to share your expertise with other divisions so they can do as well in the future.

In thanks, please arrange to take your staff out to lunch on the company.

1. **Open the document you want to convert to a merge main document.** Use *Safety Inspection Memo* for this exercise.

2. **Choose Tools ➤ Mail Merge and click Create Main Document.**

3. **Choose the type of document that you want to create.** In this case, choose Form Letters.

4. **Choose Active Window when asked if you want to use the document you have open or create a new blank document.**

5. **Click the Get Data button to open the data source.** Open *Data—Employee List.*

6. **Click Edit Main Document so that you can insert the merge codes in your open document.**

7. **Replace existing text with the desired merge codes by selecting the text you want to replace, clicking the Insert Merge Codes button, and selecting the field code you want.** Here, select "Janice," click Insert Merge Codes, and choose FirstName. Select "Jacobs," click Insert Merge Codes, and choose LastName. Select "Supervisor," click Insert Merge Codes, and choose JobTitle. Press Enter, tab once, click Insert Merge Codes and choose Department.

8. **Click View Merged Data to verify that the results are what you anticipated.**

9. **Choose File ➢ Save As to save a new name that indicates that it is a main merge document.** Save the file as *Main—Safety Inspection Memo.*

SECTION 14.3: MERGING DOCUMENTS

You have created a main document and specified a data source, so you are ready to merge the two documents. If the main document is not active, switch to the main document window.

Note: If you've closed the main document and data source windows, you will need to choose Tools ➢ Mail Merge. Choose Create and select the main document; choose Get Data and select the data source file. Follow this process whenever you need to merge two files that already exist.

Click the Merge button on the Mail Merge toolbar to open the Merge dialog box, shown in Figure 14.2. As the default settings indicate, Word will open a new document and merge all records from the data source with the main document. When the merge is complete, you can preview and then print the new, merged document. (If the results of the merge are not as you expected, see "Troubleshooting Merged Problems" later in this session.)

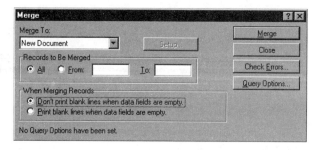

Figure 14.2

The Merge
dialog box

The first time you merge two documents, you should always merge and then view the document before you print. (You don't want fifty copies of an incorrect letter piled up on your printer.) Once you have merged a main and data source document successfully, you can choose to bypass the preview stage on successive merges and send the merged documents directly to the printer. Instead of clicking the Merge button, click the Merge to Printer button on the Mail Merge toolbar.

EXERCISE 14.4	TO MERGE A MAIN DOCUMENT WITH A DATA SOURCE

1. **Create the main document and data source.** (See Exercises 14.1 and 14.3.)

2. **Click the Merge button on the Mail Merge toolbar.**

3. **Click Merge in the Merge dialog box to create a new document with the merged records.**

4. **Preview the merge documents by using Print Preview or the Page Down button on the vertical scroll bar.**

5. **Print the merge document when you are satisfied.** For this exercise, you may choose not to print.

6. **Close the merge document without saving changes.**

A two-page main document and a 50-record data source each take up very little room on a disk. The merged file, however, will have 50 two-page letters, taking up lots of disk space. You can merge these two files any time you wish, so in the interest of preserving system resources, don't save the new merged document.

■ Specifying Records to Merge

Suppose you have a list of names and addresses, and only want to send letters to people in a certain zip code or state. Or suppose your printer can't handle printing a large number of pages at a time; it stops and prints an error message. For both problems, the solution is to merge and print records in smaller quantities.

You use the Merge dialog box to specify which records you want to include in a merge operation. After you have selected your data source and main document, click the Merge button to open the Merge dialog box. To merge a range of records, enter the data source row numbers of the first and last records you want to merge in the two text boxes in the From control.

14.2

14.3

In the database world, a **query** is a tool used to select a group of records that meet specific criteria. If you want to select records based on content rather than row number, click the Query Options button to open the Filter Records page of the Query Options dialog box, shown in Figure 14.3.

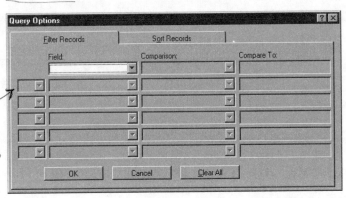

Figure 14.3
The Query Options
dialog box

Left most column And/or in
Shows after CompareTo control is defined

In the Field drop-down list, select the field you want to use to select records. If you want to merge records with zip code 48439, choose the ZipCode field. For all the customers whose last name is Jones, choose LastName.

In the Compare To control, enter the text **string** (one or more characters) you are looking for in the selected field. For records with a zip code of 48439, enter *48439*. To find all customers named Jones, enter *Jones*.

The comparison box lets you determine how the records in the data source should be compared to the text string. If you enter a ZipCode of 48439:

Comparison:	Selects Records:
Equal to (the default)	with the ZipCode 48439
Not Equal to	with a ZipCode that is not 48439
Less than	with a ZipCode in the range 00000–48438 (there are no negative zip codes)
Greater than	with ZipCodes in the range 48440–99999
Less than or Equal to	with a ZipCode 00000-48439
Greater than or Equal to	with a ZipCode 48439-99999
Is Blank	where there is no value in the ZipCode field
Is Not Blank	where any ZipCode is included

Leave the default to find a match between ZipCode and the Compared To string. (When updating the data source, you can use Is Blank to create a list of records that still need zip codes.)

Using And and Or

Once you enter a Compare To text string, the word And appears in the drop-down to the left of the Field row of the dialog box. You can enter multiple query criteria and select, for example, the records for people in California without a zip code entered in the data source. You can choose to link the two comparisons with And or Or.

Choosing And means both comparisons must be true for a match. In the comparison example given above, choosing And will select all records where the State is California *and* the ZipCode field in the data source is blank. Records for people from Arkansas, Oregon, or Massachusetts will not be selected. Records for people living in California *with* a zip code will not be selected.

Choosing Or means a match will be found if either comparison is true. In this case, *all* Californians will be selected, as well as anyone from any other state who doesn't have a zip code. Use Or when you want to select two possible values for the same field. If you select records where State is equal to California *and* State is equal to Nevada, no records will be selected (since no single record includes both states). Choosing Or will select records for both states.

■ Sorting Records in a Query

If you want to merge and print records in a different order than that used in the data source, use the other page of the Query Options dialog box: Sort Records (see Figure 14.4). Select the field you wish to sort by from the Sort By drop-down list. Ascending order is the default, but you can choose Descending by clicking the option button.

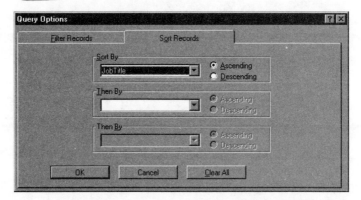

Figure 14.4

Sorting records

You may also want to add other levels of sorting. Entries in a phone book, for example, are sorted first by last name. When two or more households share the same last name, those households are sorted by first name. Only in case of a "tie" for last name (the primary sort field) is an entry sorted by first name (the secondary sort field). If you think some records in the data source may have the same value for the Sort By field, enter another field in the Then By control to handle those records.

When you have finished entering any selection or sorting information, click OK to close the Query Options dialog box and return to the Merge dialog box. Go ahead with the merge as before. When you are finished printing the merge, you can discard the merge document. If you want to save the query options, save the main document before closing it. If you plan to use this main document again and want to apply different query options next time, don't save the changes.

EXERCISE 14.5   **TO SELECT AND SORT RECORDS TO MERGE**

1. **Create or open a main document and attach a data source document.** For this exercise, create the following main document and open the *Data—Management Staff* data source file. When you are finished, save the main document as *Main - Year End Projections Memo*.

   MEMORANDUM

   December 19, 1996

   TO: <<FNAME>> <<LNAME>>, <<JOBTITLE>> <<DEPARTMENT>>

   FROM: Mary Morris, President

   RE: Year-End Sales Projections

   As we reach the end of the year, it's important for me to recognize all the people that have made this year our most successful year to date. As I'm sure you are well aware, we have exceeded all sales expectations for the year. There is no question in anyone's mind that this can be attributed in large part to the fine job that the <<DEPARTMENT>> Department has done. Thank you for a job well done.

   In appreciation, you are invited to a company dinner on December 23. Awards will be distributed to those in <<DEPARTMENT>> and all other departments who have contributed the most to this outstanding effort. I hope to see you there.

2. **Choose Mail Merge from the Mail Merge toolbar.**

3. **Click Query Options to open the Query dialog box.**

4. **Select the field you want to use to select records.** For this exercise, choose Department.

5. **Choose how you want to compare the field.** Here, select Equal to.

6. **Enter the text string you are looking for in the Compare To control.** Type Marketing.

7. **Enter other desired query criteria in the dialog box by selecting And or Or and then selecting the criteria.** Choose Or, Department, Equal To, and Finance.

8. **Click the Sort tab to sort the resulting merge document.**

9. **Select the desired sort field and indicate if you want the records to be sorted in ascending or descending order.** Here, select Department and Ascending.

10. **Select additional sort criteria.** Select LastName and Ascending.

11. **Choose OK to return to the Merge dialog box.**

12. **Click Merge to begin the merge.**

13. **Review the merge document using Print Preview or the Page Down Arrow on the vertical scroll bar.** Your merge should show one memo to Finance and three memos to Marketing beginning with Beelar and ending with Kokoska.

14. **Print the document if you are satisfied with the results.** You may choose not to print the document.

15. **Close the merged document without saving.**

16. **Close the main document. If you want to clear the query options, do not save the changes.** So that you can practice this exercise again, close *Main—Year End Projections* without saving changes.

SECTION 14.4: CREATING ENVELOPES AND LABELS

Tools → Mail/Merge
Choose → Create →
Set up main
Document →
Labels
see Box pg 223
for step by-step

Labels and envelopes are two other types of main documents. Specialty labels are available at office supply stores, allowing you to create labels for any use, including mailing labels, video tape labels, and floppy disk labels. Word can merge to various sizes of envelopes: standard, business, note card, and other sizes. If your printer can print on envelopes and labels, you can create them in Word.

To create labels, begin by choosing Labels from the Create main document drop-down list. After you select a data source, a dialog box will appear. Click the Set Up Main Document button. The Label Options dialog box (see Figure 14.5) opens, offering you a choice of label sizes. Avery is the largest manufacturer of labels in the United States, so you can select Avery labels by the number printed on the box. (Use the Label Information area to match an Avery product number to the dimensions of a non-Avery label.)

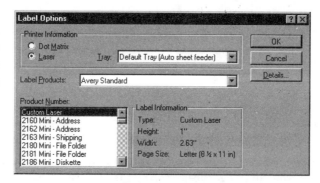

Figure 14.5

The Label Options

dialog box

There are two lists of Avery label numbers: standard (4 digit numbers) and A4 labels (numbers that begin with A4). After you select a label, click the OK button to open the Create Labels dialog box, shown in Figure 14.6.

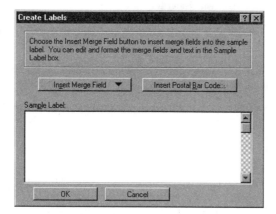

Figure 14.6

The Create Labels

dialog box

The Sample Label pane is like the main document window. Click the Insert Merge Field button to insert merge code fields in the label. Enter any other text from the keyboard. To use different fonts or paragraph formatting within a label, right-click to open the pop-up menu and make your selections. When you have created the label, choose OK to close the Create Labels dialog box and open the Mail Merge Helper so you can merge the labels with the data source.

If you want to save the label document you just created, you can close the Mail Merge Helper now and save the document, or wait until after you have merged the labels. Include the word *Labels* instead of *Main* at the beginning of the filename.

To create envelopes, choose Envelope rather than Label. Select the Envelope Size from the list provided. If you want Word to print a bar code version of the zip code (used by the Post Office to sort mail mechanically), click the Delivery Point Bar Code check box. The same Post Office machines use an FIM code to make sure the front of the envelope is facing in the right direction; click the FIM-A Courtesy Reply Mail check box if you want to help speed postal delivery. Choose OK to proceed to the Envelope Address dialog box. Insert Merge Field names just as you did in the Create Labels dialog box. When you close the Envelope Address dialog box, Word will open the Mail Merge Helper so you can merge envelopes.

EXERCISE 14.6 **TO CREATE LABELS USING MAIL MERGE**

1. **Choose Tools ➢ Mail Merge.**

2. **Create or open a main document. Choose Mailing Labels as the document type. Click New Main Document.**

3. **Get a data source.** For this exercise, open *Main—Management Staff*.

4. **Click Set Up Main Document to open the Label Options dialog box.**

5. **Scroll down the list of label options and select the label type that you want to use. Click OK.** Select No. 5383 Name Tags.

6. **Click Edit Main Document to format the main document.** Choose Edit ➢ Select All. Center the text. Change the font and font size. Arial 26 works nicely.

7. **Save the main document.** Name the document *Labels—Management Staff Name Tags*.

8. **Click View Merge Data to see how the formatted text will appear on the labels. When you are satisfied, click the Mail Merge button. Set any Query Options that you want.** Sort by LastName.

9. **Put the labels in the printer and print the merge document. Close without saving changes to the merge results document.**

10. **Close the main document.**

Tip: If you need to create a single envelope or a page of labels that are all identical (like return address labels), you don't have to use Mail Merge. Choose Tools ➢ Envelopes and Labels to open the Envelopes and Labels dialog box.

SECTION 14.5: TROUBLESHOOTING MERGE PROBLEMS

There are three basic reasons for merge problems:

- document incompatibility,

- problems with the data source, and

- problems with the main document.

Document incompatibility means Word doesn't recognize the data source or main document as a valid mail merge file. A dialog box will appear telling you that the main document has no merge codes, or that the data source is invalid. Examine the file in question. If it is a data file, make sure it has field names and that the data is in a table or is properly delimited. If the problem is the main document, open it and check to make sure you have selected the correct file and that it has merge field codes.

Even if both files seem to be OK, structural problems with individual records (like missing fields) can cause Word to stop in the middle of a merge. You can have Word check the data source for omission errors before merging. With either the data source or main document active, click the Check for Errors button on the Mail Merge toolbar to open the Checking and Reporting Errors dialog box, shown in Figure 14.6, much like checking spelling before printing.

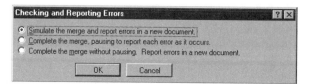

Figure 14.6

Checking for data
source errors

You can choose to have Word simulate a merge or actually merge the two documents and report errors. If you expect errors, simulation is best, as shown in Figure 14.6. If you don't think there will be errors (always the hope), go ahead and have Word merge, stopping along the way to report any errors it finds, the middle option. When Word finds an error, a dialog box will open. Depending on the type of error, you may be allowed to fix the error and then continue merging. If you cannot, note the information provided, and click the OK button to continue finding errors. When Error Checking is complete, close the merged document and fix the data source and/or main document files before merging the documents again.

Even if Word finds no errors and your documents merge, you may still find mistakes in your merged document. There is an easy way to decide if a mistake is in the main document or the data source. If the mistake appears in every merged document, look for the problem in the main document. For example, if there is no space between the first and last names in any of your merged form letters, you need to put a space between the merge codes for FirstName and LastName in the main document. Spelling errors in every merged document should lead you to suspect that you forgot to check the spelling in the main document before merging.

If a mistake appears in some but not all merged documents, the problem is in the data source. If a merged first name is spelled incorrectly in one of the merged letters, it's misspelled in the data source. Close the merged file, open the data source file and correct the error, and then merge the documents again.

Merging is a useful and time-saving tool. It can provide an easy way to personalize anything you send out but it requires thinking ahead. Create your data source files before you need them and they'll be ready for you in those crunch times. If you ever find yourself typing a list of names more than once, think "data source file" and you'll be on your way!

What You Have Learned

In this session, you have learned to create a variety of merged documents from personalized form letters to labels. You have learned how to insert merge field codes into main documents so that they can be replaced with the entries in your data source files. You now know how to convert an existing document to a main document so that you can distribute the document to a list of people. You have learned how to select specific categories of records from your data source file and sort those records by different fields using Query Options. Finally, you have learned how to produce labels and envelopes and to troubleshoot merge problems.

Focus Questions

1. What are the two documents that you need to create merge documents, and what must they contain?

2. Define each of the types of text in a main document.

3. What is the purpose of inserting a merge field code in the main document?

4. How do you convert an existing document to a merge main document?

5. Why don't you need to save the results of a merge?

6. Assuming your data source file contains fields for Age and City, how do you write a query to select records of people who are under 29 and live in Traverse City?

Reinforcement Exercises

Exercise 1   Create labels to mark the equipment that you inventoried in *Data—Computer Inventory* in Exercise 13.2. Use Avery Labels 5663 as the model for your labels. Include Description, Department, and Date Purchased. Sort the labels by Department and then by Date Purchased.

Exercise 2   Create mailing labels for a select group of your family and friends from the data source file *Data—Friends and Family*, which you created in Reinforcement Exercise 13.2. Select only those people on the list that live in the same city (or State) as yourself. Be sure to save the main document that you create.

Exercise 3   Create labels for the media collection that you organized in Reinforcement Exercise 13.3 in *Data—Media List*. Use Query Options to select the media type that corresponds to your selection of one or more of the following:

- audio labels for your CDs and tapes;

- video labels for your videos;

- book plates (*From the collection of*) labels for your books.

Exercise 4   a) Open *My Definitions* and add the following terms and your definitions for: merge field code, main document, query, labels. Save and close *My Definitions*.

b) To study the terms and their definitions, create study sheets. To do this, create a mail merge with mailing labels and a label definition that will give you four to six labels to the page. Use *My Definitions—Table* as the data source.

c) Format the labels so that the terms will be centered with a large bold font. Insert at least a couple of blank lines between the terms and the definition field codes.

d) Merge the documents. If you want, you can now print the sheets and cut the terms apart so that you have individual study cards for each term. Do not save the merged document.

PROJECT B: MERGING

Overview

The purpose of this project is to give you practical experience using mail merge, so that you can produce and personalize forms and similar documents more efficiently. In this project, you will create form letters, mailing labels, and directories for a community organization.

Description

The newly-formed Community Foundation has asked you to put together a mailing to send to various influential individuals to solicit funds for their community improvement campaign. The Foundation has received a commitment from a local corporation to match dollar for dollar any money the Foundation raises to fight drug abuse and provide job opportunities for young people. The Foundation has given you their mailing list of donors. Additionally, the Foundation has asked you to identify non-profit organizations in your community that might be interested in submitting a grant proposal to apply for these funds.

Part 1

1. Create a donor data source with the following names and addresses:

   Ms. Marsha Shilling, 3454 Sunrise, Flushing, MI, 48433, (810) 555-8584;

   Rev. Carole Huston, 455 Oak, Rochester, MI, 48307 (810) 555-6508;

   Ms. Judy Amir, 568 Oldstone Drive, Takoma Park, MD., 20912, (301) 555-6510;

   Ms. Rosemary McNatt, 999 West Adams Ave., Detroit, MI, 48214, (313) 555-8211;

   Mr. Dean Drake, 101 Parks Drive, Honolulu, Hawaii, 96782 (808) 555-6290;

   Mr. Dan Layman, 601 Margaret St., Virginia Beach, VA, 23454, (804) 555-5848;

2. Add the names and addresses of five people from your community. Save this file as *Data—Potential Donors*.

3. Write a form letter for the Community Foundation to send to prospective donors who live in your community, describing the purpose of the fund drive and asking for their generous contributions. Be sure to include merge fields for the inside address and a greeting (Dear (Mr. or Ms. ???).

4. Merge the form letter with the list of donors who live in your community.

5. Create mailing labels using Avery address labels #5160 for the people who will be receiving letters.

6. Print the letters and the labels (You can use plain paper for the labels).

Part 2

1. Create a second data source file using the local Yellow Pages or community directory, to develop a mailing list of ten community or social service organizations that might be interested in applying for the community improvement grant money. Save this file as *Data—Organizations*.

2. Create a form letter to send to the organizations describing the project and asking them to submit proposals within 90 days to apply for the grants.

3. Merge the form letters with the list of organizations.

4. Produce mailing labels using Avery address labels #5161 for the list of organizations.

5. Print the letters and the mailing labels.

Bonus

■ Create letterhead for the Community Foundation to use for their letters. Their address is 5555 3rd St., [Your Community], [Your State], [Your Zip Code].

Working with Outlines

OUTLINES HELP YOU to organize ideas when you are creating long or complex documents. Word supports outlining with toolbar buttons that let you indent or outdent text within an outline structure. Any document that includes headings and body text can be viewed and manipulated in Outline view. At the end of this session you will be able to:

- Create an outline
- Edit an outline
- Rearrange a document in Outline view
- Collapse and expand outlines
- Print an outline

Vocabulary

- body text
- collapse
- demote
- expand
- heading level
- heading numbering
- outline
- Outline view
- promote

SECTION 15.1: CREATING AN OUTLINE IN WORD

While you can create an outline in any view, there is a special Outline view that is best suited to the task. Click the Outline View button or choose View ➤ Outline to change to Outline view. The Outline toolbar is automatically displayed when you enter Outline view.

Text you enter in an outline is assigned **heading levels**. In Figure 15.1, the course title is at the highest level, Heading 1. The major topics below it are at the Heading 2 level, and the subheadings are at Heading 3 level. You can use up to 9 heading levels within an outline. One subheading has **body text**: "Remind students . . . "; body text can follow any heading level. A plus sign indicates that subheadings or body text will follow; a heading with a minus sign has no subheadings or body text.

Figure 15.1
The outline for a computer class

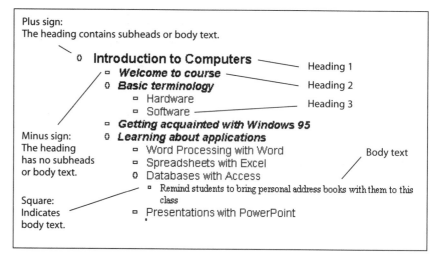

You begin by entering text at the left margin—the first heading. After typing the first heading, press Enter. Word drops down a line and keeps you on the same heading level (1).

You can continue entering all the major points in your outline, staying at heading level 1. Or, if the heading is a title, you can press Tab or click the Demote button to **demote** the next entry—move one heading lower, in this

Promote

Body Text

case to Heading 2 and enter your major points there. Pressing Tab or clicking Demote twice moves to Heading 3; and so on. Whenever you press Enter, Word moves you to a new line at the same heading level.

If you've just entered information at the Heading 3 level and the next outline entry should be at Heading 1, press Enter, hold Shift, and press Tab twice. You can also click the Promote button to **promote** the entry—move it up one level.

To enter body text, click the Body Text button on the Outline toolbar. Body text is formatted in the Normal style—the default style for document text. When you are finished typing body text, press Enter and click the Promote button to return to the previous heading level.

Word applies a different style to each heading level. To view the style name, font, size, and attributes for a heading, click anywhere in a heading and read the settings on the Formatting toolbar. You can modify the style for any heading level (see Session 12 for help on styles). Remember that Outline view is just another way to look at a document, so changing a heading style in the outline also changes the style in Normal and Page Layout views. By applying styles in Outline view, you can ensure that headings will be formatted consistently throughout a document.

EXERCISE 15.1   **TO CREATE A SIMPLE OUTLINE**

For this exercise you are going to start creating an outline, which you will edit in the next exercise. Make sure you are working in a new document.

1. Click the Outline View button to the left of the horizontal scroll bar or choose View ➤ Outline to switch to Outline view.

2. Enter Heading 1 text at the left margin, then press Enter. Type:

Introduction to Computers

3. Continue entering heading 1 text, or press Tab or click the Demote button to enter a subpoint under heading 1. Press Tab and then type the following, pressing Enter at the end of each line:

Welcome to Course

Basic Terminology

Hardware

Software

CONTINUES ON NEXT PAGE

Press Tab and type:

Word Processing with Word

Getting Acquainted with Windows 95

4. **Press Shift+Tab or click the Promote button to enter text at a higher level than the current one.** Click the Promote button and type:

Spreadsheets with Excel

Presentations with PowerPoint

Databases with Access

5. **Click the Body Text button to add body text underneath an item.** After clicking Body Text, type:

Remind students to bring their personal address books for this class

6. **View the style of each heading by clicking on the heading and looking at the Formatting toolbar.**

7. **Edit the style, if desired, as described in Session 12.** For practice with editing styles, redefine each heading's style by making the fonts 2 points larger. Set Heading 1 to 16 point; Heading 2 to 14 point; Heading 3 to 14 point; and Body Text to 12 point.

8. **Save the outline.** Name this document *Computer Class Outline.* Your finished outline should look similar to Figure 15.1.

SECTION 15.2: EDITING AN OUTLINE

To move headings or body text within an outline, begin by selecting the text you want to move. (If you move a heading, all subheadings and body text below the heading move with it.) Move the pointer to the left edge of the selection; it will change shape to a four-headed arrow (like a compass). Hold the mouse button and drag the selected text up or down to its new location in the outline. Or you can use the Move Up or Move Down buttons on the Outline toolbar to move the selected heading one level for each mouse click.

You can copy headings using the Standard toolbar or Edit menu (as you would regular text). Delete a heading by selecting it and pressing the Delete key or choosing Edit ➤ Delete.

To promote or demote an existing heading, select the heading; then click the Promote or Demote button on the Outline toolbar. When you promote or demote a heading, the headings below it are not altered. To promote or demote a heading and all subheadings associated with it, click the plus sign that appears to the left of the heading. The heading and all its subheadings will be selected, and the pointer will change to the four-headed arrow. Drag the plus symbol to the right (to demote) or left (to promote). To change a heading and subheadings to body text, drag the selected headings to the right margin.

EXERCISE 15.2	TO EDIT AN OUTLINE

1. **To move headings or text up or down in the outline: Select the text you want to move.** Select "Getting Acquainted with Windows 95."

2. **Move the pointer to the left edge of the selection. When pointer is a four-header/arrow, hold down the mouse button and drag the selected text up or down to the desired location. You can also click the Move Up or Move Down buttons on the toolbar.** Drag the text up one row so that it precedes "Word Processing with Word." Select "Presentations with PowerPoint," and click the Move Down button to move it down so that it follows "Databases with Access."

3. **To change the level of headings: Select the heading you want to change.** Select "Hardware."

4. **Drag the selection to the right to promote the heading and to the left to demote the heading. You can also click the Promote or Demote buttons on the toolbar.** Drag "Hardware" to the right so that it's a subheading under "Terminology."

5. **Insert a heading row by moving the insertion point to the desired location and pressing Enter.** Insert "Learning about Applications" as a level 2 heading in the row under "Getting Acquainted with Windows 95."

6. For more practice, select "Software" and drag it to the right, making it a subheading under "Terminology."

7. Move "Word Processing with Word," "Spreadsheets with Excel," "Databases with Access," and "Presentations with PowerPoint" as subheadings under "Learning about Applications."

8. Save the document.

SECTION 15.3: COLLAPSING AND EXPANDING THE OUTLINE

Your outline is currently fully **expanded**: all headings are visible, and all body text is displayed. You can **collapse** the outline, hiding some headings or body text. Collapsing the outline allows you to review the major ideas in the document by showing only the headings you want to see. Use the numbered Show Heading buttons on the outline toolbar to collapse or expand the outline.

| 1 | 2 | 3 | 4 | 5 | 6 | 7 | 8 | All |

Clicking the Show Heading 1 button displays only heading level 1 of the outline; the Show Heading 2 button displays levels 1 and 2. To view all the outline's headings and body text, click the Show All button. Click Show All again to hide the body text but leave all headings.

You might choose to collapse all of the outline except the section you are currently working with. Double-click the plus symbol to the left of a heading to collapse all subheadings of that heading. Double-click again on the plus sign to expand all subheadings.

To work with only one section of the outline, you may want to collapse the outline and then expand just the portion you want to work with. First, collapse the outline by clicking the Collapse button until you can see only your major headings. Click on the heading that you want to expand and click the expand button.

■ Changing Views and Printing

Any document containing paragraphs that have a heading style can be treated as an outline. Simply open the document and click the Outline View button. It may be easier to promote, demote, or move sections of the document in Outline view, and then return to Normal view for printing. You can view a document created in Outline view in the Normal or Page Layout views.

Only Outline view gives you the ability to print some, but not all headings of your document. If you are preparing a presentation, you could easily print only the headings and subheadings to pass out to the audience and still have all the detail available to you. If you collapse a document, only those headings displayed in Outline view will print. Expand the outline fully, and all headings and body text will print.

*However if
you collapse document (%)
then view to whole page (%)
you can see what the printed
pg will look like?
Yes? No?*

Note: Print Preview will not show you how a document will look printed in outline form. It assumes that you want to see how the completed document will look and shows you that instead. The only way to see how your outline will look printed is to go ahead and print it.

EXERCISE 15.3	TO VIEW AND PRINT SPECIFIC HEADINGS OF AN OUTLINE

1. **Click the Show Heading buttons to expand or collapse the desired heading levels.** Click the Show Heading 2 button to show only heading levels 1 and 2.

2. **Print the outline with only the desired heading levels showing.** Print only heading levels 1 and 2.

■ Numbering the Headings

Depending on the purpose of the outline, you may want to number the headings. You can do this using the feature called **Heading Numbering.** Move the insertion point into the outline, then choose Format ➤ Heading Numbering. Choose the type of heading numbering that you would like to apply and click OK. If you promote or demote numbered headings, the numbers will adjust automatically to their new location.

To modify the heading numbering style, click the Modify button on the Heading Numbering dialog box. The Modify dialog box is similar to the one you worked with when creating bulleted and numbered lists in Session 7. If you would like to have text appear before the number in Heading 1, enter it in the Text Before control. For example, if you need numbers that say "A-1" and "A-2," enter A- in Text Before. Click the level scroll bar on the right side of the dialog box to modify other levels. You can also change the font or starting number and adjust the distance of the numbers from the text. When you have made the appropriate modifications, click OK.

EXERCISE 15.4	TO APPLY HEADING NUMBERING TO AN OUTLINE

1. **Move the insertion point into the outline you want to number.** Move the insertion point into *Computer Class Outline.*

2. **Choose Format ➤ Heading Numbering.**

3. **Select the heading numbering style that you would like to apply.** Select the first style (I. A. 1.).

CONTINUES ON NEXT PAGE

4. **Click Modify if you would like to modify the numbering style.** Click Modify to view the Modify options but do not make any changes at this time.

5. **Click OK when you have made the selection you want.**

6. **Save the document.**

What You Have Learned

You have learned to prepare outlines to help organize your ideas when you are creating long documents or developing presentations. You can promote and demote points in outlines and enter body text under any of the headings. You know how to edit outlines by dragging headings to new locations. You can collapse and expand outlines so that you can view or print only specified levels. Finally, you know how to apply heading numbering to outlines.

Focus Questions

1. Name one advantage of working in Outline view when writing a paper or report.

2. How would you change the font for all headings at level 3?

3. What is the purpose of the four-headed arrow and how do you use it?

4. Why might you want to collapse an outline so that only one or two heading levels are visible?

5. How do you apply numbers to an outline?

Reinforcement Exercises

Exercise 1   Use the Table of Contents of this book to re-create the outline for the first four chapters. Apply Heading Numbering to level 1 by selecting "Chapter" and modifying it to say "Session." Collapse the outline so that only the Heading 1 level is showing. Expand it to show all heading levels. Print the outline.

Exercise 2 Open *We Do It Best*, which you created in Session 12. Be sure to open the *unformatted* version. Switch to Outline view. Apply the Heading 1 style to "We Do It Best Marketing Campaign" and the Heading 2 style to "Description of Campaign" and "Highlights of Campaign." Delete blank lines. Switch to normal view to view the document. Switch back to Outline view and collapse the outline to show only the headings. Save the document as *We Do It Best—Outline*.

Exercise 3 Create an outline for a presentation or report that you are working on. If you don't have a specific topic right now, create a presentation or report outline for a topic of interest to you. Make sure the outline has at least one Heading 1 heading, three Heading 2 headings under each Heading 1, and two Heading 3 headings under each Heading 2.

Exercise 4 Add the following terms and your definitions for them to *My Definitions*: *collapse, demote, Outline view, promote, expand, heading numbering*.

Harnessing the Power of Word Macros

A MACRO IS A SET of instructions that Word executes on command. These instructions can be simple or complex. If you have tasks you regularly perform that include the same series of steps, creating a macro to automate the task for you will save time and effort. At the end of this session you will be able to:

- Record a simple macro
- Create a custom toolbar button to play a macro
- Assign a macro to a keyboard shortcut
- Play macros
- Delete a macro

■ Vocabulary

- execute
- global macro
- macro
- play
- record

241

SECTION 16.1: UNDERSTANDING MACROS

You create and use macros to automate repetitive tasks that involve several steps. You **record** the series of steps you'll want to repeat later. The next time you need to complete the task, **play** the macro to repeat the series of steps in the same order.

When would you want to use macros? Here are a few examples:

- The business you work for wants all reports double-spaced, using a 12 point Arial font. But you find it easier to create the report using single line spacing (to see twice as much text on the screen), in 14 point type. You can create a macro that selects all text and changes both line spacing and font attributes. When you are ready to print the finished document, use the macro to format it according to company specifications.

- Sometimes, you forget to check the spelling on a document before you print it. You can create a macro that checks spelling, and then sends the corrected document to the printer.

- You share a computer with other users. One user likes to display all hidden text and work in Normal view with 0.5" margins. Another likes to turn off Automatic Spell Checking and work in Outline view. You prefer Page Layout view with 1" margins and no hidden text displayed. You can record a macro to turn on the settings you prefer, and then play the macro at the start of your work session.

Macros can be saved as **global macros**, which are saved with the Normal template and can be accessed from any document. Since global macros are loaded (and use some of your system resources) each time the Normal template is opened, you don't want to have hundreds of them. You can also add macros to a specific template; these macros are accessible only from documents using that template.

SECTION 16.2: RECORDING A SIMPLE MACRO

When you record a macro, you can only assign it to the template of the active document or to another open template. Before creating the macro, then, make sure that the appropriate template is open. If you want the macro to be available to all documents, create it while you are in a document created in the Normal template.

Next, determine what conditions your macro will operate under. Will the macro affect the entire document? If so, being in an active document is enough. Will you use Collapse or Expand in the macro? If you will, make sure you are in Outline view. Will the macro be used to change or format selected text? In this case, have some text selected before you begin recording the macro, just as you will when you play the macro back at a later time.

CAUTION

You may be tempted to make selecting the text one of the steps in the macro. This is a difficult step to record unless the text to be worked on will always have the same length.

When you have created the same conditions the macro will run under, choose Tools ➢ Macro to open the Macro dialog box, shown in Figure 16.1.

Figure 16.1
The Macro
dialog box

From this dialog box you can play (execute) an existing macro, delete a macro, edit a macro, or record a macro. Click the Record button to display the Record Macro dialog box, shown in Figure 16.2.

Figure 16.2

The Record Macro
dialog box

Enter a name for your macro in the Record Macro Name text box. Macro names can't include spaces, they must begin with a letter, and they should be descriptive enough that you don't have to guess what the macro does.

When you create a macro, you will be asked if you want to assign the macro to the menu bar, a toolbar, or a shortcut key combination. If you don't assign a macro to any of the three locations, it will still be accessible from a list in the Macro dialog box. Obviously, seldom-used macros shouldn't be assigned prime space on the Standard or Formatting toolbars, so you'll want to think about how important a macro is when you create it. You'll learn about assigning macros later in the session.

In the Macro Available In control, choose an active template for the macro. In the Description box, enter a brief description of the macro. Click the OK button to continue.

The message *REC* will appear on the status bar to show that you are recording a macro. The mouse pointer has a tape icon attached, and the Macro Recording toolbar with two controls will open. The Macro Recorder records commands you choose and text you enter in the order you enter them. When the macro is played back, each action you take while recording will be repeated, one after another. Since the macro recorder doesn't keep track of time, you can take as much time as you need.

If you want a macro to enter text, enter the text now. Type carefully— if you make a mistake and backspace, the same mistake and correction will be included when you replay the macro. If you want the macro to format text, choose the formatting options using the menu bar, the toolbar, or short-cut keys.

In recording a macro, you cannot use the mouse to select text or move the insertion point. Use the arrow keys, Page Up, Page Down, and the Ctrl keys to move the insertion point. Hold Shift while moving the insertion point to select text.

Tip: See the Help topics under "Navigating" and "Selecting" for lists of keystroke shortcuts.)

To pause the macro recording at any time (perhaps to look something up in this book or use Word Help), click the Pause button on the Macro Recording toolbar. When you are ready to resume, click Pause again to continue.

When you are finished recording all the steps in the macro, click the Stop button on the Macro Recording toolbar. The toolbar will close automatically.

To save the macro and discard the document, close the document without saving the changes. (You aren't discarding the macro, only the document you used while creating the macro.) If you are prompted to save changes to the template when you close Word, answer Yes.

EXERCISE 16.1   **TO CREATE A MACRO**

In this exercise, you are going to create a macro that selects all of the text in the document, changes the font to 14 point Arial, turns off the selection, and prints the document.

1. **Open the document or the template that you want to use for the tasks that you want to automate.** For this exercise, open *Executive Summary*.

2. **Choose Tools ➢ Macro to open the Macro dialog box.**

3. **Enter a name for the macro.** Type PrintForCompany.

4. **Click Record.**

5. **Click the Make Macro Available To control and select the template where you want to store the macro.** Select All Documents (Normal.dot).

6. **Click OK to begin recording the macro.**

7. **Record the steps that you want included in the macro, including any text that you want entered.** Choose Edit ➢ Select All. Choose Arial 14 point from the Formatting toolbar. Choose Format ➢ Paragraph ➢ Line Spacing ➢ Double ➢ OK. Press the Up Arrow key to deselect the text. Choose File ➢ Print ➢ OK.

8. **Click the Stop button on the macro recording toolbar when you have finished recording the steps of the macro.**

9. **Close *Executive Summary* without saving the changes.**

SECTION 16.3: RUNNING THE MACRO

To play a macro that you haven't assigned to a toolbar button, key combination, or menu, choose Tools ➤ Macro. Select the macro from the scroll list of macro names; then click the Run button. There are Word macros available on some of the templates, so don't be surprised if there are macros on the list that you did not create. The macro will **execute** (play, run) one step at a time. You can't enter text or choose menu options while the macro is executing. When the macro is done playing, Word will return control to you.

EXERCISE 16.2 | **TO PLAY A MACRO FROM THE MACRO LIST**

For this exercise, reopen *Executive Summary*.

1. **Choose Tools ➤ Macro.**

2. **Select the macro from list of available macros and click Run.**
   Select *PrintForCompany*.

SECTION 16.4: PLACING MACROS AT YOUR FINGERTIPS

Some macros you create may be used frequently. Word lets you place these macros on a toolbar button or assign them to shortcut keys when you record the macro.

Assigning a Macro to a Toolbar

Macros that you anticipate using regularly can be placed on a toolbar you always display, such as the standard or formatting toolbars. You could also create a group of macros that you use infrequently—perhaps for a particular type of document—and place them together on a toolbar of their own. (Refer to Session 11 if you need help creating a toolbar.)

After you have entered a name for the macro and selected Record, direct Word to create a macro toolbar button by choosing Assign Macro to Toolbars in the Record Macro dialog box (see Figure 16.2). The Toolbars page of the Customize dialog box will be displayed, as shown in Figure 16.3.

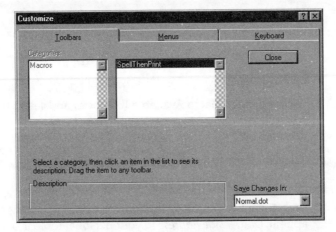

Figure 16.3
Creating a macro
toolbar button

The macro name will be displayed in the list in the center of the dialog box. Click to select the name if it is not selected; then drag the name onto the toolbar where you want the button to appear. The Custom Button dialog box appears (see Figure 16.4).

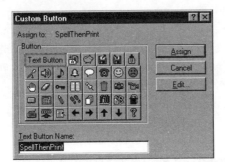

Figure 16.4
The Custom Button
dialog box

Select a button graphic or choose text for the button face. Click the Assign button to place the graphic on the button and proceed with macro recording.

EXERCISE 16.3 **TO CREATE A TOOLBAR BUTTON MACRO**

In this exercise, you will create a macro that inserts your inside address into a letter.

1. **Open the document or the template that you want to use for the tasks that you want to automate.** Create a new blank document. If available, display the personal toolbar that you created in Session 11.

CONTINUES ON NEXT PAGE

2. **Choose Tools ➢ Macro to open the Macro dialog box.**

3. **Enter a name for the macro.** Type *InsideAddress*.

4. **Click Record.**

5. **Click the Make Macro Available To control and select the template where you want to store the macro.** Select All Documents (Normal.dot).

6. **Click Toolbars to assign the macro to a toolbar.**

7. **Click OK to open the Customize dialog box.**

8. **Drag the macro name to the toolbar where you want the button to appear.** Drag *Inside Address* to your personal toolbar or to the Standard toolbar.

9. **Choose a button from the Custom Button dialog box and click Assign.**

10. **Click Close to close the Customize dialog box and begin recording your macro.**

11. **Follow Steps 5–7 in Exercise 16.1 to complete recording the macro.** For this macro, click on Align Right and enter your name and address, pressing Enter after each line. Press Enter twice at the end and click on Align Left. Stop the macro recording.

12. **Click the button on the toolbar to play the macro.**

Assigning a Macro to a Keyboard Shortcut

Instead of assigning a macro to a toolbar, you can choose to play the macro by pressing a combination of keys. In the Record Macro dialog box, choose Keyboard to open the Keyboard page of the Customize dialog box (see Figure 16.5). The macro name should be selected in the right column. To assign a shortcut, hold and press the keys you would like to assign to play the macro.

Figure 16.5

Assigning a macro shortcut

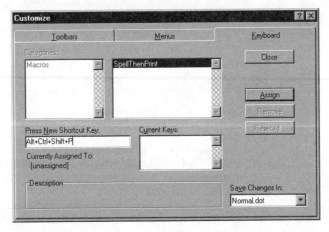

You'll need to choose a combination that is not used for anything else. You will usually need to use Alt+Shift+*letter/number*, or even Ctrl+Alt+Shift+*letter/number* to find a shortcut that is not already being used. (The combination should be easy to remember in relation to the macro, or there's no point in assigning it to shortcut keys.) The keys you pressed will be displayed in the Press New Shortcut Key text box, as shown in Figure 16.5.

If the key combination isn't assigned to another macro or function, the dialog box will say so. If the combination *is* already assigned, the current assignment will be displayed in the Current Keys box.

CAUTION

If you choose a key combination that is assigned to access the menu bar, like Alt+F to open the File menu, the Customize dialog box *will not tell you* that it is currently assigned. Don't assign macros to the Alt key in combination with F, E, V, I, O, T, A, W, or H.

To try another set of keys, delete the contents of the Press New Shortcut Key text box and try again. If you want to overwrite the current assignment or have found an unused combination, click the Assign button to begin recording the macro.

Note: If you share a machine with other users, do NOT overwrite any existing shortcuts. Make sure the key combination you select is currently unassigned.

You can also choose to assign a macro to one of the menus. Word does not make menu customization easy, so we suggest that you not add macros to menus until you are very comfortable working with Word and feel like taking on an advanced challenge. When you are ready, information on menu customization is available under "Menus" in Word Help.

EXERCISE 16.4	TO CREATE A SHORTCUT-KEY MACRO

1. **Open the document or the template that you want to use for the tasks that you want to automate.** Create a new blank document.

2. **Choose Tools ➤ Macro to open the Macro dialog box.**

3. **Enter a name for the macro.** Type InsideAddArialBold.

4. **Click Record.**

5. **Click the Make Macro Available To control and select the template where you want to store the macro.** Select All Documents (Normal.dot).

6. **Click Keyboard to assign a shortcut key to the macro.**

7. **Click OK to open the Customize dialog box.**

8. **Press a shortcut key combination in the Press New Shortcut Key control.** Press Alt+Ctrl+Shift+I.

9. **If the combination is currently assigned, delete the combination you entered and press another key combination until you find one that is available. (Do not overwrite an existing combination unless you created the macro or are sure that it is never used.)**

10. **Click Assign to assign the key combination.**

11. **Click Close to close the customize dialog box and begin recording your macro.**

12. **Follow Steps 5–7 in Exercise 16.1 to complete recording the macro.** For this macro, follow the steps below:

    ■ Click Ctrl+Home to move to the top of the document.

    ■ Click Align Right.

    ■ Change the font to Arial 12 point Bold.

    ■ Enter your name and address, pressing Enter after each line. Press Enter twice at the end and click on Align Left.

    ■ Change the font style to Regular.

    ■ Stop the macro recording.

13. **Enter the key combination to play the macro.**

SECTION 16.5: DELETING MACROS

There are two ways to delete a macro. If you have recorded a macro and are not happy with the way it executes, you can re-record the macro using the same name. You will be asked whether to overwrite (delete) the existing macro; answer Yes. You can also choose Tools ➤ Macro, select the macro from the macro list, and click the Delete button to delete the macro from the template. If you delete a macro that has a toolbar button, you also need to choose Tools ➤ Customize (or right-click on a toolbar and choose Customize) and remove the macro's button from the toolbar.

EXERCISE 16.5	TO DELETE A MACRO

1. **Choose Tools ➤ Macros.**

2. **Select the name of the macro that you want to delete.** Select InsideAddress.

3. **Click Delete and click Yes to indicate that you want to delete the existing macro.**

4. **Click Close.**

You can edit macros, copy macros from one template to another, add spots for user input or the insertion of specific information, and otherwise customize macros. Word contains extensive help information on macro creation and editing. When you have mastered the information in this session and want to learn more, choose Help ➤ Answer Wizard to find help on macros.

What You Have Learned

In this session, you learned to record simple macros using the Macro Recorder. You learned to execute your macros from the Macro dialog box and you also learned to assign a macro to the toolbar or a key combination. Finally, you have learned to overwrite a macro that you want to change or delete one that you no longer need.

Focus Questions

1. Why might you want to limit the number of global macros that you have?

2. How do you make a macro available just to the template you are working on?

3. How do you move the insertion point when you are recording a macro?

4. What are the three ways to access specific macros?

5. How do the steps for creating a macro that is assigned to a toolbar differ from the steps for creating a macro that you select from the list of macros?

Reinforcement Exercises

Exercise 1   a) Record a macro that checks the spelling in the document and then sends it to the printer. Name the macro *SpellPrint.*

b) Write a short letter to the editor of your local paper about a subject in the news this week. c) Execute the *SpellPrint* macro when you are finished. d) Save the document as *Letter to Editor.*

Exercise 2   a) Record a macro that changes top and bottom margins to 1.2" and left and right margins to 1.5", turns off Automatic Spell Checking, changes to Outline view, and sets the font to Arial 12 point. Name the macro *[YourName]* and assign it to a toolbar button.

b) Execute the macro to see that it works the way you designed it. You will have to enter some text to see that Automatic Spell Check is turned off.

c) Rewrite the macro using the same name but changing the choices for margins, spell checking, view and fonts to the way that you really like them. You might want to include other options with your macro as well. Be sure to test with a new document to see that it works as expected.

Exercise 3 a) Create a macro named *Calendar* that you assign to a toolbar. With this macro, you are going to create a monthly calendar that you can then recreate by clicking the toolbar button.

b) You might want to review the steps below so that you are sure how to do each one before recording the macro:

- Change the page to landscape orientation.

- Create a table with seven columns and six rows.

- Choose an AutoFormat that will look good with a calendar. (Grid 8 is a good choice.)

- Select the first row (use Table ➤ Select Row) and merge the cells.

- Click Center on the toolbar and type Monthly Calendar.

- Using the Tab key, move to the second row and enter the days of the week.

- Select the second row to center and bold the text.

- Turn off the Macro Recorder.

c) Create a new document and execute the macro to see that it runs correctly.

Exercise 4 Add the following terms and their definitions to *My Definitions*: *macro*, *macro recording*, *execute*. Create a macro that selects the all of the terms and sorts them alphabetically in ascending order.

PART V

Publishing Tools and Techniques

Defining and Using Columns

THIS IS THE FIRST of four sessions on the "how-to's" of desktop publishing (DTP). You have already learned a number of skills that will help you to produce eye-catching desktop publishing documents. In this session, you will learn to place text in side-by-side columns, an essential skill for creating newsletters or brochures. At the end of this session you will be able to:

- Create newspaper columns
- Adjust column widths and gutter space
- Balance columns for length
- Place vertical lines between columns of text
- Use headings that span columns
- Create locked equal columns
- Reformat columns for a section of text

Vocabulary

- balance
- column break
- End of Section marker
- gutter
- locked columns
- newspaper columns
- parallel columns
- section
- spacing

SECTION 17.1: WORKING COLUMN-WISE

You've actually been working with columns since the beginning. The text you have entered has been placed in one column that covered the page from left to right margin (give or take a few indents). Text can, instead, be formatted in multiple columns, side by side on a page. There are two types of columns: parallel and newspaper.

Parallel columns are used for text with corresponding (or parallel) information in each column. In Figure 17.1, the terms in the first column correspond to the definitions in the second column. The items in the two columns have to remain lined up. The easiest way to create parallel columns is to use Word's Table feature. (See Session 10 for more information on creating tables.)

Figure 17.1

Parallel columns

Parallel columns	A type of column used for two or more blocks of corresponding information. In Word, parallel columns are most easily constructed in tables, but can be created using tabs and indents.
Newspaper columns	A second type of column, used extensively in publishing. Text from the end of one column to the beginning of the next column. Newspaper columns are sometimes called *snaking columns*.
Gutter	In desktop publishing, the white space between the columns. Gutters must be wide enough to allow the reader to easily distinguish text in each column.

In newspaper columns, text wraps from the bottom of one column to the top of the next, as in Figure 17.2. You use **newspaper columns** to break up text on a page, making it more interesting for the reader. In Word, newspaper columns are created using the Columns feature. In the rest of this session, *columns* means newspaper columns.

You can have one, two, three, or more columns on a page. The columns can all be the same width, or you can set different widths for each column. The unoccupied white space between the columns is called a **gutter** or **spacing**.

Figure 17.2

Newspaper

columns

BUMPER SQUAD NEWS

Tournament News

The MidWest Tourney was held the last weekend in May. First place in the Men's Open was highly contested. Congratulations to Jim Compton, who finally pulled ahead with a mega score on *Double Dare*. Second place finisher Robb Morse was in first place after *Immortals*, but still is first place in the American standings after his big wins in Las Vegas and Hollywood, Florida. Patrick Cowtan finished third overall, his first placing in a major tournament.

In the Women's Open, Val Richter finished first. Val also won the Machinist's trophy with the high score for all players on *Crusin'*. Sue Kenkel took second, and third prize went to Evelyn Neumann.

The National Tournament will be held July 15-18 at the IMA Sports Arena in Flint, Michigan. A larger than usual crowd is expected. Accommodations are available at several local hostelries. To register, or for more information, call TourDex at 1-800-555-1919.

Vendor information is available by calling 1-555-777-9090. Hurry it up — limited booth space is still available.

Video Pinball

The new *Silverball Arcade III: Return of the Dead Eye* is out, and is it smooth! You'll need 8 megabytes of RAM, a CD ROM drive, and Windows 95 to run this beauty, but she's worth it. Fourteen different tables provide lots of action. *Urban Safari*, *Day at the Office*, and *Promotion!* are styled after tables with older action to appeal to the thirty and fortysomethings. *Urban Safari* places you firmly in the heart of the city. Repeated runs on the drop targets keep the rent stable on your co-op. Commute to work by scoring the left ramp. The right ramp is good for a trip home. For extended play, successfully navigate the twilight trip through the park.

There's nothing like *Day at the Office* after a day at the office. Begin by establishing the proper play mood. Choose background music from hits of the seventies and a table background from one of fourteen shades of putty gray. Then, settle in for the real action. Score extra points for schmoozing with the boss, remembering your organizer, or selling a new account. Avoid a layoff by playing the ball through the TimeClock rollover lane. Clear all the drop targets three times, then roll the upper ramp for extended play.

Several tables have obvious appeal to the younger crowd: *Teenage Mutant Hormone Rushes* and *Teenage Wannabe* feature fast moving, driving action with heavy metal and rap sound effects and background music. *Shopping Mall* is a mega-mall extravaganza. Muzak plays in the background as you drop targets for major retailers and collect friends to hang out with by clearing the rollover lanes.

To get the most out of *SA: Return of the Dead Eye*, you'll want a major multimedia machine. This package provides a great reason to buy your dream machine. And besides, in your spare time, you could learn some real software — like *Word for Windows 95*.

SECTION 17.2: CREATING EQUAL COLUMNS

 You can create columns using the Columns button on the Standard toolbar. At the beginning of the document, press the Columns button to open a column selector. Drag the pointer into the selector to choose the desired number of columns, as shown in Figure 17.3. You can select up to six columns in portrait orientation, or up to seven columns in landscape. The space between the margins will be split equally into the number of columns you selected. A 0.5" gutter will serve to separate the columns.

Figure 17.3
Choosing a number
of columns

As you type, text will be entered in the left column. When you reach the bottom of the page, Word will move the insertion point to the top of the second column.

EXERCISE 17.1 **TO CREATE COLUMNS FOR NEW TEXT**

1. **Click the Columns button on the toolbar and drag the pointer to select the number of columns that you want to use.** For this exercise, open a new, blank document and create three columns.

2. **Enter text as you normally would.** Enter the following text. Apply Heading 1 style to the heading.

Development Scores Big

This was a busy month for the Development Department, which won three major contracts totaling $4.7m. The bidding was hot but not so scorching that it could outsmart our crackerjack team. Our new clients gave the proposals rave reviews, saying that even the nontechnical people in their companies could understand them. The three projects will run concurrently, which means that everyone is going to be putting in long, hard hours; but nobody is complaining. Each of the ten developers will collect 5% of the profits as a bonus. Although they will be subcontracting some of the work, what do you want to bet that with this kind of money at stake they will be plunking away at the program code a bit themselves?

3. Save this as *Development Department Article.*

To reformat existing text, select the text you want to put into columns. Then choose the number of columns using the Columns button on the Standard toolbar.

A portion of a document with a specific number of columns is called a **section**. Each section can also have unique margins, headers and footers, and page numbering. All of the documents you created in previous sessions have had only one section. The Bumper Squad News (see Figure 17.2) has four sections. The two headings at the top of the page are in the first section, where there is only one column. The text of the Tournament News article is in section 2, separated into two unequal columns. The Video Pinball heading is back to one column, a third section. The Video Pinball article text is in two columns of equal width, a fourth section. Each time you change the number of columns within a document, you create a new section.

When you reformat existing text into columns, Word creates a section break and places an **End of Section marker** before the text to mark the end of the previous section. Another End of Section marker is placed at the end of the columns:

```
·······················End of Section·······················
```

Like page breaks, the section breaks aren't visible in Page Layout view, but you can see them in Outline or Normal view. In Page Layout view, the columns themselves are displayed side by side on the page. In Outline and Normal views, the columns are all displayed at the left margin, and are separated by **column breaks**:

```
···············Column Break···············
```

When you are creating or working with columns, it's best to remain in Page Layout view so you can best see the changes you are making to the document.

EXERCISE 17.2	TO CREATE COLUMNS FOR EXISTING TEXT

For this exercise, open *We Do It Best,* which you created in Session 12 (the unformatted version will be easier to work with). Change the top and bottom margins to 1.25" each. Select the entire document, including the headings, and apply the Normal style. Add the following text to the end of the second paragraph:

> Each of the ads appeared at least three times in the general media sources and four times in the computer periodicals.
>
> Customer Response
>
> A twenty-four hour, toll-free telephone line was included on each ad, inviting consumers to find out more about us. Throughout the course of the campaign, over 10,000 calls were received requesting information. We sent each caller a packet of information that included a letter of introduction, a description of our technical support and service departments, a catalog, order forms, and a *We Do It Best* button. In less than two months, over 25% of the callers have placed orders ranging from $29.95 to $575.00, with an average order of $79.00.

1. **Select the text that you want to convert to columns.** Select all of the text, including the headings and title. (Edit ➤ Select All works nicely.)

2. **Click the Columns button on the toolbar and drag the numbers of columns that you want.** Select three columns for this exercise.

3. **Save this document as** *We Do It Best—Columns.*

SECTION 17.3: ADJUSTING COLUMN WIDTHS

The margins and tab stops in columnar text are displayed on the ruler bar. Move the insertion point into a section that includes multiple columns, and you can read the column widths and gutter width on the ruler, shown in Figure 17.4. There is only one set of indent markers; they move from column to column with the insertion point.

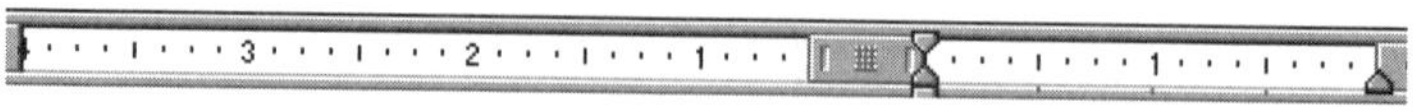

Figure 17.4

The ruler bar in a section with columns

The inch measurements also change, so that the 0" position is always at the left margin of the current column. When the insertion point is in the first column, the ruler begins at 0" and continues to the right margin. In Figure 17.4, the insertion point is in the second column. The ruler bar numbers for column 1 are negative numbers, measuring backwards from the left margin of column 2.

There are two settings that affect the amount of space available for text in a section of columns: the page margins and the gutter(s). If you want narrower columns, you can increase the left and right page margins, or increase the width of the gutter(s). Decreasing page margins and gutter space leaves more room for text on the page.

The gray spacing marker between two columns shows the width and position of the gutter. To increase the gutter between columns and change its width, point to either side of the gutter spacing marker. The pointer will change to a double-headed arrow. Drag the edge of the gutter to the left to widen the gutter and make the left column narrower. Use the right edge of the spacing marker to alter the width of the right column.

The gutter spacing marker includes a gutter position tool, which looks like a small grid in the center of the marker. You can change equal columns to unequal columns by dragging the entire gutter to the left or right using the gutter position tool.

EXERCISE 17.3   **TO ADJUST COLUMNS WIDTHS AND GUTTER POSITION**

1. **Point to the gutter spacing marker to get a double-headed arrow and drag it left or right to increase or decrease the width of the gutter and the column.** Using *Development Department Article,* drag the gutter spacing markers left and right to see the difference it makes in gutter size and column width.

2. **To change column width without affecting gutter size, point to the gutter positioning tool in the center of the spacing marker and drag it to the right or to the left.** Drag the gutter position tool to the left and to the right to see how it affects column width.

SECTION 17.4: MIXING COLUMN FORMATS

Many documents include a mixture of multicolumn text and headings that span more than one column. A report title or newsletter masthead should be centered on the page, not over just one column. Word's section breaks make it easy to mix column formats within a document. To create a heading that spans all columns, first select the heading; then click the Columns button on the Standard toolbar and select 1 Column. (You remove columns in the same way. Position the insertion point in the section or select the text to be reformatted, and choose 1 column.)

SECTION 17.5: BALANCING AND BREAKING

The text in columns doesn't always fill an entire page. The last column may be only half full, giving the document an unfinished look. When you **balance** columns within a section, Word takes the text in the section and divides it evenly between the columns. (See Figure 17.2 for two examples of balanced column lengths.) To balance the columns in a section, move the insertion point to the end of the text you want to balance. Choose Insert ➤ Break to open the Break dialog box, shown in Figure 17.5. Choose Continuous to balance the columns.

Figure 17.5

The Break
dialog box

The other section breaks can be used in multi- or single-column documents. Next Page ends the section and goes to the top of the next page. To go to a new page *and* balance columns, you must balance columns first and then insert a hard page break (Ctrl + Enter). Even Page and Odd Page end the current section, and begin the new section at the top of the next even or odd page. The Odd section break is used in publishing to ensure that new chapters begin on the odd, or right-hand page of a book.

You can choose to have a column end at a particular point. For example, suppose you have a three-line address that needs to be kept together, but the column automatically breaks after the first line of the address. To insert a manual (hard) column break, move the insertion point to the desired break point and press Ctrl+Shift+Enter. Text following the insertion point will move to the top of the next column. Hard column breaks override column balancing. If you want to balance columns and keep a block of text together, select the address, choose Format ➤ Paragraph, and use the Keep Text Together control on the Text Flow page of the dialog box.

EXERCISE 17.4	TO BALANCE COLUMN LENGTH

1. **Move the insertion point to the end of the column that you want to balance.** Using *Development Department Article,* move the insertion point to the end of the last line, " . . . pat on the back."

2. **Choose Insert ➢ Break and click Continuous.**

For more practice with columns,

3. Select the article heading "Development Scores Big," click the Columns button on the toolbar, and choose one column.

4. Click the Center button to center the heading over the columns.

5. Move the insertion point to the end of the heading and press Enter once or twice to insert a blank line between the heading and the article.

6. Delete any extra lines at the beginning of the article to reposition the text so that it fills the columns.

7. To move the heading back into the column, select it again, click Align Left, and drag the heading back to the first line of the column. Press Enter to insert a line between the heading and the article.

SECTION 17.6: USING THE COLUMN DIALOG BOX

You can easily create most of the columns you want to construct using the Column button on the toolbar. Sometimes, however, you may need to use the Column dialog box. You should use the dialog box to create columns when:

■ You may need to adjust column widths but want them to remain equal to each other.

■ You want more columns than you can select from the toolbar: 6 columns in portrait orientation or 7 in landscape orientation.

■ The columns and/or gutters in a document must be of a specific width (for example, 2.3" wide) rather than some fraction of the total page width.

Choosing Format ➤ Columns opens the Columns dialog box, shown in Figure 17.6. The Presets control has five sample column formats: one, two, or three equal columns; two unequal columns with the narrower on the left; and two unequal columns with the narrower on the right. (If you want more than three columns, use the Number of Columns spin arrows.) The default settings for the selected preset are displayed in the Width and Spacing portion of the dialog box, and a sample of the selected column format is shown in the Preview pane.

Figure 17.6
The Columns
dialog box

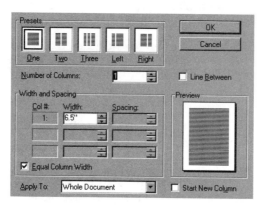

Locked Equal Columns

The Equal Column Width check box is the most important control in the Columns dialog box. Think of it as a **column lock**. If Equal Columns is turned on when you create columns, you will not be able to adjust the width of individual columns later on.

When you create locked columns using the Columns dialog box, the gutter spacing marker won't include a position tool. With Equal (locked) Columns enabled, adjusting one column or gutter affects all columns and gutters.

Entering Specific Column Widths

When Equal Column Width is on, you can enter only one column width and one gutter spacing width in the Width and Spacing area of the dialog box. If you turn Equal Column Width off, you can enter specific values for individual columns and gutters. There is a fixed amount of space between the margins when you open the dialog box, so as you increase the width of column 1, the widths of the remaining columns shrink. With only two or three columns, be sure you retain at least 0.5" spacing between the columns. With less than half an inch, it's hard to tell where one column ends and the next begins. (You can decrease the gutter spacing to as little as 0.25" if you justify the text in the columns or are using more than 3 columns.)

The Apply To choices depend on whether you are creating new columns or working with selected text or existing columns. When you are creating new columns, you can apply the columns to the Whole Document or from This *(Insertion)* Point Forward. If you have text selected, choose between Selected Text and Whole Document. If you are working with existing columns, you can choose between This Section and This Point Forward.

The Line Between check box places a line in the gutter between the columns (see the first section of columns in Figure 17.2). If you are creating new columns, this line does not appear until you have moved into the second column. Choosing Start New Column moves the text following the insertion point to the top of the next column. (You must have chosen From This Point Forward in the Apply To control for this to work.)

EXERCISE 17.5   **TO CREATE OR ADJUST COLUMNS USING THE COLUMNS DIALOG BOX**

1. **To create columns, choose Format ➢ Columns. To adjust existing columns, move the insertion point into the columns to be affected before choosing Format ➢ Columns.** For this exercise, move the insertion point into the columns in *Development Department Article.*

2. **Click one of the preset columns to select a preset design or enter the number of columns in the Number of Columns control.** Click the preset for three columns.

3. **Click Equal Column Width to lock and unlock the column width.** To see how locked equal columns appear, click Equal Column Width and then OK to return to the document. Drag the spacing markers left or right and notice that all three columns are now adjusted at once. Choose Format ➢ Columns to reopen the Columns dialog box. Click the Equal Column Width box again to unlock the columns.

4. **When the Equal Column Width box is not checked, enter column widths and gutter spacing in the Widths and Spacing control.** Enter 1.2" for column 1 and press Tab. Enter 0.5" for Spacing and press Tab. Enter 2.6" and 0.5" for Column 2. Column 3 should say 1.2" and 0.5".

5. **Check the Line Between box to place a vertical line between columns.**

CONTINUES ON NEXT PAGE

6. In the Apply To control, choose the part of the document in which you want to change column widths. Choose This Section.

7. If you want to move the text following the insertion point to the top of the next column, choose Start New Column and Apply To: From This Point Forward. For now, leave these boxes unchecked.

8. Click OK to return to the document when you've entered all settings.

You may notice that the heading "Development Scores Big" doesn't fit very nicely in the column now with the new column widths. For more practice, correct this.

9. Use the Columns dialog box and follow Step 4 to change the column width settings to 1.3", 2.4", and 1.3", respectively, still maintaining 0.5" gutters.

10. Save the document with changes.

What You Have Learned

In this session, you have learned the difference between parallel and newspaper columns. You have learned how to create newspaper columns to enter new text and to convert existing text into columns. You now know how to adjust column width and adjust the spacing between columns using the ruler and using the Columns dialog box. Finally, you now know how to insert a vertical line between columns and how to lock the columns so that they are always of equal width.

Focus Questions

1. What is the difference between parallel and newspaper columns? What feature can you use to create parallel columns?

2. How do balanced columns differ from unbalanced columns? What are the steps to create balanced columns from existing text?

3. What is the gutter position tool and how do you use it?

4. How do you view the End of Section marker?

5. Name at least two adjustments that you can make to a document to increase the amount of space available for text on the page.

Reinforcement Exercises

Exercise 1 a) You are planning a holiday party for all of your co-workers. Develop a shopping list that contains at least twenty items. (Use paragraph numbering to make the job of counting easier.)

b) Select the list and convert it to four columns using the Columns button on the toolbar.

c) Now, change it to a two-column list.

d) Using the ruler, adjust the column widths so that there is only about 0.5" of gutter between the columns.

e) Go to the Columns dialog box to verify the spacing size. Adjust it here if necessary. Note how wide the two columns are.

f) Save the list as *Shopping List*.

Exercise 2 a) Create a new document with three columns of equal width with a 0.6" gutter between them.

b) Write a short opinion paper about what you think should be done about the problem of alcohol and drug abuse in schools or in the workplace. (Make the essay about 250–350 words; you can use Tools ➤ Word Count to check the length.)

c) Balance the columns when you are finished.

d) Center a title over the columns.

e) Make the center column wider than the other two.

f) Check the spelling and then print your essay.

g) Save the essay as *Substance Abuse*.

Exercise 3 a) Create a new document using one of the two Preset column widths for two columns.

b) You have just been appointed to plan the annual company picnic. Write a short article for the company newsletter about what you are planning to make this year's picnic memorable.

c) Center a title over the columns.

d) Check the spelling and then print the article.

e) Save the article as *Company Picnic.*

Exercise 4   a) Open *My Definitions.* Convert the document into two equal columns with a line between them.

b) Balance the columns for length. Center the heading over the two columns.

c) When you are satisfied with the appearance, add the following terms and your definitions to the end of the document: *parallel columns, newspaper columns, End of Section marker, gutter,* and *column break.*

d) Save the changes.

Adding Impact with Graphic Objects

THIS SESSION FOCUSES on inserting clip art and other imported graphics into documents. In Session 19, you'll learn to move and position graphics on a page and other ways that you can use graphics to spruce up your documents. At the end of this session you will be able to:

- Use clip art
- Size and crop pictures
- Copy, paste, and delete pictures
- Add borders to pictures
- Insert other graphic images in your document
- Link and embed graphic files
- Turn off graphics display for faster scrolling

Vocabulary

- clip art
- crop
- dynamic
- embed
- filter
- graphics
- handles
- import
- link
- object
- picture placeholders
- pictures
- thumbnail

SECTION 18.1: USING GRAPHICS

Visual images can draw attention to your document. Never underestimate the power of pictures—when a reader feels your publication's design is engaging, he or she is more likely to read the text that surrounds the pictures. You can place **graphics** or **pictures** from a variety of sources in a Word document:

- Clip art images from the Microsoft ClipArt Gallery or any of the hundreds of clip art collections available on disk or CD;

- files created in graphic art packages like Windows Paint or Corel DRAW;

- pictures captured from paper using a scanner;

- objects from other Office applications like Excel;

- photographs stored on disk/CD;

- drawings created in Word with the drawing tools; and

- picture objects you create using other Microsoft programs accessible from Word.

You can also place text in a box and treat it as a graphic. Graphics can be resized or trimmed if you want to use just part of the picture in a document.

SECTION 18.2: USING CLIP ART IN A DOCUMENT

Clip art is a generic term for graphics, often simple line drawings or cartoons, that can be used in publications. (Before computers, clip art came on sheets of paper. Using scissors, you clipped art from the paper and glued it into a newsletter or brochure.) The clip art that comes with Word is kept in the ClipArt folder. To place clip art in a document, choose Insert ➤ Picture to open the Insert Picture dialog box, shown in Figure 18.1.

Figure 18.1
The Insert Picture
dialog box

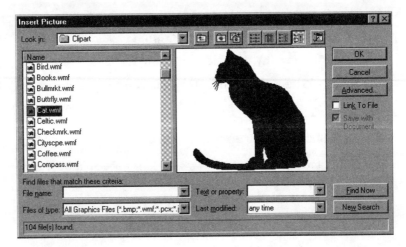

Placing Clip Art

Clip art files are listed in the Name scroll box. Select a picture, and a preview appears to the right of the scroll box. Spend a minute previewing the available clip art. To insert a selected image in the document, click the OK button. The image appears in the document at the insertion point, as shown in Figure 18.2. Any text that followed the insertion point moves to a new position below the graphic.

Figure 18.2
Inserting clip art

CAT-ASTROPHE

Last week, our cat crawled out a second story window and up onto the roof. Then, he couldn't get down! We called the fire department, but the dispatcher said that they don't rescue cats any more.

EXERCISE 18.1   **TO INSERT CLIP ART**

1. **Place the insertion point where you want the graphic to appear.** For this exercise, open a new blank document and leave the insertion point at the top.

2. **Choose Insert ➢ Picture to open the Insert Picture dialog box.**

CONTINUES ON NEXT PAGE

> **3.** Scroll down the list of graphics available in the Name box.
>
> **4.** View any graphic by clicking its name on the list.
>
> **5.** Select the graphic that you want to insert and click OK.

▨ Sizing and Cropping Pictures

Once the clip art is in place, clicking once on the image selects the image. A line will appear around the image. Eight **handles** appear on the sides and corners of the picture:

The handles are used to resize the picture. To make the picture larger or smaller, move the pointer to a handle. The pointer will change to a two-headed sizing arrow. Drag the handle to expand or contract the box surrounding the picture. When you release the mouse button, the picture will be resized to fit the box.

If you want the graphic to remain in proportion as you resize it, drag any corner handle. The height and width of the graphic will move together so that it stays even. The handles on the four sides of the graphic will stretch the graphic either horizontally or vertically out of proportion.

Note: If the graphic you are working with is too small or too big to work with easily, you may want to change the editing view using the Zoom button on the Formatting toolbar.

You can also use the handles to **crop** the picture—trim it so that only part of it appears. To crop the picture, move the pointer to a handle and press Shift. The sizing arrow will change to a cropping tool. Continue to hold Shift while you drag the handle. When you drop the handle, only the parts of the image remaining in the box will be displayed:

You can recover the parts of the graphic that you cropped off by holding Shift and dragging it in the reverse direction. To restore the graphic to its original shape and size, click Undo until all of the changes are reversed. You can also delete the graphic and reinsert it.

Copying, Pasting, and Deleting a Picture

You copy or delete a picture just as you would text. Begin by selecting the picture. To copy, click the Copy button on the toolbar or choose Edit ➤ Copy. Once a picture has been copied to the clipboard you can paste it in another location using the toolbar or the Edit menu. To delete, click the Delete button on the keyboard.

EXERCISE 18.2 | **TO SIZE AND CROP A PICTURE**

Click on the graphic that you inserted in the first exercise to select it. Press the Delete key so that you can have a blank screen for this exercise. Following the instructions in Exercise 18.1, insert the graphic named *Cityscpe.wmf*. If *Cityscpe* is not available, choose any other graphic.

1. **Select the graphic that you want to size or crop.**

2. **To resize the graphic, point to one of the handles and drag it with the two-headed sizing arrow.** Stretch the width of the graphic by dragging the handle on the right side. Drag the handle in either bottom corner to resize the graphic in both directions.

3. **To crop the graphic, point to one of the handles, hold down the Shift key and drag it with the cropping arrow.** Point to the handle in the bottom center of *Cityscpe* and drag it so that there is no longer a reflection of the city visible at the bottom.

4. **Release the mouse button when the part of the graphic you want remains.**

Adding Borders

You can add a border to separate a picture from the text above and below it. To apply a regular border, select the picture and then use the Borders button on the Formatting toolbar to open the Borders toolbar. Select a border, and it will be added to the picture. (For a review of applying borders, see Session 7.)

Special picture border formatting is also available. With a picture selected, choose Format ➤ Borders and Shading or right-click and select Borders and Shading from the pop-up menu to open the Picture Borders dialog box, shown in Figure 18.3.

Figure 18.3

The Picture Borders dialog box

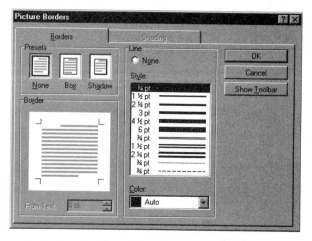

Begin by selecting either the Box or Shadow preset format. (If you leave None selected, you won't get a border on your picture, regardless of other choices you make in this dialog box.) A preview of the border appears in the Border area. Use the Style box to select a line style for the entire border. You can choose a Border color from the Color drop-down list.

You can use different line styles and colors on individual sides of the border. Set a line style and color; then click on one of the four sides illustrated in the Border control to apply the line style and color to that side. When you are finished constructing the border, click OK to apply the border to the picture. (You may have to click somewhere else in the document to deselect the picture so you can see the border.)

EXERCISE 18.4 | **TO ADD A BORDER TO A PICTURE**

1. **Select the picture to which you want to add a border.** Select *Cityscpe*.

2. **Click the Borders button on the Formatting toolbar.**

3. **Select the border size and type you want to apply, just as you would a text border.**

4. **For additional border formatting, choose Format ➢ Borders and Shading to open the Borders dialog box.**

5. **Select Box or Shadow preset format.** Select Shadow.

6. **Select a Border color from the Color drop-down.** Choose any color that appeals to you.

7. **Click OK.**

SECTION 18.3: IMPORTING OTHER GRAPHICS

Graphics programs save images using different file formats. Each format uses a unique file extension. Word includes **filters** that translate graphic images saved in a variety of formats into formats that Word can work with. When you insert a graphic created in another application, Word uses the filter to **import** the file. The clip art you used earlier in this session was imported: most clip art is saved in either a Windows Metafile or Bitmap format.

Filters are selected during the Word installation process, and a Typical installation includes:

Tag Image File Format (TIF)

Windows Bitmaps/Windows Paint (BMP)

WordPerfect Graphics (WPG)

Macintosh PICT (PCT)

Windows Metafile (WMF)

JPEG File Interchange format (JPG)

You can find out what filters have been installed with Word in the Insert Picture dialog box. Choose Insert ➢ Picture, then click the List Files of Type drop-down list to see the types of graphic files you can import.

If the graphic you want to use is saved in a file type you can import, you insert the graphic the same way you inserted clip art. If the picture file isn't located in the Clipart folder, click the Look In drop-down list in the Insert Picture dialog box and select the drive and folder where the file is located. (See *Appendix A: Managing Word Files in Windows 95* for help on locating files in drives and folders.)

■ Linking and Embedding Pictures

When you initially insert a picture in a document, you can choose how the picture will be saved with the document. By default, Word **embeds** the picture, saving it with the document when the document is saved. If the picture is complex, the document will take up a lot of space on disk. However, since the picture is saved within the document, it is there whenever and wherever you open the document.

You can choose to have Word save a **link** to the picture instead of embedding the picture. With a link, each time you open the document, Word goes to the picture's location on disk and loads the picture into the document. If the picture isn't in the proper location, Word will give you an error message and the document will load without the picture. This means you should be careful to not delete or move files that are linked to documents. It also means that you can only successfully open the Word document on the computer the document was created on or another computer with the same picture file in the same location.

Despite the potential problems, linking is important. Linking definitely saves disk space. While clip art files are typically small because they are simple, it isn't unusual for an Encapsulated Postscript or Tagged Image picture to take up more than half the space on a floppy disk. Perhaps you will decide to use an image at the top of a weekly employee newsletter. If you embed the picture, at the end of a year you will have 53 copies of the picture on disk—the original and the copy embedded in each week's newsletter. If you know you will always open the newsletters on the same computer, it's better to link rather than embed.

Linking is also **dynamic**, meaning that the current version of the linked image is loaded each time the document is opened. If the image changes, the change is reflected in all documents linked to the image. For example, suppose your company is in the process of changing its logo. If each time you create a document using the logo you link the picture file, then when the new logo is ready, you will only have one file to change—the file that contains the logo. When you open any document that contains the link, the changed logo file will be loaded.

☐ Link To File

If you want to link a file, you must create the link when you select the picture from the Insert Picture dialog box. To instruct Word to link rather than embed the picture file, check the Link to File check box before choosing OK.

SECTION 18.4: FASTER WORK WITH GRAPHICS

As you scroll through a document, Word redraws the entire document window with each scroll increment. When you have graphics in a document, it takes longer to scroll because it takes longer to redraw a picture than to redraw text. To speed up scrolling during the editing process, you can have Word display **picture placeholders** rather than the pictures themselves.

To substitute placeholders for graphics, choose Tools ➢ Options to open the Options dialog box. On the View page (see Figure 18.4), select Picture Placeholders. With this option selected, you will see empty boxes rather than pictures. This only affects the view, not the document itself. If you printed the document now, the pictures would still print. To display the pictures again, return to the Options dialog box and turn Picture Placeholders off.

Figure 18.4

The View Options dialog box

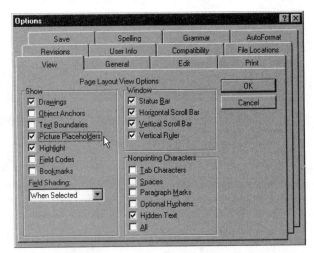

EXERCISE 18.6   **TO HIDE GRAPHICS FOR FASTER SCROLLING**

1. **Choose Tools ➢ Options to open the Options dialog box.**

2. **Click the View tab and select Picture Placeholders.** Click OK. Empty boxes should be visible rather than the graphics.

3. **Close Word without saving the documents you created in this session.**

What You Have Learned

In this session, you learned how to insert clip art into documents using Insert Picture and how to place colorful borders around graphics. You understand that there are various file formats for graphics and how Word can use filters to import graphics in different formats. You now know how to link a graphic so that you save disk space and simplify changes to regularly used graphics. Finally, you learned how to hide graphics to use less memory so that you can work faster.

Focus Questions

1. What is the purpose of the handles that appear around a selected graphic, and how do you use them?

2. List three examples of objects.

3. What is a graphic filter?

4. What is the difference between embedding and linking a graphic? Which one saves space on the hard drive?

5. What does it mean to say that linking is dynamic? Give an example where this might be useful to you.

6. Why might it be faster to work with picture placeholders?

Reinforcement Exercises

Exercise 1 a) Create a new blank document. Insert a graphic using Insert ➢ Picture. Link it to the document rather than embedding it.

b) Change the picture by cropping it.

c) Resize the new cropped graphic proportionally so that it fills about half of the document window.

d) Copy the graphic using the Copy button on the toolbar and paste it into another blank document.

e) Close both documents without saving.

Exercise 2 a) Open a new document. Open the Insert Picture dialog box. Change the type of file so that you are only viewing graphics that are Windows Metafiles. Select one and link it to the document.

b) Practice increasing and decreasing the size of the graphic. Stretch it horizontally across the page. Click in the page so the graphic is no longer selected, tab once and type *Windows Metafile (*.wmf)*. Press Enter twice.

c) Open the Insert Picture dialog box. Change the type of file again so that you are only viewing graphics that are Windows Bitmaps. Select one and link it to the document.

d) Change the size of this graphic so that it is approximately the same size as the graphic above it. Click off of the graphic so that it is no longer selected, tab once, and type Windows Bitmap (*.bmp).

e) Save the file as *Graphic Formats.*

Exercise 3 a) Open *Company Picnic,* which you wrote in Reinforcement Exercise 17.3.

b) Review the graphics available to you and select one to illustrate the article.

c) Position the insertion point at the beginning of the first paragraph and link the graphic to the article.

d) Resize the graphic so that it looks good. (You will learn how to reposition graphics in Session 19.

e) Save the document as *Company Picnic with Graphic.*

Exercise 4 a) Open *My Definitions* and add the following terms and definitions: *crop, handles, import, link, embed, dynamic, clip art.*

b) Sort the list again so it is alphabetical.

c) Choose four terms and find graphics to illustrate them. Insert the graphics between the terms and their definitions. Resize them so that they fit appropriately on the page.

d) Choose one of the divider graphics (*Divider1.wmf)* and insert it between the heading and the columns. Stretch and resize it so that it extends across the page.

e) Save the changes.

Advanced Graphic Features in Word

THIS SESSION FOCUSES on graphics in desktop publishing. You'll learn how to move pictures, wrap text around graphics, and work with documents once objects have been inserted. You'll even see how to create simple graphic images yourself using Word's drawing tools. At the end of this session you will be able to:

- Frame a picture
- Position frames on a page
- Add shading to frames
- Wrap text around frames
- Put text in a frame
- Make your own graphics using Draw
- Create text boxes
- Layer text and graphics

Vocabulary

- add-in
- anchor
- callout
- fill
- frame
- layer
- pull quote
- text box
- wrap

281

SECTION 19.1: POSITIONING OBJECTS IN DOCUMENTS

When you insert a picture into a document, you can size it and crop it. However, to move the picture once it's been placed you have to insert it into a frame. In Figure 19.1, a picture has been inserted in the Bumper Squad Newsletter. When the graphic was inserted, the text moved below the graphic. The newsletter's appearance would be improved if the text began to the right of the graphic and flowed or **wrapped** around it.

Figure 19.1

A newsletter with a picture inserted

Tournament News

The National Tournament will be held July 15-18 at the IMA Sports Arena in Flint, Michigan. A larger than usual crowd is expected. Accommodations are available at several local hostelries. To register, or for more information, call TourDex at 1-800-555-1919.

The MidWest Tourney was held the last weekend in May. First place in the Men's Open was highly contested. Congratulations to Jim Compton, who finally pulled ahead with a mega score on *Double Dare*. Second place finisher Robb Morse was in first place after *Immortals*, but still is first place in the American standings after his big wins in Las Vegas and Hollywood,

Vendor information is available by calling 1-555-777-9090. Hurry it up — limited booth space is still available.

Tip: Pictures and other objects are easiest to manipulate if you work in Page Layout view.

A **frame** is a movable container in which you can place pictures, text, or other objects. The frame and its contents can be moved and positioned on the page. Text can be wrapped around a frame. You can either place a frame around an existing object or insert a frame and place something in it later. To frame a picture, select it, right-click, and choose Frame Picture from the pop-up menu. The frame (see Figure 19.2) is a wide box filled with diagonal lines. Now that the picture is framed, text automatically wraps around it.

Figure 19.2

A framed picture

Tournament News

The MidWest Tourney was held the last weekend in May. First place in the Men's Open was highly contested. Congratulations to Jim Compton, who finally pulled ahead with a mega score on *Double Dare*. Second place finisher Robb Morse was in first place after *Immortals*, but still is first place in the American standings after his big wins in Las Vegas and Hollywood, Florida. Patrick Cowtan finished third overall, his first placing in a major tournament.

In the Women's Open, Val Richter finished first. Val also won the Machinist's trophy with the high score for all

The National Tournament will be held July 15-18 at the IMA Sports Arena in Flint, Michigan. A larger than usual crowd is expected. Accommodations are available at several local hostelries. To register, or for more information, call TourDex at 1-800-555-1919.

Vendor information is available by calling 1-555-777-9090. Hurry it up — limited booth space is still available.

To move the frame to another location, position the pointer over the frame. A four-headed move arrow will be added to the pointer. Hold the mouse button down and drag the frame to its new location before releasing the button. You can place the frame anywhere in the document—even in a location where you could not enter text, like the gutter between columns.

EXERCISE 19.1 — **TO MOVE A PICTURE**

For this exercise, open *We Do It Best*, which you created in Session 12. Be sure to open it in Page Layout view. Place the insertion point at the beginning of the first paragraph. Insert a graphic into the document.

1. **Select the graphic that you want to move.** Select the graphic that you just inserted.

2. **Choose Insert ➢ Frame to frame the graphic.**

3. **Move the pointer inside the graphic and drag to the new location.** For practice, drag the graphic to various locations around the document. Notice how text moves to surround the graphic. Resize the graphic to make it look better. When you find an attractive position, drop the graphic there.

You can change the border of the picture, as you did when it was unframed. But with a framed picture you can also shade the border. With the picture selected, right-click and choose Format ➢ Borders and Shading to open the Borders and Shading dialog box. Click the Shading tab to open the Shading page, shown in Figure 19.3. Select a pattern or density that will be used to **fill** (color in) the frame border by clicking Custom and then selecting from the Shading scroll box. (Choosing None turns the border off.) You can apply colors to the background and foreground of the border using the Foreground and Background drop-down controls.

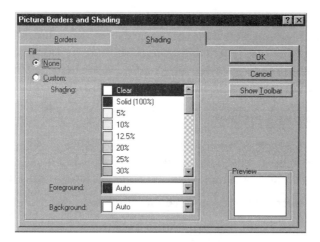

Figure 19.3

The Shading page of the Borders and Shading dialog box

■ Relating Frames to Text and Margins

When a frame is created, it is attached or **anchored** to a nearby paragraph. The frame's anchor is hidden. Make sure the frame is selected, and click the Show/Hide Hidden Text button on the Standard toolbar to view hidden text. The anchor is somewhere nearby. It is only visible when the frame is selected. In Figure 19.4, the anchor is above the frame in the empty lines between the title and text of the Tournament News article.

Figure 19.4

A frame anchor (hidden text visible)

You can use the anchor to make sure a paragraph and the picture that illustrates it stay together during editing by locking the frame's anchor to the paragraph. To anchor a frame to a specific paragraph, first drag the anchor and drop it on the appropriate paragraph. Now, you need to lock the anchor in place; otherwise it will move if you move the frame. With the frame selected, right-click and choose Format Frame (or choose Format ➤ Frame from the menu bar) to open the Frame dialog box, shown in Figure 19.5. In the Vertical section of the dialog box, click the Lock Anchor check box to lock the frame's anchor in its current paragraph. Word will add a lock to the anchor icon so you can see that it is locked.

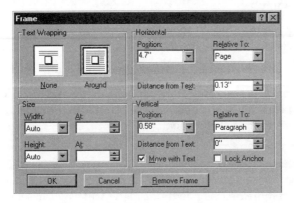

Figure 19.5

The Frame

dialog box

It's the relationship between the frame and paragraph that's locked, not the frame itself. If you select the paragraph, the frame will also be selected. The frame will print in its vertical and horizontal position on the page—but if you move its paragraph to another page, the frame will print in that same vertical and horizontal position on the new page. You can still reposition the frame on the page.

The other check box, Move with Text, relates the frame to surrounding text. When you are still editing a document, selecting Move with Text relates the frame to the text above and below it. If you insert text above the frame's position, both the text and the frame will move. Move with Text and Lock Anchor both move a frame if text is inserted or moved. If you want a frame to stay put regardless of how the text around it is adjusted, turn Move with Text and Lock Anchor off.

EXERCISE 19.2 | **TO ATTACH A FRAME TO TEXT**

1. **Select the graphic that you want to attach to a paragraph.** Select the graphic you inserted in Exercise 19.1.

2. **Click the Show/Hide button on the toolbar to locate the anchor.**

3. **Drag the anchor to the desired paragraph.** Here, drag the anchor to the first paragraph.

4. **Choose Format ➢ Frame to open the Frame dialog box.**

CONTINUES ON NEXT PAGE

5. Click the Lock Anchor check box to lock the frame's anchor to the paragraph.

6. Click Move With Text to relate the frame to the text above and below it. Click OK to close the dialog box.

7. Click the Show/Hide button again to turn it off.

8. For more practice, select the first paragraph and move it below the second. Notice that the graphic is selected with the paragraph and moves with it to the new location.

There are some other useful settings in the Format Frame dialog box. If you want more precision in frame placement, you can set the position of the frame exactly on the page. Use the Horizontal and Vertical sections to place the frame precisely relative to the Page, Margin, or Column margin. You can increase the measurement in the Distance from Text spin box to leave more white space around the frame.

Use the Text Wrapping control to specify either None (no wrapping) or Around (the default setting). In the Size section, you can specify exactly how large the frame should be.

SECTION 19.2: ADDING PICTURES AND TEXT TO FRAMES

When you insert a picture and then frame it, Word makes the frame the size of the picture. If you know where you want to put a graphic but haven't selected it yet, you can insert a frame first, and then place a picture in it. You can also use text as a graphic element. Put text in a frame to create a **text box** in a document, like the **pull quote** shown in Figure 19.6.

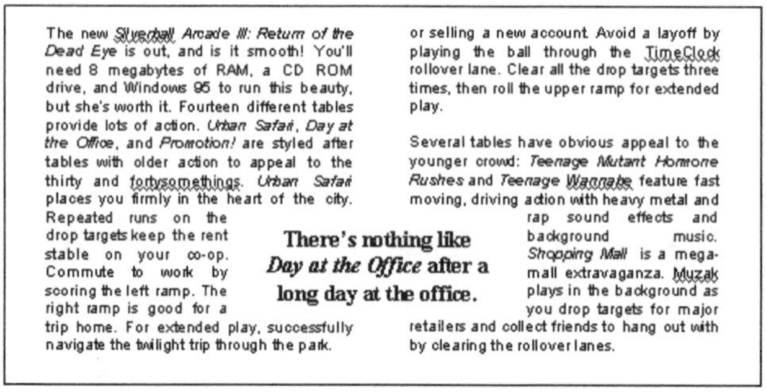

Figure 19.6

Framed text

The new *Silverball Arcade III: Return of the Dead Eye* is out, and is it smooth! You'll need 8 megabytes of RAM, a CD ROM drive, and Windows 95 to run this beauty, but she's worth it. Fourteen different tables provide lots of action. *Urban Safari*, *Day at the Office*, and *Promotion!* are styled after tables with older action to appeal to the thirty and fortysomethings. *Urban Safari* places you firmly in the heart of the city. Repeated runs on the drop targets keep the rent stable on your co-op. Commute to work by scoring the left ramp. The right ramp is good for a trip home. For extended play, successfully navigate the twilight trip through the park.

There's nothing like *Day at the Office* after a long day at the office.

or selling a new account. Avoid a layoff by playing the ball through the TimeClock rollover lane. Clear all the drop targets three times, then roll the upper ramp for extended play.

Several tables have obvious appeal to the younger crowd: *Teenage Mutant Hormone Rushes* and *Teenage Wannabe* feature fast moving, driving action with heavy metal and rap sound effects and background music. *Shopping Mall* is a mega-mall extravaganza. Muzak plays in the background as you drop targets for major retailers and collect friends to hang out with by clearing the rollover lanes.

To insert an empty frame, choose Insert ➤ Frame. The pointer will change to cross-hairs (like a large plus sign). Point to where you want one corner of the frame to be; hold down the mouse button and move to the opposite corner, laying out a rectangle. Release the mouse button to insert the frame.

The insertion point is active in the frame. Choose Insert ➤ Picture or Insert ➤ Object to import a graphic or place a picture from the ClipArt Gallery. Text is even easier to insert. Simply type, edit, and format text in the frame. When you are finished entering text or inserting objects, position the frame in the document.

EXERCISE 19.3 **TO INSERT TEXT IN A FRAME**

1. **Choose Insert ➤ Frame to change the pointer to cross-hairs.**

2. **Move the insertion point to where you want a corner of the frame to appear.** Move the insertion point to the beginning of the second paragraph.

3. **Hold down the mouse button and drag to create a box. Release the mouse button when the box is of the desired size.** Make the box about 2" wide and three lines high.

4. **Enter and format text as you normally would.** Change to Center alignment, Arial 24 point Bold, and type *We Do It Best*.

5. **Point inside the text box and then drag it to the correct position.** Drag the text box to the center of paragraph so that there are two lines above it and two lines below it.

6. **Resize the frame if necessary so that the text fits nicely in the frame.**

7. **Close** *We Do It Best* without saving changes.

SECTION 19.3: DRAWING YOUR OWN GRAPHIC OBJECTS

You can create lines and shapes using tools on Word's Drawing toolbar and then combine them to make a graphic of your own design. To display the Drawing toolbar, right-click on any toolbar and select Drawing, or choose View ➤ Toolbars and select the toolbar in the Toolbars dialog box. The Drawing toolbar includes five groups of buttons:

You're going to learn about the first two groups right now. Buttons in the first group are used to create shapes, lines, and objects. Use buttons in the second cluster to format lines and objects.

■ Creating and Formatting Lines and Shapes

 To draw a line, click the Line button. Move the cross-hair pointer to one end of the line you want to draw. Hold the mouse button and drag to draw the line. Release the button to create the line and turn the Line tool off. The line has handles, allowing you to move, cut, or delete it as you would any graphic object. If you want a line that is absolutely horizontal or vertical, hold the Shift key while dragging the line.

The Line and other object buttons work like the Format Painter button: When you have more than one object to draw, begin by double-clicking on its button. The button will stay depressed, allowing you to draw more objects, until you click any button. The objects created in Draw are placed in a separate **layer** on top of the text in a document.

 Change the color of a selected line by clicking the Line Color button to open a color palette. If there is no line selected, the color you choose is the new default color and will be applied to lines you create in the future (until you change it again).

 The Line Style button opens a palette of line styles: various widths and styles, including arrows. Selecting More from the palette opens the Drawing Defaults dialog box, shown in Figure 19.7.

Figure 19.7

The Drawing Defaults dialog box

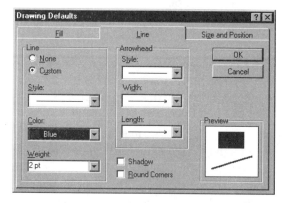

You can also open this dialog box by double-clicking on a line or any other object you have drawn. The Drawing Defaults dialog box is a convenient place to change several of the line's attributes at one time. Your choices are applied to the selected line (or other object), or used for future lines if no line is selected.

Use the Rectangle button on the Drawing toolbar to draw boxes. Click the button, and then lay out a rectangle just as you did when you inserted a frame. With rectangles and other two-dimensional objects you can set a Fill Color for the area inside the object as well as attributes for the line that surrounds the object.

Clicking the Fill Color button opens the fill palette. If you just want a rectangle without any "filling," choose None. (This is *not* the same as the colorless sample on the bottom row of the palette—that's the color white.)

Use the Ellipse tool to draw circles and ellipses. The Arc tool creates curved line segments. With the Freeform tool, you can draw irregular shapes. Click once to anchor the end of a line, then click again to draw one side of a shape. Click again, and you have two sides. Hold down the mouse button to draw freely with the Freeform tool. It takes a lot of practice to master the Freeform tool. Make sure that Fill Color is set to None if you want only the lines of your drawing to show. Unlike the other line and shape tools, the Freeform tool will stay on, even if you only click it once, until you do one of the following:

- click once after forming a closed shape

- press the Escape key on the keyboard

- double-click at the point you want to finish drawing.

Note: If you need several objects of the same size and shape, draw the first one and select it. Copy the object using the Copy button and then paste it as many times as you need it.

EXERCISE 19.5 | **TO DRAW LINES AND OBJECTS**

For this exercise, open a new, blank document.

1. **Right-click on any toolbar and select Drawing from the list of available toolbars (or choose View ➢ Toolbars).**

2. **Click on a drawing tool to change the pointer to cross-hairs for drawing lines and shapes. Double-click the tool to draw more than one of the selected object.** Click the Line tool.

3. **Drag the cross-hairs from a starting point to the point where you want the line or shape to end, and release the mouse button.** Drag a line across the top of the page.

CONTINUES ON NEXT PAGE

4. **Select a drawing tool and hold down the Shift key while dragging to create a straight line, square, or circle.** Select the line again and hold down the Shift key while dragging to create a second line below the first.

5. **Select the object to change its color, line style, or position using the toolbar buttons.** Select the first line, click the Line Color button, and choose a different color. Click the Line Style button and choose an arrow style.

6. **Double-click the object to open the Drawing Object dialog box so you can set several attributes at once.** Click the Line tab and change the style, color, and weight to your liking.

8. **Use the Fill button on the toolbar to change the fill color or double-click to open the Drawing Object dialog box and select the Fill tab, to change the fill color and the patterns and pattern colors of shapes.** Click the Rectangle button and drag the cross-hairs to create a rectangle. Open the Drawing Object dialog box. Change the fill colors, and select a pattern and a pattern color.

9. **Move an object by selecting it and dragging it to a new location.** Move each of the lines so that they both touch the rectangle.

For more practice, draw each of the five shapes: line, rectangle, ellipse, arc, and freeform. (Remember to hold Shift to draw a circle, square, or straight line.) Try filling each shape with a color. If you end up with a masterpiece, save it before continuing.

■ Text Boxes and Callouts

The text boxes you create using the Text Box tool differ from text in a frame in one important respect. Since a text box is a Draw object, the other text in the document doesn't wrap around it. You can still move the Draw text box as you would any other graphic object.

A **callout** is a combination of a line and a text box used to label or explain text or an object in a document, as shown in the callout for the Elba Center in the map in Figure 19.8. (The interstate labels are simple text boxes.) To create a callout, click the Callout button. Drag from the object to wherever its callout should appear. Word will create the line and place a text box at the end so you can enter the callout text.

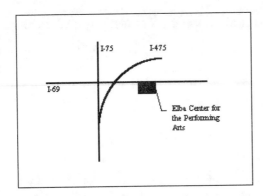

Figure 19.8

Map with callout

 To change the appearance of the callout, click the Format Callout button to open the Callout Defaults dialog box. For more information on callouts, click the Help button in the Callout Defaults dialog box.

■ Selecting and Manipulating Objects

 You can select a group of objects and apply a different line style or fill to all objects in the group. To select multiple objects, click the Select Drawing Objects button. Using the cross-hair pointer, drag a rectangle that includes all the objects you want to select.

  The Bring to Front and Send to Back buttons move the selected object(s) in relation to text and other graphic objects. If you create a rectangle and place an ellipse over the right half of it, the ellipse covers part of the rectangle. If you want the entire rectangle to show, covering part of the ellipse, either send the ellipse to the back or bring the rectangle to the front.

  The shapes created in Draw are placed in a separate **layer** on top of the text in a document. The next two buttons are used to place graphics behind or in front of document text. In this example, a rectangle was created on top of the Video Pinball heading, and then sent behind the text:

Video Pinball

To create a watermark effect (like those seen in some kinds of paper), select a lightly shaded graphic, center it on the page, and send it behind the text.

EXERCISE 19.6 | **TO SEND OBJECTS TO BACK OR BRING THEM TO FRONT**

1. **Select the object that you want to bring forward or move behind.** Type your name and address in the document that you created in Exercise 19.5. Cover the text with one of the objects that you drew by dragging it on top of the text you just entered.

2. **Click the Bring in Front of Text or Send Behind Text button on the Drawing toolbar if you want to position text on a graphic.** Click Send Behind Text.

3. **Click the Bring to Front or Send to Back button if you want to switch the position of one graphic on top of another.** Move one of the objects you created on top of another. Click Send to Back to bring the other object forward.

 When you are done creating a drawing, you may want to have document text flow around the drawing. To place a drawing in a frame, first use the Select Drawing Objects tool to select all the objects to be framed. Then click the Insert Frame button (or choose Insert ➤ Frame from the menu bar) to place your drawing in a frame.

EXERCISE 19.7 | **TO FRAME A DRAWING**

1. **Click the Select Drawing Objects tool on the Drawing toolbar.**

2. **Drag a box around all of the objects that you want to include in the drawing.** Move several of the objects you have created close together. When you are ready, select them using the Select Drawing Objects tool.

3. **Click the Insert Frame button (at the far right of the toolbar) or choose Insert ➤ Frame from the menu bar.**

■ Editing the Picture

Once you have placed several objects in a frame, Word treats them as a single picture rather than independent objects. If you want to edit the picture, double-click to open the image. The Picture toolbar will be displayed:

The cross-hairs that surround the picture are the picture boundaries. Click the Reset Picture Boundary button on the Picture toolbar to move the boundaries as close to the image as possible.

Here, you can work with the objects as a unit or as independent objects again. Select the object that you want to edit and you can change colors and line styles just as you did before they were part of a picture.

You may have noticed that there is an insertion point within the picture boundaries. You can add text to the picture, as shown in Figure 19.9. (The text will type right through the picture, so you don't have a lot of room.) When you have reset boundaries and edited the picture, click the Close Picture button to return to the main document.

Figure 19.9
Adding Text
to a Picture

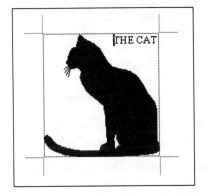

What You Have Learned

You have learned all about framing objects and pictures so that you can position them within a document. You now know how to apply borders and shades to framed pictures. You are also able to anchor a frame to a paragraph so that it can be locked into position to move where that paragraph moves. Additionally, you have learned how to create text boxes and to insert graphics into frames. You have created your own drawing objects using the drawing features of Word. With a little practice, you can turn those objects into pictures that can be used just like imported clip art.

Focus Questions

1. List three advantages to putting a frame around imported clip art.

2. What's the primary purpose of anchoring a frame to a paragraph?

3. Why might you want to put text inside a frame?

4. What is the Freeform tool and how do you use it?

5. What do you need to do if you want text to flow around a drawing that you have created?

6. How do you edit a picture when you can no longer select individual objects?

Reinforcement Exercises

Exercise 1 a) Create a new blank document. Insert a clip art image. Insert a frame around the picture.

b) Insert another frame that is at least twice as large as the clip art picture you just inserted. Insert the same clip art image into this frame. Notice the size difference between the two pictures.

c) Change the Border around the larger graphic so that it is 2¼ points and a color other than black.

d) Delete the smaller graphic.

e) Write a paragraph describing the graphic you chose to insert.

f) Resize and position the graphic in the paragraph so that the text flows around it and your paragraph looks engaging.

g) Save this document as *Paragraph with Graphic.*

Exercise 2 a) Open *Substance Abuse,* which you wrote in Session 17 Reinforcement Exercise 2. Drag a frame that spans part of column 1, all of column 2, and part of column 3.

b) Identify a sentence or part of the sentence to use as a pull quote. Select the text and copy it into the text box. Change the font to Arial 12 point.

c) Move the text box about halfway into the essay. Resize the text box to fit the quote.

d) Change the border (Format ➢ Borders and Shading) to a 1½ point shaded border.

e) Save the changed document.

Exercise 3 a) Open *Company Picnic*, which you created in Session 17 Reinforcement Exercise 3. Insert two frames into the article where you would like to place graphics.

b) Insert a picture to enhance the article.

c) Create a picture in the second frame using the drawing tools.

d) Group the objects together to make them one picture.

e) Edit the picture if you want by double-clicking it to open the image. Close the picture when you are finished editing.

f) Resize and reposition the frames if needed. Size the frames appropriately.

g) Save the changes.

Exercise 4 a) Open *My Definitions*. Add the following terms and your defni-tions for them to the list and then sort the list alphabetically: *frame, anchor, pull quote, text box,* and *wrap*.

b) Insert frames around each of the four graphics that you inserted in Session 18.

c) Reposition and resize the graphics so that they are not all in line down the column.

d) Identify one definition on each page to use as a pull quote. Set each one off in a frame between columns.

e) Save the changes.

Putting It All Together: Publishing with Word

YOU'VE ALREADY learned the core skills necessary for **desktop publishing (DTP)**. In this final session, you will pull together all the skills from the last three sessions, along with everything else you know about formatting text, to create exciting publications using Word. At the end of this session you will be able to:

- Use drop caps to add emphasis to text
- Create logos using WordArt
- Use kerning to space characters
- Use leading to increase space before lines of text
- Apply guidelines and rules for desktop publishing
- Construct publications in Word

■ Vocabulary

- desktop publishing (DTP)
- drop cap
- leading
- kerning
- WordArt

SECTION 20.1: SPECIAL EFFECTS FOR TEXT

Word includes two tools used to turn text into graphics: Drop Caps and WordArt. A **drop cap** is special treatment for the first character of a paragraph, as shown in Figure 20.1. Drop caps are usually used for the first paragraph of an article or section, not every paragraph in a document.

Figure 20.1

A paragraph with a drop cap

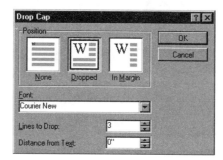

The drop-capped character is pulled out of the paragraph and placed in a text box. You could do this manually, but Word automates the process. To create a drop cap, begin by placing the insertion point at the beginning of the paragraph. Choose Format ➤ Drop Cap to open the Drop Cap dialog box, shown in Figure 20.2.

Figure 20.2

The Drop Cap dialog box

Choose a position for the drop cap from the samples at the top of the dialog box. The character's current font is displayed in the Font control. If you wish, you can choose a more decorative font for the drop cap. The Lines to Drop determines how large the drop cap will be. The Distance from Text control is used to increase the white space between the drop cap and the remaining text in the paragraph.

TO CREATE A DROP CAP

For this exercise, open *Development Department Article*.

1. **Select the first letter of the word that you want to contain the drop cap.** Here, select the "T" in "This," the first word of the first paragraph.

2. **Choose Format ➢ Drop Cap to open the Drop Cap dialog box.**

3. **Select the type of Drop Cap you would like: Dropped or In-Margin.** Choose Dropped.

4. **Change the font if you would like the Drop Cap to appear in a different font.** For now, leave the font the same.

5. **Adjust the number of Lines to Drop.** Leave this set to 3.

6. **Adjust the Distance from Text.** Change this to 0.1".

7. **Choose OK when you have made all the selections.**

8. For more practice, change the first letters of the other two paragraphs to drop caps. So that you can see both types of drop caps available, make one of them an In-Margin drop cap. Adjust the Lines to Drop and the Distance from Text to see what you think looks best.

WordArt is used to create a graphic object from an entire word or phrase. WordArt is a separate program that is included with Word as an **add-in**. Use WordArt to create logos, emphasize titles, and add excitement to a document. Because it can make text difficult to read, use it sparingly for that extra added effect.

To create WordArt, place the insertion point where you want the graphic, and choose Insert ➢ Object from the menu bar. From the Insert Object dialog box, select Microsoft WordArt to launch the WordArt program. (If WordArt is not a choice, it isn't installed on your computer.) Depending on the version of WordArt that you are running, you may see a Word Art dialog box or a WordArt toolbar with an Enter Your Text Here text box. In either case, type the text you want to turn into WordArt in the Enter Your Text Here box, as shown in Figure 20.3. Then, click the Update Display button to place the text in the document. After you edit the text, click Update Display again to apply the change to the WordArt text.

Figure 20.3

Entering text

for WordArt

Most of the buttons and controls for formatting WordArt text will be familiar. However, the first drop-down control, labeled Shape, is unique to WordArt. Click the arrow to open a palette of shapes for your graphic, as shown in Figure 20.4.

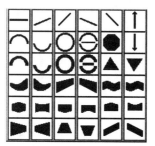

Figure 20.4

The WordArt

shape palette

Select a shape from the palette, and the text you entered is **poured** into the shape, resulting in a graphic that is a mixture of text and an object, as shown in Figure 20.5. Click the formatting buttons to enhance the object. Clicking anywhere outside the text box or dialog box closes WordArt and returns you to the document window in Word.

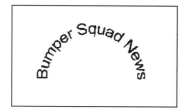

Figure 20.5

A logo created

in WordArt

If you need to change or edit the WordArt graphic later, just double-click it to open WordArt again. Like any other object, WordArt can be framed for positioning within the document. If you don't frame it, you can still size and crop it.

EXERCISE 20.2   **TO CREATE WORDART**

1. **Place the insertion point where you want the WordArt to appear.** Create a new document.

2. **Choose Insert Object to open the Object dialog box.**

3. **Select Microsoft WordArt 2.0 from the Create New list to launch WordArt.**

4. **Type the text that you want to convert to WordArt in the Enter Your Text Here box.** Type your full name.

5. **Select a shape from the WordArt shape palette.** Select any shape that appeals to you.

6. **Click the formatting buttons to change the font and font attributes, rotation, alignment, borders, shading, and shadows.** Experiment with different effects and attributes to see how they impact the text.

7. **Click outside the text box or dialog box to close WordArt and return to the normal editing screen.**

8. **To position the WordArt, add a frame to the object by selecting it and choosing Insert ➢ Frame.**

9. **Double-click the graphic to edit it.**

10. **Close the document without saving.**

WordArt is just one of the add-ins available that you can use in Word. Microsoft Graph and other packages that come with Microsoft Office can be used to create objects to better communicate the ideas in a document. Most of the add-in programs listed include a Help feature on the menu bar that you can use to get more information about using the program. Scroll the list in the Insert Object dialog box (Insert ➢ Object) to see the add-ins you can use in Word.

SECTION 20.2: TEXT SPACING

Word includes two desktop publishing tools used to control the spacing of regular text: kerning and leading.

■ Applying Kerning

Kerning increases or decreases the space between characters, expanding or contracting text. There are two reasons to use kerning. You may decide there is too much or too little space between certain characters in the font and size you have selected. Or, you may need to squeeze a few more characters into a space or adjust a heading to fill a space. To adjust the space between characters, first select the text to be adjusted. Then choose Format ➤ Font to open the Font dialog box. Click the Character Spacing tab (see Figure 20.6). Use the Spacing control to Expand or Compress the selected text by the number of points in the By control. You can manually adjust the spacing by increasing or decreasing the number in the By control. To raise or lower the position of the text in relation to the rest of the line, use the Position and By controls.

Figure 20.6
Adjusting Character
Spacing

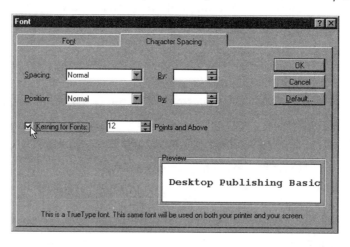

Checking the Kerning for Fonts box instructs Word to apply kerning automatically. Word will evaluate the space between characters and, if necessary, adjust the space to be consistent. Most text fonts are designed for use at 10–12 points; at larger sizes, they can look too "spaced out." Use the Points and Above spin box to adjust the sizes of fonts you want Word to kern automatically.

EXERCISE 20.3 | **TO APPLY KERNING**

Switch to *Development Department Article* if it is not already active.

1. **Select the text to be adjusted.** Select "Development Scores Big."

2. **Choose Format ➤ Font to open the Font dialog box.**

3. **Click the Character Spacing tab at the top of the dialog box.**

4. **Choose Normal, Condensed, or Expanded from the Spacing drop-down.** Choose Expanded.

5. **Use the spin box to adjust the number of points to condense or expand the spacing.** For this exercise, change this number to 3.5 points.

6. **Click the Position drop-down and use the By spin box to change the position of the text in relation to the rest of the line.** Leave this at Normal.

7. **Check the Kerning for Fonts check box to have Word automatically apply kerning to fonts over the point size you specify.**

8. Click OK to return to the main document window.

Using Leading

Leading (pronounced "ledding") is the space between lines of text. The term comes from the days when type was set manually with letters made of lead. To create more space above or below a line, the typesetter would add extra strips of lead between the lines.

You adjust leading in the Paragraph dialog box. Begin by selecting the text to be adjusted; then choose Format ➤ Paragraph and choose the Indents and Spacing tab, as shown in Figure 20.7. Use the Before and After spin boxes to add leading in 6-point ($\frac{1}{12}$") increments.

Figure 20.7

Adding leading

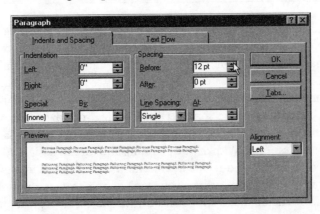

Leading is commonly applied to headings. Many of the Word heading styles include some leading adjustment. You may want a bit more space around a heading, but not the extra half line or line that you can select from the Line Spacing drop-down. When you create styles for headings or titles, you might consider leading the heading style to set the headings apart from the text above and below.

EXERCISE 20.4 **TO ADD LEADING TO A HEADING**

1. **Select the text to which you want the leading applied.** For this exercise, delete the blank line between the heading and the first paragraph of *Development Department Article.* Select the heading.

2. **Choose Format ➤ Paragraph and select the Indents and Spacing tab.**

3. **Use the Before and After Spin box controls to apply leading in 6 point increments or type in an amount if you want another number. Click OK to return to the main document.** Change these to 12 points before and after.

4. Close the document without saving.

Leading cannot be decreased below 0 points. If you want to *decrease* the amount of space between lines, change the Line Spacing control to Exactly. In the At control, choose a point size smaller than the current font size:

SECTION 20.3: DESKTOP PUBLISHING IN WORD

There are many reasons to do your own desktop publishing. You don't have to worry about a typesetter's schedule; you can work at your own pace. You don't have to pay someone else to implement your vision for a finished document. You have much greater control over the accuracy of the text. And perhaps most importantly, you get the satisfaction of creating a product from start to finish.

There is great personal reward in doing your own desktop publishing even though it may take you longer and you may not have the same equipment as a professional. With a little planning and careful design, you can produce a professional looking document. Allow more time to create your initial publications. If you are rushed, you won't be able to give your document the attention to detail that distinguishes an adequate from a great publication.

■ Guidelines for Desktop Publishing

Desktop publishing includes implementing the skills you have learned and developing a sense of how a publication should be constructed. The final design of the documents you create will improve as you do more desktop publishing. There are some steps you can follow when creating documents:

- Think about the type of document you intend to create. Is it a newsletter? Brochure? Business card? Invitation? Handbill? Poster?

- Identify your audience. A Brownie troop? Potential clients? Current contributors? Students in a college class? The length and layout of the document should reflect the readership.

- Create a basic layout. How many pages will be included in the newsletter? If it's a poster or handbill, how much room do you want to use for text? If you're creating a brochure, will it be a bi-fold or a tri-fold? The layout will dictate your paper orientation and outline.

- Outline and create the text that will fit in your tentative layout.

- Format the text. Use headings, styles, and columns to implement your basic layout. If you know that some text requires illustration, insert empty frames to use as placeholders.

- Select or create graphic objects that enhance the text. Place and frame the pictures, drawings, and pull quotes, and anchor them to the text where appropriate.

- Preview the document. Adjust kerning and leading to improve character spacing and separate headings from text.

- Save and print your completed publication.

These are, of course, only guidelines. Not every document comes together in this sequence. The layout may already be established, or you may begin with text that you need to find a way to present. Use the guidelines, but be flexible.

■ Rules for Page Layout

It's often easy to spot the work of a novice desktop publisher: all the tricks he or she has just learned are used in each and every document, whether or not they fit. While it is wonderful to have an opportunity to show off new skills, too many fonts or graphics can quickly clutter a document. There are some basic rules for beginning desktop publishing:

Fonts: Limit yourself to three fonts within a publication. Of these three, only use one or two for body text. Use text fonts for blocks of text. Save the decorative display fonts for wedding invitations and graduation announcements. Don't mix text fonts within a paragraph or newsletter article.

Graphics: If the connection between a graphic and the publication won't be immediately apparent to the user, omit the graphic. Graphics can easily overpower text, so limit yourself to two graphics per standard page. Graphics shouldn't compete with text. If the most important text is in the upper-left corner, don't place a stunning graphic in the lower-right corner, drawing the reader's attention to less important material. Use a style of graphic that supports the type of document you are creating. The more cartoon-like clip art rarely enhances a formal report.

Layout: The front page of a newsletter includes a masthead or banner, and can have a different layout from the other, inside pages. Inside pages should share a layout. Choose a number of columns, and stick with it. Choose one alignment for each heading type and one text alignment. Mixing justified and unjustified text is rarely attractive.

White Space: Resist the urge to fill every nook and cranny with text and graphics. Some blank space makes a publication friendlier and easier to read.

Consistency: If you publish a weekly newsletter, you want to establish a look that readers will recognize. Develop a standard format, and stick with it. Keep regular features in the same place in each issue, so readers know where to find them.

As you gain experience, you will know when and where you can safely stray from these rules. To evaluate your work, listen carefully to see if the newsletter, report, or brochure accomplished its job by communicating your message. Although desktop publishing is fun and can be personally enjoyable, don't expect lots of direct praise from those who receive your publications. Truly great design often goes unnoticed because it doesn't call attention to itself.

What You Have Learned

In this session, you have learned about two text-related graphic design features of Word, drop caps, and WordArt. Additionally, you have learned about kerning and leading and how to apply them to your text. You have also learned the guidelines for creating high quality desktop publishing on your own.

Focus Questions

1. What are drop caps and how would you create them without the aid of the Drop Caps feature of Word?

2. Why doesn't it make sense to apply WordArt to an entire paragraph of text?

3. What is the difference between kerning and leading?

4. List three advantages to doing your own desktop publishing. Identify two disadvantages.

5. List five skills you have learned that you can use in desktop publishing.

6. What is the maximum number of fonts that you should use in a document and why?

7. Is it a good idea to try to fill all of the available space on a page? Why or why not?

Reinforcement Exercises

Exercise 1 a) Open *We Do It Best—columns*. Change the first letter of each section to Drop Caps, dropping 2 lines.

b) Select the title "Results of We Do It Best Marketing Campaign," and apply kerning of 18 points after the heading. Create a new style and name it *Title*.

c) Select the "Description of Campaign" and apply 6 points of kerning after the heading. Redefine the style to include these changes.

    d) Using what you know about columns, styles, graphics, and text enhancement, improve the appearance of this document.

    e) Save the changes as *We Do It Best—DTP*.

Exercise 2 Open *Substance Abuse—Graphics*, which you saved in Reinforcement Exercise 2 in Session 19. Apply drop caps, kerning, and leading as appropriate to improve the appearance of the document. Save the changes.

Exercise 3 Open *Company Picnic—Graphics*, which you saved in Reinforcement Exercise 3 in Session 19. Apply drop caps, kerning, and leading as appropriate to improve the appearance of the document. Save the changes.

Exercise 4 a) Open *My Definitions*. Add the following terms and your definitions for: *kerning, leading, drop caps, white space*, and *desktop publishing*.

    b) Make any changes that you want to make the document suitable for printing: sorting, adjusting columns, changing heading styles, enhancing text, applying drop caps, and/or editing headers and footers.

    c) Check the spelling, save the changes, and print the document.

PROJECT C: CREATING AN ELECTRIFYING NEWSLETTER

Overview

In this project, you are going to design a weekly company newsletter. The purpose of this newsletter is to inform employees of the news from various departments, special events that are being planned, new employees, employees who are leaving, awards, etc.

Description

You can decide to write your own articles from scratch or you can incorporate documents from previous exercises into the two-page company newsletter. Use the guidelines for desktop publishing outlined in Session 20 to help develop your newsletter.

1. Plan the layout of the newsletter on paper first. Decide how many columns it will have. What size will the columns be? What fonts will you use for the headings and body text? How will you use lines and graphics to enhance the text? How many articles will it contain? What will be the average length of the articles?

2. Design a heading that can be repeated from week to week. Come up with a name for the newsletter that reflects its identity and its audience. You may want to use WordArt or graphics to develop a logo.

3. Identify what articles you are going to include. Edit the articles using Thesaurus and Grammar so that the headings are clear and the text is interesting. If you want to use articles from the book, you may want to use *Development Department*

Article, We Do It Best, Company Picnic (Reinforcement Exercise 17.3), *Safety Inspection,* or *Sales Projections* as the source material for your articles. You will have to do some writing to convert some of these documents into news articles. Add any others of your own choosing. Be creative.

4. Input (or copy) the text into the newsletter format that you designed.

5. Insert pull-quotes and graphics where appropriate.

6. Edit for length and review the design to make sure it's not too crowded.

7. Print the newsletter after you have checked the spelling and saved it.

PROJECT D: PRODUCING HIGH-IMPACT PROMOTIONAL MATERIALS

Overview

In this project, you are going to use the desktop publishing skills you've developed to produce a one page promotional flyer and other promotional materials for a brand new veterinary clinic that is opening in your community. Your job is to develop promotional materials that will be sent out to all of the residents in a ten-mile radius of the clinic.

Part 1

1. Create a letterhead for this new clinic. Use WordArt or other graphic tools to make the letterhead look professional but distinctive. (Invent a name for the clinic and locate it on a likely street in your community.)

2. Save it as a template.

3. Write a short letter from the clinic staff introducing themselves to the community.

4. Save and print the letter.

Part 2

1. Create business cards for this new business using the same design as you used on the letterhead. (Use the Envelopes and Labels feature under Tools and select Avery Business Card labels #5371.)

2. Save the document as *Vet—Business Cards*. Print the cards on plain paper.

Part 3

1. Develop a one-page promotional flyer to invite residents and their pets to a special open house to be held in the next month.

Decide when the open house is going to be, and what kinds of special services you'll be offering that day.

2. Write the text for the flyer.

3. Identify two or three graphics that will enhance the flyer.

4. Decide on the fonts that you will use in the headings and body text.

5. Create the flyer, paying attention to spacing, layout, and design concerns. Be careful not to clutter it up too much.

6. Save the flyer before printing it.

Part 4

1. Create a page of coupons (6 to a page) that provide a different service each month for the next six months at drastically reduced prices. (Use the Envelopes and Labels feature under Tools and Avery Shipping Labels #5664 to give you 2 across and 3 down on one page) Services could include: Heartworm exam for a dog, spaying or neutering a dog or cat, flea baths, Rabies vaccination, teeth-cleaning, and grooming.

2. Use the same text design that you used in the letterhead, business cards, and flyer to create a common look for the business.

3. Save the coupons and print them on plain paper.

Glossary

active window The window containing the application or document currently in use, indicated by the highlighted title bar.

add-in A program added to an application for additional functionality, like the Spelling tool.

align To place text either to the left, center, or right relative to the margins.

anchor In desktop publishing, to secure the location of a graphic relative to a character, line, paragraph, or page.

application window A container within the Windows 95 interface that displays a program.

applications (apps) Programs that allow you to complete specific tasks such as word processing.

AutoCorrect A Word feature that automatically corrects commonly misspelled words based on entries in a dictionary.

AutoFormat The Word tool that automatically formats headings, borders, numbered and bulleted lists, and certain symbols.

automatic save A feature of Word and other word processing programs that automatically saves a backup copy of active documents for recovery in the event of an unexpected shutdown.

AutoText A Word innovation that allows you to store frequently used text and graphics and quickly insert them into documents.

backspace The key above the Enter key that is often represented by a left arrow. When pressed, backspace deletes the character to the left of the insertion point.

balance To divide text in a section evenly between columns.

block Any word or group of consecutive words in a word processing document.

boldface A font style in which printed text is darker than normal for the typeface.

border Printable lines around text or cells in a table.

bullet character A special character like a dot or an asterisk that is used to identify separate points or items in a list.

callout In desktop publishing, text that describes and points to an area in a graphic.

Caps Lock A key on a computer keyboard that can be toggled on or off to type uppercase or lowercase letters.

cell A division of a table; the intersection of a row and a column.

center Text alignment that positions text midway between the left and right margins.

character map A Windows feature that shows the letters, numbers, and other symbols available in a font.

click To press the left mouse button to select an object.

clip art In desktop publishing, commercially available graphics and other images you can import into an application and then position, resize, and edit for use in various documents.

clipboard An area of memory reserved by Windows for the temporary storage of text and images so they can be moved or copied within or between documents and applications.

close To remove a window and its contents (application or document) from the desktop when you are finished working with it. Closing does not remove programs or documents from your disks or hard drive.

collapse In Outline view, to hide body text and subheadings under other headings to focus on higher-level topics.

column A vertical division of a page between the margins.

column break A code you can insert into a column to indicate the point where text should wrap to the next column.

context-sensitive Features that become available in an application based on what task is being performed.

Control Panel A Windows 95 program that allows users to customize various Windows settings. The Control Panel is accessed from the Start menu and is located under Settings.

convert To change a document's internal format so that an application other than the original can work with it.

copy To create a duplicate of a file, text, or graphics for use elsewhere in the same or another document.

crop To cut off unwanted parts of a graphic image.

cursor The flashing line in the document window that indicates where the next character will be inserted. Also referred to as the *insertion point.*

Custom dictionary A list of correctly spelled words created by the user that were not included in the Microsoft dictionary.

customize To change default settings of an application according to user preferences.

cut To move text or graphics to the clipboard so that they can be pasted to another location.

data source The file that contains information broken down into specific fields for use in a merge.

database A collection of information organized into categories for fast and easy retrieval.

default A preexisting setting for hardware or software that the user can choose to accept or change.

Delete (Del) A key on a computer keyboard used to erase unwanted text.

demote To move an item to a lower level of an outline.

desktop The control center for Windows 95.

desktop publishing (DTP) The use of a computer to produce printed material that contains text and graphics.

dialog box A window that appears when a Windows-based program requires more information from the user to complete a task.

document A word processing file created by a user.

document incompatibility In mail merging, a condition where Word doesn't recognize either the data source or the main document as a valid merge file.

document window The space defined by and contained within an application window where the user enters text to create a document.

double-clicking Pressing and releasing the primary mouse button twice in rapid succession without moving the mouse between clicks.

drag-and-drop A method of moving or copying selected text or files. You hold down the mouse button and move the pointer to the new location before releasing the button.

drive A device used to transfer programs and information such as document files between disk storage and a computer's memory. A computer system may contain several drives, for example, a hard drive, a floppy drive, and a CD-ROM drive.

drop cap In desktop publishing, enlarging the first letter of a paragraph to extend over several lines.

dynamic Subject to change. Describes object linking, in which changes made to an object in one application are reflected in any other application to which it is linked.

embed To copy a file created in one application into a document created in a different application.

End-of-Section marker A marker inserted by Word to distinguish the end of a section (such as a change in column layout, header/footers, or orientation) within a document.

execute To launch an application, macro, or other program.

expand In Outline view, to display previously hidden body text and subheadings, to view lower levels of a document's organization.

face (typeface) The design shared by a set of characters.

field A category of information in a database, like first name or address.

field names The names given to various categories of information in a database.

fill A color or pattern inside a drawn object.

filter A program that translates a particular type of file (such as TIFF or EPS graphic images) so that the file can be used in a specific application.

Find A Windows 95 and Word feature that locates files, text strings, formatting, or special codes in a document or folder.

first-line indent An indent applied to the first line of a paragraph.

first-line indent marker
A marker displayed on the ruler to indicate that a line is indented.

font A complete set of characters in a specific typeface including design, weight, size and style; typeface.

font style Within a font, variations such as italic or boldface.

footer Text or graphics automatically repeated at the bottom of each designated page.

format Broadly, all the elements that define the appearance of a document; to control or change any of these elements is to format the document; a set of specifications used to save a file, also known as file type; a process for initializing a floppy or hard disk so that it can used to save files.

frame A container that holds an object so that it can be repositioned on a page.

global macro An automated series of steps that can be run in any documents that share the Normal template.

graphics Pictures or images that can be imported into documents.

gridlines Nonprinting vertical and horizontal lines that designate rows and columns in a table.

gutter The white space that separates columns of text.

gutter margin Extra space added to inside margins of a document that will be bound.

handles Markers that appear around a selected graphic object. Handles are used to resize the object.

hanging indent A paragraph formatting style with the first line of a paragraph aligned with the left margin, and subsequent lines indented.

hard return A code inserted when the Enter key is pressed to designate a new paragraph.

hardware The physical components of the computer system.

header Text or graphics that are automatically repeated on the top of designated pages.

Highlight Transparent color applied by the user to text for the purpose of emphasis.

highlighting Contrasting color applied by Word to text or menu options to indicate that the item has been selected.

I-beam The form the mouse pointer takes when it is located within a document window. The I-beam is used to position the insertion point.

icons Small pictures that represent programs and files used in a graphical user interface.

import To bring a file created in one application into another application.

indent To position text in from the left or right margins.

Insert (Ins) A key on the keyboard that allows toggling between Insert and Overtype modes of text entry.

insertion point The place where text will be entered in a word processing document, designated by a flashing vertical line.

italics A font style where text is slanted to the right.

justify To align text evenly with both the left and right margins.

kerning Used to increase or decrease the space between characters, expanding or contracting text.

landscape A page orientation where text is rotated so that it prints parallel to the long side of the paper.

launch To start a program.

layering Placement of objects "on top of" text or other objects in a document, as if the objects were on printed transparency sheets.

leader A type of tab that inserts dots or other characters to help the reader follow to the tabbed text.

leading (pronounced "ledding") the space above or below one or more lines of text. In Word, specified as line spacing.

left indent marker A marker on the Ruler Bar that indicates where the left indent is located relative to the left margin.

line spacing The number of lines separating lines of text.

link To connect two files from different applications, such as a Word document and an Excel worksheet.

locked columns Columns whose widths cannot be adjusted.

Main dictionary A file supplied with Word, containing a list of thousands of words used to check spelling.

main document In merging, the document that contains the field codes and formatted text that will be merged with a data source.

margin The white space around the edges of a document.

maximize To make a window fill the entire desktop.

menu bar The bar containing lists of options available in a program or window.

merge To combine a data file with a form document to produce mass mailings, labels, and lists.

merge field code A code representing data in a data file; it is replaced with actual data as the result of a merge.

microcomputer (PC) A computer designed to fit on a desktop.

minimize To reduce an application or document window to the size of an icon, allowing it to continue running in the background while another program has priority.

mirror margins Margins that are the same on opposite sides of the page for back-to-back printing.

mouse An input device used to activate commands and select text by pointing and clicking.

move To reposition text or objects from one location to another.

navigation buttons Controls located on the bottom of a data form used to move to the previous and next records in a data source.

new document A document, just created, that is blank.

newspaper columns Segments of text arranged vertically on a page. When text reaches the end of a segment, it wraps to the top of the next segment.

normal view A screen display available in Word that does not show margins, to allow for maximum width and editing area.

Num Lock The toggle key on a computer keyboard that allows the calculator keypad to be used for numeric entry or insertion point movement.

object Anything that can be created in another application and inserted into Word.

open To make available for use, as in a dialog box or document.

operating system Software that manages computer resources (such as memory, disk space, processor time, and peripherals) and allows application programs to run. Windows 95 is an operating system.

orientation Determines whether a page will be printed with text running horizontally or vertically.

orphan A first line of a paragraph left alone at the bottom of a page.

outline A document structured by topic headings from major topics through minor topics.

Outline view A screen display available in Word that shows the structure (headings and titles vs. regular text) of the document.

overtype mode The opposite of insert mode. New keystrokes replace existing text.

page break A code that indicates the end of a physical page.

Page Layout view A Word screen display that shows the document as it will be printed with headers, footers, and margins.

paragraph formatting The indents, line spacing, text flow, and tabs related to a paragraph.

parallel columns Two or more segments of text that are arranged vertically on a page and correspond to each other.

password A secret word entered by a user to secure a document so that others can't open it.

paste To copy text or objects from the clipboard into a document.

personal computer (pc) A computer, designed for use by an individual, that contains its own central processing unit and memory.

picture placeholders Empty boxes that can be inserted into a Word document to represent the eventual placement of a graphic.

picture A piece of art that can be inserted into a Word document.

play To run or execute a macro.

point A measurement unit used to describe the size of type; 1/72 of an inch.

pop-up menu A context-sensitive menu that appears when you right-click the mouse.

portrait A page orientation where text is printed parallel to the short side of the paper.

printer font A font that is available to a printer but for which there is no matching screen display font.

promote To move an item to a higher level in a outline.

pull quote In desktop publishing, a quote that is pulled out of a document, often framed in a box for special emphasis.

query A method of retrieving specific information from a database.

record In a database, a collection of related items such as an individual's name, address, and city in a mailing list.

Redo A Word tool that restores the previously undone action.

repagination A Word feature that automatically reassigns page breaks when text has been entered or deleted.

replace An operation that substitutes one text string or formatting type for another.

reverse video A display mode where the background and foreground colors of surrounding text are reversed to highlight text.

revert To return to a previously saved version of a file.

right-click To click the right mouse button (to open a context menu).

right indent marker A marker located on the ruler bar that indicates where the right indent is located relative to the right margin.

row A horizontal group of cells in a table.

ruler bar A Word feature that shows page measurements, left and right margins, tabs, and indents.

save To copy information from the computer's active memory to permanent storage such as a floppy disk.

scalable Describes a font that can be resized. All TrueType fonts are scalable.

screen font A font that is available only for display on a monitor.

scroll bar The horizontal and vertical bars to the right of a document window and below it that allow you to see parts of the document that are not included in the current screen display.

section A portion of a document that includes a page, a column, or some formatting variation.

select To designate a text string or an object by clicking or dragging to highlight it; the next operation will affect the selected item.

shading Gray background tones added to text or table cells.

shortcut key A combination of keys that can be pressed in place of using the mouse to initiate an action.

Shut Down An option on the Windows 95 Start menu that closes all applications and prepares your computer to be turned off or restarted.

size To reduce or enlarge a window on the desktop.

soft (page break) A page break inserted automatically when text overflows to the next page.

software All the instructions that a computer can execute. Software includes both application programs (like Word) that carry out specific tasks, and operating systems (like Windows 95) that make the computer's resources available to applications.

sort To reorder words, lines, or paragraphs in alphabetical or numerical order.

source document A document that contains information for one or more records that will be entered into a data source file.

spacing The unoccupied area between margins in columns; also called gutter.

spin box A type of control used in a Windows dialog box to increase or decrease numeric values.

split To divide a cell in a table into two or more cells; to divide the screen between two or more document windows.

Start menu The menu that appears when you click on the Start button; it enables you to access Windows 95 features and applications.

static Unchanging; the opposite of *dynamic*. Formulas in Word tables are described as static because once a formula has been entered in a table cell, the result does not change, even if the contents of the cells in the column or row change.

status bar The bar at the bottom of a document window that gives you information about the current document, such as page number and cursor position.

style Paragraph and text formatting that is saved so that it can be applied to other text.

symbol Any character, available in a font, that is not a letter, numeral, or punctuation mark.

tab stops Measurements on the ruler that indicate where the insertion point will move when the Tab key is pressed.

table Text that is entered in rows and columns.

taskbar A Windows 95 desktop feature that that contains the Start button and buttons for any applications currently running.

template A pattern for the text, graphics, and formatting of a document.

text box A graphic frame that contains text.

text string One or more consecutive characters.

Thesaurus A built-in feature of Word that provides a list of synonyms for a selected word.

Tip Wizard A Word feature that provides tips to help you learn about the software's many features.

toggle To switch between two options by pressing a key or a toolbar button.

tool tip The name of a toolbar button, displayed when you point to the button.

toolbar A bar containing buttons that carry out specific functions such as saving and printing.

typeface (face) The design shared by a set of characters.

underline An attribute of a font that appears as a line underneath characters.

undo To reverse an action.

vertical centering To position text on a page so that it is midway between the top and bottom margins.

weight A characteristic of a typeface based on the thickness of the individual characters.

widow The last line of a paragraph at the top of a new page.

wildcards Characters that can be used in a Find operation to replace unidentified characters.

Windows 95 The newest version of Microsoft's graphical user interface developed to take advantage of faster, more powerful PCs.

Wizard A program that walks you through a series of steps to accomplish a certain task.

word processing programs Applications that are designed to produce text-based documents that are easy to edit, format, and print.

WordArt A program used to create special visual effects with text.

wrap To flow from one line to the next automatically without the user entering a return.

zoom To increase or decrease the size of the text or objects on the display.

Index

Note to the Reader:
Boldfaced numbers indicate pages where you will find the principal discussion of a topic or the definition of a term. *Italic* numbers indicate pages where topics are illustrated in figures.

A

activating an inactive window, 53
active window, 52–53
Add Field Name button on Create Data Source dialog box, *201*, 201–202
Add to Template check box in New Style dialog box, 188
add-ins, 299, 301
adding color to a border, 283–284, *284*
adding entries to dictionary, 56
adding records to a data source, 204
adjusting character spacing, 301–304
adjusting column widths, *260*, 260–261
adjusting gutter position, 261
aligning text, *77*, 77–78
alignment buttons on Formatting toolbar, 78
alignment, changing, 78
Always Create Backup Copy option, 171
anchor, *284*, **284–286**
AND, using in a comparison, 218
antonyms, finding, *130*, 130–131
application window, **8**, *8*
applications, **4**
applying styles in Outline view, 233
Arc tool, 289, *289*

ascending order when sorting, 205
assigning a macro to a keyboard shortcut, 248–250, *249*
assigning a macro to a list, 244
assigning a macro to a toolbar, 246–248, *247*
creating a macro toolbar button, 246–248, *247*
Custom Button dialog box, *247*, 247–248
AutoCorrect, **157, 164**
AutoCorrect dialog box, 164–166, *165*
AutoCorrect feature, 55
AutoCorrect, customizing, 164–166, *165*
AutoFit, using to adjust column width, 147–148
AutoFormat, 177, 182–186
reviewing and rejecting changes, 183, *183*, 185
AutoFormat As You Type option, 99
AutoFormat dialog box, 183, *183*
AutoFormat of a table, 143–145
automatic bullets, 99
automatic numbering, 99
automatic save, 172
Automatic Save option, 172
automatic spell-check, 55–60, 128
Automatic Word Selection option, 169
AutoText, 177, **191**, *191*
creating an AutoText entry, 191–192
pasting in a document, 191–192
AutoText dialog box, 191, *191*

B

back-to-back page printing, 115
Background Repagination option, 167
balancing columns within a section, *262*, 262–263
bar code version of zip code, 223
Beep on Error Actions option, 167

block of text, **37**
Blue Background, White Text option, 167
body text, 232
bold font style, 69–71
book icon, 57
Borders toolbar, *107*, 107–109
borders, adding, *107*, 107–109, 273–274, *274*
borders, adding color, 283–284, *284*
borders, removing, 108
borders, shading, 283–284, *284*
Break dialog box, 262, *262*
built-in style, 186
bullet character, 100
bulleted lists, **98–103**
automatic bullets, 99
bullet characters, 100
Bullets and Numbering dialog box, 100, *100*
changing bullet position, 101
changing format, 100
character map, 101
creating, 99–100
Modify Bulleted List dialog box, 100–101, *101*
modifying the format, *100*, 100–103, *101*
removing bullets from the text, 102
Symbol dialog box, 101, *101*
Bullets and Numbering dialog box, 100, *100*

C

callout, **290–291**, *291*
Callout Defaults dialog box, 291
Caps Lock key, 33
cell, *140*, *140*
centering, vertical, 122
changing column width, 147–148
character map, 101
character spacing, adjusting, 301–304
character style, 186

Checking and Reporting Errors
    dialog box, 224, *224*
checking spelling, 55–60
clicking, **6**
clip art, 270–274
    borders, 273–274
    copying, 273
    cropping, 272–273
    deleting, 273
    Insert Picture dialog box,
        271, *271*
    inserting, 271–272
    pasting, 273
    Picture Borders dialog box,
        273–274, *274*
    placing, 271
    sizing, 272–273
clipboard, **39**
Close button, 11, *11*
closing a document, 24
closing a document without saving
    changes, 33, 52
closing print preview window, 44
Closing the Word application, 11
collapsing an outline, **236**
column border, adjusting width
    manually, 147–148
column break, 259, 262
column break, hard
    inserting, 262
Column dialog box, using,
    263–266, *264*
column width, changing, 147–148
column widths, adjusting, *260*,
    260–261
columns, **140,** *140,* 255–266
    adjusting column widths, *260*,
        260–261
    adjusting page margins, 261
    balancing, 262–263
    Break dialog box, 262, *262*
    breaking, 262–263
    column breaks, 259, 262
    Column dialog box, using,
        263–266, *264*
    creating, *258,* 258–260
    creating equal, *258,* 258–260
    End of Section marker, 259
    gutter, 257
    gutter position tool, 261, *261*

gutter position, adjusting, 261
gutter spacing marker, 261, *261*
hard column break, inserting, 262
keeping text together, 262
Line Between check box, 265
locked equal columns, 264
maximum number per page, 258
mixing column formats within a
    document, 261–262
multicolumn text, 261–262
newspaper, *256,* 256–257
parallel, 256, *256*
Presets control of Columns dia-
    log box, 264
reformatting existing text into,
    259–260
ruler bar in section with
    columns, *260,* 260–261
section, **259**
section break, 259
spacing, 257
specifying column widths,
    264–266
commas as delimiters in a data
    source, 198–200
comparisons, list of, 218
context-sensitive, 48
convert, 169
converting an existing document
    to a main document, *213,*
    213–214
converting text to table, 153, 199
converting Word table to data
    source table, 197
copying text, 39–40, 48–51
copying text between documents,
    53–54
copying text using drag-and-drop,
    49–51
Create Data Source dialog box,
    201, *201*
    Add Field Name button, *201,*
        201–202
    Remove Field Name button,
        201, *201*
Create Labels dialog box, 222, *222*
creating a delimited data source,
    198, 198–200, *199*
creating a macro toolbar button,
    246–248, *247*

creating a main document for
    merge, 210–213
creating a new document, 25–26
creating a new toolbar, *163,*
    163–164
creating a style from formatted
    text, 190
creating envelopes, 221–223
creating equal columns, *258,*
    258–260
creating labels, 221–223
creating logos. *See* WordArt
cross-hairs pointer, 287
cross-hairs surrounding picture,
    293, *293*
Current Keys box in assignment of
    macros, 249, *249*
cursor, **21**
cursor, moving, 34–35
Custom button dialog box, *247,*
    247–248
Custom dictionary, 55. *See also*
    dictionary
customize, **161**
Customize dialog box, *162,*
    162–164
customizing AutoCorrect, 164–166,
    165
customizing toolbars, 161–164, *162*
    adding buttons, 161–163
    deleting buttons, 161–163
    restoring default toolbar set-
        tings, 162
cut, **39–40,** 48, 50

D

Data Form dialog box, 202–203,
    203
data source, **196**
data source file types, 199
data source table
    converting Word table to, 197
    creating, *196,* 196–198
    rules when creating, 197
data source, sorting, *205,* 205–206
    ascending order, 205
    descending order, 205
database, **196**

Database toolbar, using, *204, 204–206*
  adding records to a data source, 204
  deleting records from a data source, 204–205
  finding records, 205
  sorting records in a data source, 205–206
Date and Time dialog box, *82, 82–84*
date formats, 82
date placeholder, 82–83
date, adjusting system, 82
date, inserting as text, 83–84
date, inserting as updatable field, 82–83
Date/Time Properties dialog box, 82
dates, inserting in documents, 82–84
decreasing leading, 304, *304*
decreasing space between lines, 304, *304*
deleting macros, 251
deleting records from a data source, 204–205
deleting rows and columns in a table, 146–147
deleting text, 35–36
delimited data source, creating, *198,* 198–200, *199*
demote, 232–233
descending order when sorting, 205
desktop publishing guidelines, 305
desktop, Windows 95, **5–6,** *6*
dialog box, **22**
dictionary, 55, 56
display font, 67
displaying nonprinting characters, 113
displaying toolbars, *158,* 158–161, *159, 160*
document incompatibility, 224
document window, **20,** *20*
document, creating, 25–26
Documents menu, accessing, 6
double-click, 23
downsizing the Word application window, 9, *9*
drag-and-drop, 49–51

Drag-and-Drop Text Editing option, 169
dragging, 37–38
dragging text, 49–51
Drawing Defaults dialog box, *288,* 288–289
drawing graphics, 287–293. *See also* Drawing toolbar
  cross-hairs surrounding picture, 293, *293*
  editing the picture, *292,* 292–293, *293*
  framing drawings, 292, *292*
  picture boundaries, 293
  Reset Picture Boundary, 293, *293*
  selecting and manipulating objects, *291,* 291–292
Drawing toolbar, *287,* 287–290, *288, 289*
  Arc tool, 289, *289*
  callout, **290–291,** *291*
  Ellipse tool, 289, *289*
  filling in color, 289, *289*
  Freeform tool, 289, *289*
  layer, 288
  line color, 288, *288*
  line style, 288, *288*
  lines, 288, *288*
  rectangles, 289, *289*
  Text Box tool, 290
drives, drop-down list of, 23, *23*
drop cap, *298,* 298–299
Drop Cap dialog box, 298–299, *299*
dropping text, 49–51
dynamic linking, 276
dynamic program results, **150**

E

Edit options. *See* options, edit
Edit the Data Source, 202
editing an outline, 234–235
editing and closing a document without saving changes, 33
Ellipse tool, 289, *289*
Embed TrueType Fonts option, 171
embedding, **171**
embedding pictures, 275–276
End of Section marker, 259
ending the recording of macros, 245

ending your Word session, 11
entering body text in an outline, 233–234
entering records in a data source, 202–204
envelopes, creating, 221–223
executing macros, 246
exiting a table, 143
exiting print preview, 44
expanding an outline, **236**
external file, 196, 199

F

face. *See* typeface
field, 196
field names, 196–197
  syntax requirements, 197
file formats for graphics, 275
File menu, 30, *30*
file name control, 23
file name, valid characters in, 23
file names, maximum length of, 5, 23
File Sharing option, 172
file, created using Word, 196
file, external, 196
file, shared, 196
filename, 23
fill, 283
filling in color, 289, *289*
filter, 275
Filter Records page of Query Options dialog box, 217, *217*
filters, list of installed, 275
FIM code, 223
Find dialog box, 131–133, *132*
  closing, 133
  Find All Word Forms, 132
  Find Whole Words Only, 132
  Format, 132
  Match Case, 132
  No Formatting, 133
  Sounds Like, 132
  Special, 132–133
  special codes, 133
  unformatted text, 133
  Use Pattern Matching, 132
  wildcards, 132
Find menu, accessing, 6

find, using, 131–133
finding text, 131–133
fonts, **66**
    attributes of, 66–74
    changing, 68, 73–74
    color of, 73
    default, setting the, 74–75
    display, 67
    effects, 72–73
    Font dialog box, 71–72, *72*
    icons for, 71
    monospaced, 67
    printer, 67
    proportionally spaced, 67
    scalable, 69
    screen, 67
    size of, 68–69
    style, 66, 69–71
    styles, turning off, 69
    symbol, 67
    text, 67
    TrueType, 67
    WYSIWYG, 67
footers
    creating, 118–121, *119*
    deleting, 121
    editing, 121
    omitting from first page of doc-
        ument, 119
Format Painter, 76–77
formats, altering, 135–136
Formatting toolbar, 19, *19*, 66, *66*
formatting, defined, **66**
Formula dialog box, 150, *150*
four-headed arrow, 234–235, 283
fractions, creating, 103
frame, *282*, **282–287**, *284, 285, 286*
    four-headed arrow, 283
    inserting empty, 287
    moving, 283
frame anchor, *284*, **284–286**
Frame dialog box, 284–286, *285*
    horizontal position, 286
    size, 286
    Text wrapping control, 286
    vertical position, 286
framing pictures, 286–287
framing text, *286*, 286–287
Freeform tool, 289, *289*
full alignment, 77

G
General options. *See* options,
    General
global macros, 242
graphics, 270–277. *See also* clip art
    borders, 273–274, *274*
    clip art, 270–274
    dynamic linking, 276
    embedding pictures, 275–276
    filter, 275
    filters, list of installed, 275
    handles, 272
    hiding for faster scrolling,
        276–277, *277*
    importing other, 275
    Insert Picture dialog box,
        271, *271*
    linking pictures, 275–276
    moving, 283
    picture placeholders, 276–
        277, *277*
    sources, 270
    View Options dialog box,
        277, *277*
graphics file formats, 275
    JPEG File Interchange format
        (JPG), 275
    Macintosh PICT (PCT), 275
    Tag Image File Format (TIF), 275
    Windows Bitmap, 275
    Windows Bitmaps/Windows
        Paint (BMP), 275
    Windows Metafile (WMF), 275
    WordPerfect Graphics
        (WPG), 275
graphics, drawing, 287–293. *See
    also* Drawing toolbar
    cross-hairs surrounding pic-
        ture, 293
    editing the picture, *292*,
        292–293, *293*
    framing drawings, 292, *292*
    picture boundaries, 293
    Reset Picture Boundary, 293, *293*
    selecting and manipulating
        objects, *291*, 291–292
gridlines, 142
guidelines for desktop publish-
    ing, 305

gutter, 257
gutter margins, 115
gutter position tool, 261, *261*
gutter position, adjusting, 261
gutter spacing marker between
    columns, 261, *261*

H
handles, 272
hard column break, inserting, 262
hard return, defined, **86**
hardware, **4**
Header and Footer toolbar, 119, *119*
headers
    creating, 118–121, *119*
    deleting, 121
    editing, 121
    omitting from first page of doc-
        ument, 119
heading levels, 232
heading numbering, 237–238
Heading Numbering dialog box,
    237–238
Help menu, accessing, 6
Help question mark, using,
    167, *167*
Help system, using to view a para-
    graph's style, 189–190, *190*
Hide Marks button of Review
    AutoFormat Changes dialog
    box, 183
hiding graphics for faster scrolling,
    276–277, *277*
highlighted entries, 23
highlighting text, 75–76
homonyms, finding, 132
horizontal lines for added empha-
    sis, 78–79
horizontal row, **140**, *140*
horizontal scroll bar, 20

I
icon, **5**
importing files, 275
inactive window, 53
indent markers,
    first-line, 91

left, 91
right, 91
indents, **90–93**, *91, 92*
 creating, using the Formatting
  toolbar, 91
 creating, using the Paragraph
  dialog box, 92, *92*, 93
 creating, using the ruler bar,
  91, 92
 dual, 90
 first-line, 90
 hanging, 90
 left, 90
 outdent, 90
 right, 90
Ins key, 34
Insert mode of insert key, 34
Insert Picture dialog box, 271, *271*
Insert Table dialog box, **141**, *141*
inserting rows and columns in a
  table, 146–147
inserting text, 35–36
insertion point, **21**
insertion point, moving, 34–35
italics, 69–71

J

JPEG File Interchange format
  (JPG), 275
justification, 77

K

Keep Text Together control, 262
kerning, 301–303, *302*

L

Label Options dialog box, 221–222,
  222
labels, creating, 221–223
landscape orientation, *116*,
  116–117
layer, 288
leading, 301, *303*, 303–304
Letters and Faxes Wizard, using to
  create a document, 182
Line Between check box, 265

line color, 288, *288*
line spacing, changing, *104*,
  104–105
line style, 288, *288*
lines, drawing, 288, *288*
link, 167–168
linking pictures, 275–276
List control of the Style dialog
  box, 186
locked equal columns, 264
locking an anchor, 284–286, *285*
logos, creating. *See* WordArt
Look In text box, 31

M

Macintosh PICT (PCT), 275
Macro dialog box, 243, *243*
macro names, rules for, 244
macros, **241–251**
 assigning to a keyboard shortcut, 248–250, *249*
 assigning to a list, 244
 assigning to a toolbar, 246–
  248, *247*
 Current Keys box, 249, *249*
 deleting, 251
 ending the recording of, 245
 examples of use, 242
 executing, 246
 global, 242
 Macro dialog box, 243, *243*
 macro names, rules for, 244
 overwriting, 251
 pausing the recording of, 245
 playing, 242, 244, 246
 Record Macro dialog box, *244*,
  244–245
 recording, 242–245
 running, 246
 saving, 245
magnifying glass, 43–44
mail merge, 196–205
Mail Merge Helper, *200*, 200–
  202, 213
Mail Merge toolbar, 210, *210*
Main dictionary, 55. See also
  dictionary
main document for merge, creating, 210–213

margins, 20, **114**
 changing, *114*, 114–116
 gutter, 115
 mirror, 115
 Page Setup dialog box, 114,
  114, 115
master document view, 112, *112*
mathematical operations in a table,
  performing, 150–151
Maximize button, 10, *10*
maximizing the Word application
  window, 11
Measurement Units option, 168
menu bar, 17–18
menu bar, accessing items on, 17–18
Merge dialog box, 215–217, *216*
merge field code, **211**
merge problems, troubleshooting,
  224–225
merge simulation, 224
merge, mail, 196–205
merge, sorting records to, 220–221
merged document, previewing, 213
merged documents, printing, 216
merging, **196**
merging a main document with a
  data source, 216
merging documents, 215–225
merging table cells, 148–149, *149*
Microsoft Graph, 301
Microsoft Office folder, opening, 7
Microsoft Word for Windows 95,
  starting, 7
Microsoft Word menu bar, 17–18
Microsoft Word window, 17, *17*
Minimize button, 8, *8*
minimizing an application, 8
minimizing the Word application
  window, 9
mirror margins, 115
mixing column formats in a document, 261–262
Modify Bulleted List dialog box,
  100–101, *101*
Modify dialog box, 237–238
Modify Style dialog box, 190
monospaced font, 67
mouse, **6**
mouse buttons, changing settings
  of, 16

mouse pointer, shape of, 34, 49
Mouse properties sheet, opening, 16
mouse, changing settings, 16
Move with Text check box, 285
moving a frame, 283
moving a graphic, 283
moving a picture, 283
moving text, 39–40, 48–51
moving text between documents, 53
moving text using drag-and drop, 49–51
moving text using pop-up menu, 48
moving the Word application window, 10
multicolumn text, 261–262
multiple documents, working with, 51–54
multiple page button when previewing, 43–44

N

navigation buttons, 213, *213*
New dialog box, 178, *178*
New Document dialog box, 25, *25*
new document window, 25
New Style dialog box, *188*, 188–189
New Toolbar dialog box, 163, *163*
Newsletter Wizard, *179*, 179–181, *180, 181*
newspaper columns, 256–257, *257*
Nonprinting Characters option, 170
nonprinting characters, displaying, 113
normal view, 112, *112*
Num Lock key, 34
numbered lists, **98–99**
    AutoFormat As You Type option, 99
    automatic numbering, 99
    Bullets and Numbering dialog box, 100, *100*
    creating, 98–99
    modifying the format, 100, *100*, 102–103
    removing numbers from the text, 102
numbering the headings of an outline, 237–238

O

Office folder, opening, 7
Open dialog box, **30–31,** *31*
open files listed on Window menu, 51, *51*
opening a document as a read-only copy, 43
opening a document from the Start menu, 33
opening a document saved on a floppy disk, *31,* 31–32
opening a document using the file menu, 32
opening a document using the toolbar, 33
opening an existing document, *30,* 30–33, *31*
opening multiple documents, 51–53
operating systems, **4**
Options dialog box, 128, *128, 166,* 166–172
    Compatibility options, 169
    Edit options, 168–169
    General options, 167–168
    Revisions options, 171
    Save options, *171,* 171–172
    User Info options, 169–170
    View options, 170, *170*
options, Edit
    Automatic Word Selection, 169
    Drag-and-Drop Text Editing, 169
    Overtype Mode, 169
    Typing Replaces Selection, 168
    Use Smart Cut and Paste, 169
    Use Tab and Backspace Keys to Set Left Indent, 169
    Use the INS key for Paste, 169
options, General
    Background Repagination, 167
    Beep on Error Actions, 167
    Blue Background, White Text, 167
    Measurement Units, 168
    Recently Used File List, 168
    TipWizard Active, 168
    Update Automatic Links at Open, 167–168

options, Save, 171–172
    Always Create Backup Copy, 171
    Automatic Save, 172
    Embed TrueType Fonts, 171
    File Sharing, 172
options, setting Word, 166–172
options, View
    Nonprinting Characters, 170
    Show, 170
    Window, 170
OR, using in a comparison, 218
orientation, paper, *116,* 116–117
orphan line control, 106
Outline toolbar, 232, *232*
outline view, 112, *112*
Outline view, 236
outlines, 231–238
    applying styles in Outline view, 233
    body text, 232
    collapsing, **236**
    creating, 232
    demote, 232–233
    editing, 234–235
    entering body text, 233–234
    expanding, **236**
    four-headed arrow, 234–235
    heading levels, 232
    Modify dialog box, 237–238
    numbering the headings, 237–238
    Outline toolbar, 232, *232*
    outline view, 236
    printing, 236–237
    promote, 233
    Show Heading button on Outline toolbar, 236, *236*
Overtype mode of insert key, 34
Overtype Mode option, 169
overwriting macros, 251
OVR indicator on status bar, 34

P

page break, 106
    hard, 106
    soft, 106
page layout rules, 305–306
Page Layout view, 112, *112*

Page Number Format dialog box, 117–118, *118*
Page Numbers dialog box, 117, *117*
page numbers, adding, *117,* 117–118, *118*
page numbers, format of, 117–118, *118*
page orientation, *116,* 116–117
Page Setup dialog box, 114, *114,* 115, *116,* 116–117, 119, *120*
Page Setup Layout page, 119–120, *120*
pagination, managing, 106–107
paper orientation, *116,* 116–117
Paragraph dialog box, opening Tabs dialog box from, 88
paragraph formatting, 86
paragraph style, 186
paragraph's style, viewing, 189
paragraph, defined, **86**
parallel columns, 256, *256*
password, 172
paste, **39–40,** 48, 50
pausing the recording of macros, 245
Picture Borders dialog box, 273–274, *274*
picture placeholder, 276–277, *277*
Picture toolbar, *292,* 292–293
placeholder, date, 82–83
placeholder, picture, 276–277, *277*
placeholder, time, 82–83
playing a macro, 242, 244, 246
point, **68,** *68*
pointer, magnifying glass, 43–44
pointing and clicking, **6**
pop-up menu, 48
portrait orientation, *116,* 116–117
positioning objects in documents, *282,* 282–286, *284, 285*
poured text, 300, *300*
Presets control of Columns dialog box, 264
preview window, 43, *44*
previewing a document, 43–44, *44*
previewing merged documents, 213, 216
Print dialog box, 60, *60*
print parameters, setting, 61
print percentage, 43

print preview, *43,* 43–44
Print Preview toolbar, 43, *43*
print preview window, closing, 44
print preview, exiting, 44
printer font, 67
printing a range of pages, 61
printing an entire document, 61
printing an outline, 236–237
printing back-to-back pages, 115
printing documents, 60–62
    setting print parameters, 61
printing merged documents, 216
printing multiple copies, 61
printing odd and even pages, 61
Programs menu, *7*
Programs menu, accessing, 6
promote, 233
proportionally spaced font, 67
pull quote, 286, *286*

Q

query, **217**
Query Options dialog box, 217, *217*

R

read-only, 43
Recently Used File List option, 168
record, 196
Record Macro dialog box, *244,* 244–245
recording steps of a macro, 242–245
records, entering in a data source, 202–204
rectangles, 289, *289*
red wavy line, purpose of, 21, 55–56
redo, 41–42
redo button on toolbar, *41,* 41–42
redo history, *41,* 41–42
reformatting existing text into columns, 259–260
regular text, 210
Remove Field Name button on Create Data Source dialog box, 201, *201*
repagination, 167
Replace dialog box, *134,* 134–136

replace, using, 134–136
    altering formats, 135–136
replacing all occurrences of a word, 135
replacing text, 134–136
Reset Picture Boundary button on Picture toolbar, 293, *293*
Reset Toolbar dialog box, 162
resizing the Word application window, 10
Restore button, **9,** *9*
reverse video, **37**
Review AutoFormat Changes dialog box, 183, *183*
right mouse button to open pop-up menu, 48
row, **140,** *140*
ruler, 20
ruler bar in a section with columns, *260,* 260–261
ruler bar, viewing, 85, *85*
rules for page layout, 305–306
running macros, 246

S

sans-serif, 67
sans-serif typeface, example of, 67
Save As dialog box, 22, *22*
Save options. *See* options, Save
saving a document, 22–25, 42–43
    as a copy, 42–43
    to a floppy disk, 24
saving as, 22–23, 42–43
saving macros, 245
scalable fonts, 69
screen font, 67
scroll bar, 20
searching for text using find and replace, 131–136
section, **259**
section break, 259
selecting records to merge, 217–218, 220–221
selecting text, 37–39
serif, 67
serif typeface, examples of, 67
setting print parameters, 61
shading a border, 283–284, *284*
shading, adding, *107,* 107–109

shading, removing, 108
shared file, 196
shortcut keys, **18**
Show Heading button on Outline
    toolbar, 236, *236*
Show option, 170
Show/Hide button on the Standard
    toolbar, 113, 120
shutting down the computer, 11–12
size, 66, 68–69
sizing the Word application win-
    dow, 10
sizing tool, 10
software, **4**
    applications, **4**
    operating systems, **4**
    system, **4**
Sort Records page of the Query
    Options dialog box, 219, *219*
sorting a data source, *205,* 205–206
    ascending order, 205
    descending order, 205
sorting records to merge, 220–221
source document, **202,** *202*
sources of graphics, 270
spacing between columns, 257
spacing of text, 301–304, *302, 303*
special keys, 33–34
specifying column widths, 264–266
spell-check, 55–60
spell-check and book icon, 57
spell-check, automatic, 55–60, 128
spell-check, correcting misspelled
    words when using, 56
spell-check, ignoring flagged words
    when using, 56
spell-checking an entire document,
    58–60
Spelling dialog box, 59, *59*
spelling options, changing,
    128–129
splitting table cells, 148–149, *149*
Standard toolbar, 19, *19*
Start menu, **6,** *6*
starting Windows 95, 5
static program results, **150**
status bar, *19,* **19–20**
style, 66, 69–71, **184**
Style dialog box, 186–187, *187*
Style drop-down list, 186

Style Gallery dialog box, 184, *184*
style, built-in, 186
style, character, 186
style, creating from formatted
    text, 190
style, font, 66, 69–71
    bold, 69–71
    italics, 69–71
    normal, 69
    underline, 69–71, 72, *72*
    unemphasized, 69
style, paragraph, 186
styles, applying, 186–187
styles, applying in Outline view, 233
styles, creating, *188,* 188–190, *190*
Symbol dialog box, 101, *101*
symbol font, 67
symbols, using, 103, *103*
synonyms, finding, *130,* 130–131
system clock, adjusting, 82
system software, **4**

T

tab leader, 88–89, *89*
tab stops, 84–90
    bar, 88
    changing, 86, 89
    clearing, using Tabs dialog box,
        89
    clearing, using the ruler bar, 87
    moving, 86–87
    setting, 86–90
    setting, using the ruler bar,
        86–88
    setting, using the Tabs dialog
        box, 88–90
    types, 86
Table AutoFormat, 143–145
Table AutoFormat dialog box,
    143–145, *144*
table cells, merging, 148–149, *149*
table cells, splitting, 148–149, *149*
table data source
    converting Word table to, 197
    creating, *196,* 196–198
    rules when creating, 197
Table menu, 141
Table Wizard, 141
tables, 139–151, *140*

AutoFit, using to adjust column
    width, 147–148
AutoFormat, 143–145, *144*
column border, adjusting width
    manually, 147–148
column width, changing,
    147–148
converting text to table, 153
creating a new row, 143
deselecting cells, 146
deleting rows and columns,
    146–147
entering text, 142–143
exiting, 143
formatting table cells, 145–146
formatting, using AutoFormat,
    143–145
Formula dialog box, 150, *150*
gridlines, 142
Insert Table dialog box, 141, *141*
inserting rows and columns,
    146–147
mathematical operations, per-
    forming, *150,* 150–151
merging table cells, 148–149, *149*
moving between rows, 143
moving from cell to cell, 142
moving to the next line of a
    cell, 142
selecting table cells, 145–146
setting orientation, *116,* 116–117
splitting table cells, 148–149, *149*
Table AutoFormat dialog box,
    143–145, *144*
Table menu, 141
using Standard toolbar, 141–
    142, *142*
using Table Wizard, 141
tabs as delimiters in a data source,
    198–200
Tabs dialog box, *88,* 88–90
Tag Image File Format (TIF), 275
taskbar, **5**
template, **5, 178**
templates, using to create a docu-
    ment, 182
text box, 286, *286*
Text Box tool, 290
Text Flow page of Paragraph dialog
    box, 106, *106*

text flow, managing, 106–107
text font, 67
text spacing, 301–304, *302, 303*
text string, **131,** 217–218
text types in main document, 210
text, poured, 300, *300*
Thesaurus dialog box, 130, *130*
thesaurus, using the, *130,* **130–131**
time formats, 82
time placeholder, 82–83
time, adjusting system, 82
time, inserting in document, 82–84
    as text, 83–84
    updatable field, 82–83
Tip of the Day, 19
Tip Wizard toolbar, 19, *19*
TipWizard Active option, 168
title bar, **8,** *8*
titles, emphasizing. *See* WordArt
tool tips, 19
toolbar display options, 158
Toolbar pop-up menu, 159, *160*
Toolbar Preferences dialog box,
    160, *160*
toolbars, **18–19,** *19*
    browsing, 19
    closing, 159
    creating, *163,* 163–164
    customizing, 161–164, *162*
    displaying, *158,* 158–161,
        159, 160
    displaying all, 158
    hiding, 159
    moving, 159
    setting defaults, 160, *160*
    Toolbars dialog box, 158,
        158, 163
troubleshooting merge problems,
    224–225
TrueType font, 67
type font, 67
typeface, **66–68.** See also font

Typing Replaces Selection
    option, 168

U

underline font style, 69–71, 72, *72*
undo, 41–42
undo button on toolbar, *41,* 41–42
undo history, *41,* 41–42
Update Automatic Links at Open
    option, 167–168
Use Smart Cut and Paste
    option, 169
Use Tab and Backspace Keys to Set
    Left Indent option, 169
Use the INS key for Paste
    option, 169

V

variable text, 210
vertical centering, 122
vertical column, **140,** *140*
vertical scroll bar, 20
View Data as Source button on
    Data Form dialog box, 202,
    203, 204
View Merged Data button on the
    Mail Merge toolbar, 213
View options. *See* options, View
View Options dialog box, 277, *277*
viewing a paragraph's style, 189
viewing all open documents simul-
    taneously, 52, *52*
viewing documents, 112–114
    master document view, 112, *112*
    normal view, 112, *112*
    outline view, 112, *112*
    page layout view, 112, *112*
viewing two copies of same
    document, 53

W

wavy red line, purpose of, 21,
    55–56
widow line control, 106
wildcards, 132
Window menu, open files listed
    on, 51, *51*
Window option, 170
Windows 95 desktop, **5–6,** *6*
Windows Bitmap, 275
Windows Bitmaps/Windows Paint
    (BMP), 275
Windows Metafile (WMF), 275
wizard, **5**
Wizard categories, 179
    general, 179
    letters and faxes, 179
    memos, 179
    other documents, 179
    publications, 179
    reports, 179
Wizard, Letters and Faxes, using to
    create a document, 182
Wizard, Newsletter, *179,* 179–181,
    180, 181
Wizard, previewing documents
    created by, 179, *179*
Wizards, **177–182**
Word file, 196, 199
Word menu bar, 17–18
Word window, 17, *17*
word wrap, **21**
Word, starting, 7
WordArt, 299–301, *300*
WordPerfect Graphics (WPG), 275
wrapping text, 282
WYSIWYG font, 67

Z

zooming in, 112–113, *113*

TOP TWENTY WORD COMMANDS

To carry out any of these operations, either click the toolbar button or follow the menu path (the ➤ symbol points to your next choice). For some operations you'll make further choices once you reach the appropriate dialog box. For a few of these operations, Word provides no toolbar buttons.

---

1. Save a File

File ➤ Save

2. Open a File

File ➤ Open

3. Create a New File

File ➤ New

4. Close a File
File ➤ Close

5. Print Preview

File ➤ Print Preview

6. Print the Current Document

File ➤ Print

7. Check Spelling

Tools ➤ Spelling

8. Cut the Current Selection

Edit ➤ Cut

9. Copy the Current Selection

Edit ➤ Copy

10. Paste from the Clipboard

Edit ➤ Paste